Praise for *Modern Software Engineering*

"*Modern Software Engineering* gets it right and describes the ways skilled practitioners actually engineer software today. The techniques Farley presents are not rigid, prescriptive, or linear, but they are disciplined in exactly the ways software requires: empirical, iterative, feedback-driven, economical, and focused on running code."

—Glenn Vanderburg, Director of Engineering at Nubank

"There are lots of books that will tell you how to follow a particular software engineering practice; this book is different. What Dave does here is set out the very essence of what defines software engineering and how that is distinct from simple craft. He explains why and how in order to master software engineering you must become a master of both learning and of managing complexity, how practices that already exist support that, and how to judge other ideas on their software engineering merits. This is a book for anyone serious about treating software development as a true engineering discipline, whether you are just starting out or have been building software for decades."

—Dave Hounslow, Software Engineer

"These are important topics and it's great to have a compendium that brings them together as one package."

—Michael Nygard, author of *Release IT*, professional programmer, and software architect

"I've been reading the review copy of Dave Farley's book and it's what we need. It should be required reading for anyone aspiring to be a software engineer or who wants to master the craft. Pragmatic, practical advice on professional engineering. It should be required reading in universities and bootcamps."

—Bryan Finster, Distinguished Engineer and Value Stream Architect at USAF Platform One

T0253118

MODERN SOFTWARE ENGINEERING

MODERN SOFTWARE ENGINEERING

DOING WHAT WORKS TO BUILD

BETTER SOFTWARE FASTER

David Farley

✦Addison-Wesley

Boston • Columbus • New York • San Francisco • Amsterdam • Cape Town
Dubai • London • Madrid • Milan • Munich • Paris • Montreal • Toronto • Delhi • Mexico City
São Paulo • Sydney • Hong Kong • Seoul • Singapore • Taipei • Tokyo

For information about buying this title in bulk quantities, or for special sales opportunities (which may include electronic versions; custom cover designs; and content particular to your business, training goals, marketing focus, or branding interests), please contact our corporate sales department at corpsales@pearsoned.com or (800) 382-3419.

For government sales inquiries, please contact governmentsales@pearsoned.com.

For questions about sales outside the U.S., please contact intlcs@pearson.com.

Visit us on the Web: informit.com/aw

Library of Congress Control Number: 2021947543

Copyright © 2022 Pearson Education, Inc.

Cover image: spainter_vfx/Shutterstock

ISBN-13: 978-0-13-731491-1
ISBN-10: 0-13-731491-4

17 2023

Pearson's Commitment to Diversity, Equity, and Inclusion

Pearson is dedicated to creating bias-free content that reflects the diversity of all learners. We embrace the many dimensions of diversity, including but not limited to race, ethnicity, gender, socioeconomic status, ability, age, sexual orientation, and religious or political beliefs.

Education is a powerful force for equity and change in our world. It has the potential to deliver opportunities that improve lives and enable economic mobility. As we work with authors to create content for every product and service, we acknowledge our responsibility to demonstrate inclusivity and incorporate diverse scholarship so that everyone can achieve their potential through learning. As the world's leading learning company, we have a duty to help drive change and live up to our purpose to help more people create a better life for themselves and to create a better world.

Our ambition is to purposefully contribute to a world where:

- Everyone has an equitable and lifelong opportunity to succeed through learning.

- Our educational products and services are inclusive and represent the rich diversity of learners.

- Our educational content accurately reflects the histories and experiences of the learners we serve.

- Our educational content prompts deeper discussions with learners and motivates them to expand their own learning (and worldview).

While we work hard to present unbiased content, we want to hear from you about any concerns or needs with this Pearson product so that we can investigate and address them.

- Please contact us with concerns about any potential bias at https://www.pearson.com/report-bias.html.

I would like to dedicate this book to my wife Kate and to my sons, Tom and Ben.

Kate has been unfailingly supportive of my writing and my work over many years and is always an intellectually stimulating companion as well as my best friend.

Tom and Ben are young men whom I admire as well as love as a parent, and it has been my pleasure, while working on this book, to have also had the privilege to work alongside them on several joint ventures. Thanks for your help and support.

Contents

Foreword

I studied computer science at university, and of course I completed several modules called "software engineering" or variations on the name.

I was not new to programming when I started my degree and had already implemented a fully working inventory system for my high school's Careers Library. I remember being extremely confused by "software engineering." It all seemed designed to get in the way of actually writing code and delivering an application.

When I graduated in the early years of this century, I worked in the IT department for a large car company. As you'd expect, they were big on software engineering. It's here I saw my first (but certainly not my last!) Gantt chart, and it's where I experienced waterfall development. That is, I saw software teams spending significant amounts of time and effort in the requirements gathering and design stages and much less time in implementation (coding), which of course overran into testing time and then the testing...well, there wasn't much time left for that.

It seemed like what we were told was "software engineering" was actually getting in the way of creating quality applications that were useful to our customers.

Like many developers, I felt there must be a better way.

I read about Extreme Programming and Scrum. I wanted to work in an agile team and moved jobs a few times trying to find one. Plenty said they were agile, but often this boiled down to putting requirements or tasks on index cards, sticking them on the wall, calling a week a *sprint*, and then demanding the development team deliver "x" many cards in each sprint to meet some arbitrary deadline. Getting rid of the traditional "software engineering" approach didn't seem to work either.

Ten years into my career as a developer, I interviewed to work for a financial exchange in London. The head of software told me they did Extreme Programming, including TDD and pair programming. He told me they were doing something called *continuous delivery*, which was like continuous integration but all the way into production.

I'd been working for big investment banks where deployment took a minimum of three hours and was "automated" by the means of a 12-page document of manual steps to follow and commands to type. Continuous delivery seemed like a lovely idea but surely was not possible.

The head of software was Dave Farley, and he was in the process of writing his *Continuous Delivery* book when I joined the company.

I worked with him there for four life-changing, career-making years. We really did do pair programming, TDD, and continuous delivery. I also learned about behavior-driven development, automated acceptance testing, domain-driven design, separation of concerns, anti-corruption layers, mechanical sympathy, and levels of indirection.

I learned about how to create high-performance, low-latency applications in Java. I finally understood what big O notation really meant and how it applied to real-world coding. In short, all that stuff I had learned at university and read in books was actually used.

It was applied in a way that made sense, worked, and delivered an extremely high-quality, high-performance application that offered something not previously available. More than that, we were happy in our jobs and satisfied as developers. We didn't work overtime, we didn't have crunch times close to releases, the code did not become more tangled and unmaintainable over those years, and we consistently and regularly delivered new features and "business value."

How did we achieve this? By following the practices Dave outlines in this book. It wasn't formalized like this, and Dave has clearly brought in his experiences from many other organizations to narrow down to the specific concepts that are applicable for a wider range of teams and business domains.

What works for two or three co-located teams on a high-performance financial exchange isn't going to be exactly the same thing that works for a large enterprise project in a manufacturing firm or for a fast-moving startup.

In my current role as a developer advocate, I speak to hundreds of developers from all sorts of companies and business domains, and I hear about their pain points (many of them, even now, not dissimilar to my own experiences 20 years ago) and success stories. The concepts Dave has covered in this book are general enough to work in all these environments and specific enough to be practically helpful.

Funnily enough, it was after I left Dave's team that I started being uncomfortable with the title *software engineer*. I didn't think that what we do as developers is engineering; I didn't think that it was engineering that had made that team successful. I thought engineering was too structured a discipline for what we do when we're developing complex systems. I like the idea of it being a "craft," as that encapsulates the idea of both creativity and productivity, even if it doesn't place enough emphasis on the teamwork that's needed for working on software problems at scale. Reading this book has changed my mind.

Dave clearly explains why we have misconceptions of what "real" engineering is. He shows how engineering is a science-based discipline, but it does not have to be rigid. He walks through how scientific principles and engineering techniques apply to software development and talks about why the production-based techniques we thought were engineering are not appropriate to software development.

What I love about what Dave has done with this book is that he takes concepts that might seem abstract and difficult to apply to the real code we have to work with in our jobs and shows how to use them as tools to think about our specific problems.

The book embraces the messy reality of developing code, or should I say, software engineering: there is no single correct answer. Things will change. What was correct at one point in time is sometimes very wrong even a short time later.

The first half of the book offers practical solutions for not only surviving this reality but thriving in it. The second half takes topics that might be considered abstract or academic by some and shows how to apply them to design better (e.g., more robust or more maintainable or other characteristics of "better") code.

Here, design absolutely does not mean pages and pages of design documents or UML diagrams but may be as simple as "thinking about the code before or during writing it." (One of the things I noticed when I pair programmed with Dave was how little time he spends actually typing the code.

Turns out, thinking about what we write before we write it can actually save us a lot of time and effort.)

Dave doesn't avoid, or try to explain away, any contradictions in using the practices together or potential confusion that can be caused by a single one. Instead, because he takes the time to talk about the trade-offs and common areas of confusion, I found myself understanding for the first time that it is precisely the balance and the tension between these things that creates "better" systems. It's about understanding that these things are guidelines, understanding their costs and benefits, and thinking of them as lenses to use to look at the code/design/architecture, and occasionally dials to twiddle, rather than binary, black-and-white, right-or-wrong rules.

Reading this book made me understand why we were so successful, and satisfied, as "software engineers" during that time I worked with Dave. I hope that by reading this book, you benefit from Dave's experience and advice, without having to hire a Dave Farley for your team.

Happy engineering!

—Trisha Gee, developer advocate and Java champion

Preface

This book puts the *engineering* back into *software engineering*. In it, I describe a practical approach to software development that applies a consciously rational, scientific style of thinking to solving problems. These ideas stem from consistently applying what we have learned about software development over the last few decades.

My ambition for this book is to convince you that engineering is perhaps not what you think it is and that it is completely appropriate and effective when applied to software development. I will then proceed to describe the foundations of such an engineering approach to software and how and why it works.

This is not about the latest fads in process or technology, but rather proven, practical approaches where we have the data that shows us what works and what doesn't.

Working iteratively in small steps works better than not. Organizing our work into a series of small, informal experiments and gathering feedback to inform our learning allows us to proceed more deliberately and to explore the problem and solution spaces that we inhabit. Compartmentalizing our work so that each part is focused, clear, and understandable allows us to evolve our systems safely and deliberately even when we don't understand the destination before we begin.

This approach provides us with guidance on where to focus and what to focus on, even when we don't know the answers. It improves our chances of success, whatever the nature of the challenge that we are presented with.

In this book, I define a model for how we organize ourselves to create great software and how we can do that efficiently, and at any scale, for genuinely complex systems, as well as for simpler ones.

There have always been groups of people who have done excellent work. We have benefitted from innovative pioneers who have shown us what is possible. In recent years, though, our industry has learned how to better explain what really works. We now better understand what ideas are more generic and can be applied more widely, and we have data to back up this learning.

We can more reliably build software better and faster, and we have data to back that up. We can solve world-class, difficult problems, and we have experience with many successful projects, and companies, to back those claims, too.

This approach assembles a collection of important foundational ideas and builds on the work that went before. At one level there is nothing that is new here in terms of novel practices, but the approach that I describe assembles important ideas and practices into a coherent whole and gives us principles on which a software engineering discipline may be built.

This is not a random collection of disparate ideas. These ideas are intimately entwined and mutually reinforcing. When they come together and are applied consistently to how we think about, organize, and undertake our work, they have a significant impact on the efficiency and the quality of that work. This is a fundamentally different way of thinking about what it is that we do, even though each idea in isolation may be familiar. When these things come together and are applied as guiding principles for decision-making in software, it represents a new paradigm for development.

We are learning what software engineering really means, and it is not always what we expected.

Engineering is about adopting a scientific, rationalist approach to solving practical problems within economic constraints, but that doesn't mean that such an approach is either theoretical or bureaucratic. Almost by definition, engineering is pragmatic.

Past attempts at defining *software engineering* have made the mistake of being too proscriptive, defining specific tools or technologies. Software engineering is more than the code that we write and the tools that we use. Software engineering is not production engineering in any form; that is not our problem. If when I say *engineering* it makes you think bureaucracy, please read this book and think again.

Software engineering is not the same thing as computer science, though we often confuse the two. We need both software engineers and computer scientists. This book is about the discipline, process, and ideas that we need to apply to reliably and repeatably create better software.

To be worthy of the name, we would expect an engineering discipline for software to help us solve the problems that face us with higher quality and more efficiency.

Such an engineering approach would also help us solve problems that we haven't thought of yet, using technologies that haven't been invented yet. The ideas of such a discipline would be general, durable, and pervasive.

This book is an attempt to define a collection of such closely related, interlinked ideas. My aim is to assemble them into something coherent that we can treat as an approach that informs nearly all of the decisions that we make as software developers and software development teams.

Software engineering as a concept, if it is to have any meaning at all, must provide us with an advantage, not merely an opportunity to adopt new tools.

All ideas aren't equal. There are good ideas, and there are bad ideas, so how can we tell the difference? What principles could we apply that will allow us to evaluate any new idea in software and software development and decide if it will likely be good or bad?

Anything that can justifiably be classified as an engineering approach to solving problems in software will be generally applicable and foundational in scope. This book is about those ideas. What criteria should you use to choose your tools? How should you organize your work? How should you organize the systems that you build and the code that you write to increase your chances of success in their creation?

A Definition of Software Engineering?

I make the claim in this book that we should think of software engineering in these terms:

> **Software engineering** is the application of an empirical, scientific approach to finding efficient, economic solutions to practical problems in software.

My aim is an ambitious one. I want to propose an outline, a structure, an approach that we could consider to be a genuine engineering discipline for software. At the root this is based in three key ideas.

- Science and its practical application "engineering" are vital tools in making effective progress in technical disciplines.

- Our discipline is fundamentally one of learning and discovery, so we need to become **experts at learning** to succeed, and science and engineering are how we learn most effectively.

- Finally, the systems that we build are often complex and are increasingly so. Meaning, to cope with their development, we need to become **experts at managing that complexity**.

What Is in This Book?

Part I, "What Is Software Engineering?", begins by looking at what engineering really means in the context of software. This is about the principles and philosophy of engineering and how we can apply these ideas to software. This is a technical philosophy for software development.

Part II, "Optimize for Learning," looks at how we organize our work to allow us to make progress in small steps. How do we evaluate if we are making good progress or merely creating tomorrow's legacy system today?

Part III, "Optimize for Managing Complexity," explores the principles and techniques necessary for managing complexity. This explores each of these principles in more depth and their meaning and applicability in the creation of high-quality software, whatever its nature.

The final section, Part IV, "Tools to Support Engineering in Software," describes the ideas and approaches to work that maximize our opportunities to learn and facilitate our ability to make progress in small steps and to manage the complexity of our systems as they grow.

Sprinkled throughout this book, as sidebars, are reflections on the history and philosophy of software engineering and how thinking has progressed. These inserts provide helpful context to many of the ideas in this book.

Register your copy of *Modern Software Engineering* on the InformIT site for convenient access to updates and/or corrections as they become available. To start the registration process, go to informit.com/register and log in or create an account. Enter the product ISBN (9780137314911) and click Submit. Look on the Registered Products tab for an Access Bonus Content link next to this product, and follow that link to access any available bonus materials. If you would like to be notified of exclusive offers on new editions and updates, please check the box to receive email from us.

Acknowledgments

Writing a book like this takes a long time, a lot of work, and the exploration of numerous ideas. The people who helped me through that process helped me in all sorts of different ways, sometimes agreeing with me and reinforcing my convictions and sometimes disagreeing and forcing me either to strengthen my arguments or to change my mind.

I'd like to start by thanking my wife, Kate, who has helped me in all sorts of ways. Even though Kate is not a software professional, she read large parts of this book, helping me correct my grammar and hone my message.

I'd like to thank my brother in-law, Bernard McCarty, for bouncing ideas around on the topic of science and making me dig deeper to think about why I wanted to talk about experimentation and empiricism as well as lots of other things.

I'd like to thank Trisha Gee for not only writing such a nice foreword, but also being enthusiastic about this book when I needed a boost.

I'd like to thank Martin Thompson for always being there to bounce around opinions on computer science and for usually responding to my rather random thoughts in minutes.

I'd like to thank Martin Fowler, who despite being over-committed to other projects, gave me advice that helped to strengthen this book.

Many more of my friends have contributed indirectly over the years to help me shape my thinking on these topics, and many more: Dave Hounslow, Steve Smith, Chris Smith, Mark Price, Andy Stewart, Mark Crowther, Mike Barker, and many others.

I'd like to thank the team at Pearson for their help and support through the publication process of this book.

I would also like to thank a whole bunch of people—not all of whom I know—who have been supportive, argumentative, challenging, and thoughtful. I have bounced many of these ideas around on Twitter and on my YouTube channel for some years now and have been involved in some great conversations as a result. Thank you!

About the Author

David Farley is a pioneer of continuous delivery, thought leader, and expert practitioner in continuous delivery, DevOps, TDD, and software development in general.

Dave has been a programmer, software engineer, systems architect, and leader of successful teams for many years, from the early days of modern computing, taking those fundamental principles of how computers and software work and shaping groundbreaking, innovative approaches that have changed how we approach modern software development. He has challenged conventional thinking and led teams to build world-class software.

Dave is co-author of the Jolt award-winning book *Continuous Delivery*, is a popular conference speaker, and runs the highly successful and popular "Continuous Delivery" YouTube channel on the topic of software engineering. He built one of the world's fastest financial exchanges and is a pioneer of BDD, an author of the Reactive Manifesto, and a winner of the Duke award for open source software with the LMAX Disruptor.

Dave is passionate about helping development teams around the world improve the design, quality, and reliability of their software by sharing his expertise through his consultancy, YouTube channel, and training courses.

Twitter:	@davefarley77
YouTube Channel:	https://bit.ly/CDonYT
Blog:	http://www.davefarley.net
Company Website:	https://www.continuous-delivery.co.uk

I

WHAT IS SOFTWARE ENGINEERING?

Introduction

Engineering—The Practical Application of Science

Software development is a process of discovery and exploration; therefore, to succeed at it, software engineers need to become experts **at learning**.

Humanity's best approach to learning is science, so we need to adopt the techniques and strategies of science and apply them to our problems. This is often misunderstood to mean that we need to become physicists measuring things to unreasonable, in the context of software, levels of precision. Engineering is more pragmatic than that.

What I mean when I say we should apply the techniques and strategies of science is that we should apply some pretty basic, but nevertheless extremely important, ideas.

The scientific method that most of us learned about in school is described by Wikipedia as:

- **Characterize**: Make an observation of the current state.

- **Hypothesize**: Create a description, a theory that may explain your observation.

- **Predict**: Make a prediction based on your hypothesis.

- **Experiment**: Test your prediction.

When we organize our thinking this way and start to make progress on the basis of many small, informal experiments, we begin to limit our risk of jumping to inappropriate conclusions and end up doing a better job.

If we start to think in terms of controlling the variables in our experiments so that we can achieve more consistency and reliability in our results, this leads us in the direction of more deterministic systems and code. If we start to think in terms of being skeptical about our ideas and explore how we could falsify them, we can identify, and then eliminate, bad ideas more quickly and make progress much faster.

This book is deeply grounded in a practical, pragmatic approach to solving problems in software, based on an informal adoption of basic scientific principles, in other words, **engineering!**

What Is Software Engineering?

My working definition for software engineering that underpins the ideas in this book is this:

> *Software engineering* is the application of an empirical, scientific approach to finding efficient, economic solutions to practical problems in software.

The adoption of an engineering approach to software development is important for two main reasons. First, software development is always an exercise in discovery and learning, and second, if our aim is to be "efficient" and "economic," then our ability to learn must be sustainable.

This means that we must manage the complexity of the systems that we create in ways that maintain our ability to learn new things and adapt to them.

So, we must become **experts at learning and experts at managing complexity**.

There are five techniques that form the roots of this focus on learning. Specifically, to become *experts at learning*, we need the following:

- Iteration
- Feedback
- Incrementalism
- Experimentation
- Empiricism

This is an evolutionary approach to the creation of complex systems. Complex systems don't spring fully formed from our imaginations. They are the product of many small steps, where we try out our ideas and react to success and failure along the way. These are the tools that allow us to accomplish that exploration and discovery.

Working this way imposes constraints on how we can safely proceed. We need to be able to work in ways that facilitate the journey of exploration that is at the heart of every software project.

So as well as having a laser-focus on learning, we need to work in ways that allow us to make progress when the answers, and sometimes even the direction, is uncertain.

For that we need to become **experts at managing complexity**. Whatever the nature of the problems that we solve or the technologies that we use to solve them, addressing the complexity of the problems that face us and the solutions that we apply to them is a central differentiator between bad systems and good.

To become **experts at managing complexity**, we need the following:

- Modularity

- Cohesion

- Separation of Concerns

- Abstraction

- Loose Coupling

It is easy to look at these ideas and dismiss them as familiar. Yes, you are almost certainly familiar with all of them. The aim of this book is to organize them and place them into a coherent approach to developing software systems that helps you take best advantage of their potential.

This book describes how to use these ten ideas as tools to steer software development. It then goes on to describe a series of ideas that act as practical tools to drive an effective strategy for any software development. These ideas include the following:

- Testability

- Deployability

- Speed

- Controlling the variables

- Continuous delivery

When we apply this thinking, the results are profound. We create software of higher quality, we produce work more quickly, and the people working on the teams that adopt these principles report that they enjoy their work more, feel less stress, and have a better work-life balance.[1]

These are extravagant claims, but again they are backed by the data.

Reclaiming "Software Engineering"

I struggled over the title of this book, not because I didn't know what I wanted to call it, but because our industry has so redefined what *engineering* means in the context of software that the term has become devalued.

In software it is often seen as either simply a synonym for "code" or something that puts people off as being overly bureaucratic and procedural. For true engineering, nothing could be further from the truth.

---

1. Based on findings from the "State of DevOps" reports as well as reports from Microsoft and Google

In other disciplines, *engineering* simply means the "stuff that works." It is the process and practice that you apply to increase your chances of doing a good job.

If our "software engineering" practices don't allow us to build better software faster, then they aren't really engineering, and we should change them!

That is the fundamental idea at the heart of this book, and its aim is to describe an intellectually consistent model that pulls together some foundational principles that sit at the roots of all great software development.

There is never any guarantee of success, but by adopting these mental tools and organizing principles and applying them to your work, you will certainly increase your chances of success.

How to Make Progress

Software development is a complex, sophisticated activity. It is, in some ways, one of the more complex activities that we, as a species, undertake. It is ridiculous to assume that every individual or even every team can, and should, invent how to approach it, from scratch, every time we begin a new piece of work.

We have learned, and continue to learn, things that work and things that don't. So how can we, as an industry and as teams, make progress and build on the shoulders of giants, as Isaac Newton once said, if everyone has a veto on everything? We need some agreed principles and some discipline that guides our activities.

The danger in this line of thinking is that, if misapplied, it can lead to draconian, overly directive, "decision from authority"–style thinking.

We will fall back on previous bad ideas, where the job of managers and leaders is assumed to be to tell everyone else what to do and how to do it.

The big problem with being "proscriptive" or overly "directive" is, what do we do if some of our ideas are wrong or incomplete? They inevitably will be, so how can we challenge and refute old, but well-established, bad ideas and evaluate novel, potentially great, untried ideas?

We have a very strong example of how to solve these problems. It's an approach that allows us the intellectual freedom to challenge and refute dogma and to differentiate between fashion, plain-old bad ideas and great ones, whatever their source. It allows us to replace the bad ideas with better ideas and to improve on the good ideas. Fundamentally we need some structure that allows us to grow and to evolve improved approaches, strategies, processes, technologies, and solutions. We call this good example *science*!

When we apply this kind of thinking to solving practical problems, we call it *engineering*!

This book is about what it means to apply scientific-style reasoning to our discipline and so achieve something that we can genuinely and accurately refer to as *software engineering*.

The Birth of Software Engineering

Software engineering as a concept was created at the end of the 1960s. The term was first used by Margaret Hamilton who later became the director of the Software Engineering Division of the MIT Instrumentation Lab. Margaret was leading the effort to develop the flight-control software for the Apollo space program.

During the same period, the North Atlantic Treaty Organization (NATO) convened a conference in Garmisch-Partenkirchen, Germany, to try to define the term. This was the first **software engineering** conference.

The earliest computers had been programmed by flipping switches, or even hard-coded as part of their design. It quickly became clear to the pioneers that this was slow and inflexible, and the idea of the "stored program" was born. This is the idea that, for the first time, made a clear distinction between software and hardware.

By the late 1960s, computer programs had become complex enough to make them difficult to create and maintain in their own right. They were involved in solving more complex problems and were rapidly becoming the enabling step that allowed certain classes of problems to be solved at all.

There was perceived to be a significant gap between the rate at which progress was being made in hardware compared to the rate at which it was being made in software. This was referred to, at the time, as the *software crisis*.

The NATO conference was convened, in part, in response to this crisis.

Reading the notes from the conference today, there are many ideas that are clearly durable. They have stood the test of time and are as true today as they were in 1968. That should be interesting to us, if we aspire to identify some fundamental characteristics that define our discipline.

A few years later, looking back, Turing award–winner Fred Brooks compared the progress in software with that in hardware:

> *There is no single development, in either technology or management technique, which by itself promises even one order of magnitude improvement within a decade in productivity, in reliability, in simplicity.*[2]

Brooks was saying this in comparison with the famous Moore's law,[3] which hardware development had been tracking for many years.

---

2. Source: Fred Brooks' 1986 paper called "No Silver Bullet." See https:// bit.ly/2UalM4T.

3. In 1965, Gordon Moore predicted that transistor densities (not performance) would double every year, later revised to every two years, for the next decade (to 1975). This prediction became a target for semiconductor producers and significantly exceeded Moore's expectations, being met for several more decades. Some observers believe that we are reaching the end of this explosive growth in capacity, because of the limitations of the current approaches and the approach of quantum effects, but at the time of writing, high-density semiconductor development continues to track Moore's law.

This is an interesting observation and one that, I think, would surprise many people, but in essence it has always been true.

Brooks goes on to state that this is not so much a problem of software development; it is much more an observation on the unique, staggering improvement in hardware performance:

> We must observe that the anomaly is not that software progress is so slow but that computer hardware progress is so fast. No other technology since civilization began has seen six orders of magnitude price-performance gain in 30 years.

He wrote this in 1986, what we would today think of as the dawn of the computer age. Progress in hardware since then has continued at this pace, and the computers that seemed so powerful to Brooks look like toys compared to the capacity and performance of modern systems. And yet...his observation on the rate of improvement in software development remains true.

Shifting the Paradigm

The idea of *paradigm shift* was created by physicist Thomas Kuhn.

Most learning is a kind of accretion. We build up layers of understanding, with each layer foundationally under-pinned by the previous one.

However, not all learning is like that. Sometimes we fundamentally change our perspective on something, and that allows us to learn new things, but that also means we must discard what went before.

In the 18th century, reputable biologists (they weren't called that then) believed that some animals spontaneously generated themselves. Darwin came along in the middle of the 19th century and described the process of natural selection, and this overturned the idea of spontaneous generation completely.

This change in thinking ultimately led to our modern understanding of genetics and our ability to understand life at a more fundamental level, create technologies that allow us to manipulate these genes, and create COVID-19 vaccines and genetic therapies.

Similarly, Kepler, Copernicus, and Galileo challenged the then conventional wisdom that Earth was at the center of the universe. They instead proposed a heliocentric model for the solar system. This ultimately led to Newton creating laws of gravitation and Einstein creating general relativity, and it allowed us to travel in space and create technologies like GPS.

The idea of paradigm shift implicitly includes the idea that when we make such a shift, we will, as part of that process, discard some other ideas that we now know are no longer correct.

The implications of treating software development as a genuine engineering discipline, rooted in the philosophy of the scientific method and scientific rationalism, are profound.

It is profound not only in its impact and effectiveness, described so eloquently in the *Accelerate Book*,[4] but also in the essential need to discard the ideas that this approach supersedes.

This gives us an approach to learning more effectively and discarding bad ideas more efficiently.

I believe that the approach to software development that I describe in this book represents such a paradigm shift. It provides us with a new perspective on what it is that we do and how we do it.

Summary

Applying this kind of engineering thinking to software does not need to be heavyweight or overly complex. The paradigm shift in thinking differently about what it is that we do, and how we do it, when we create software should help us to see the wood for the trees and make this simpler, more reliable, and more efficient.

This is not about more bureaucracy; it is about enhancing our ability to create high-quality software more sustainably and more reliably.

---

4. The people behind the "State of DevOps" reports, DORA, described the predictive model that they have created from their research. Source: *Accelerate: The Science of Lean Software and DevOps* by Nicole Fosgren, Jez Humble, and Gene Kim (2018)

2

What Is Engineering?

I have been talking to people about software engineering for some years now. As a result I regularly get involved in a surprising number of conversations about bridge building. They usually start with the phrase "Yes, but software isn't bridge building" as though this was some kind of revelation.

Of course, software engineering is not the same as bridge building, but what most software developers think of as bridge building isn't like real bridge building, either. This conversation is really a form of confusion between production engineering and design engineering.

Production engineering is a complex problem when the discipline involved is dealing with physical things. You need to get those physical things created to certain levels of precision and quality.

You need your widgets delivered to some specific location in space, at a particular time, to a defined budget, and so on. You need to adapt theoretical ideas to practical reality as your models and designs are found to be lacking.

Digital assets are completely different. Although there are some analogs to these problems, for digital artifacts these problems either don't really exist or can be made trivially simple. The cost of production of digital assets of any kind is essentially free, or at least should be.

Production Is Not Our Problem

For most human endeavor, the production of "things" is the hard part. It may take effort and ingenuity to design a car, an airliner, or a mobile phone, but taking that initial prototype design and idea into mass production is immensely more expensive and complicated.

This is particularly true if we aim to do it with any kind of efficiency. As a result of these difficulties, we, products of the industrial age and industrial age thinking, automatically, almost unthinkingly, worry about this aspect, the production, of any significant task.

The result of this, in software, has been that we have fairly consistently tried to apply "production-style thinking" to our industry. Waterfall[1] processes are production lines for software. They are the tools of mass production. They are not the tools of discovery, learning, and experimentation that are, or at least should be, at the heart of our profession.

Unless we are foolish in our software development choices, for us, production consists of triggering the build!

It is automatic, push-button, immensely scalable and so cheap that it is best considered free. We can still make mistakes and get it wrong, but these are problems that are understood and well addressed by tools and technology.

"Production" is not our problem. This makes our discipline unusual. It also makes it subject to easy misunderstanding and misapplied thinking and practices, because this ease of production is so unusual.

Design Engineering, Not Production Engineering

Even in the real world, what most people think of as "bridge building" is different if the bridge-builders are building the first of a new kind of bridge. In this circumstance you have two problems: one that is relevant to software development and one that is not.

First, the one that is not—when building even the first of a new kind of bridge, because it is physical, you have all of the production problems, and many more, that I mentioned. From a software perspective, these can be ignored.

The second, in the case of bridge-building, is that in addition to those production problems, if you are building the first of a new kind of bridge, the second really difficult part is the design of your new bridge.

This is difficult because you can't iterate quickly when your product is something physical. When building physical things, they are difficult to change.

As a result, engineers in other disciplines adopt modeling techniques. They may choose to build small physical models, and these days probably computer simulations of their design or mathematical models of various kinds.

In this respect, we software developers have an enormous advantage. A bridge-builder may create a computer simulation of their proposed design, but this will only be an approximation of the real thing. Their simulation, their model, will be inaccurate. The models that we create as software, our computer simulations of a problem, are our product.

---

1. Waterfall, as applied to software development, is a staged, sequential approach to organizing work by breaking it down into a series of distinct phases with well-defined handovers between each phase. The idea is that you tackle each phase in turn, rather than iterate.

We don't need to worry if our models match reality; our models are the reality of our system, so we can verify them. We don't need to worry about the cost of changing them. They are software; thus, they are dramatically easier to change, at least when compared to a bridge.

Ours is a technical discipline. We like to think of ourselves in this context, and my guess is that the majority of people who think of themselves as professional software developers probably have had some science in their education.

Despite this, little software development is practiced with scientific rationalism in mind. In part, this is because we took some missteps in our history. In part this is because we assume that science is hard, expensive, and impossible to achieve within the scope of normal software development schedules.

Part of the mistake here is to assume some level of idealistic precision that is impossible in any field, let alone the field of software development. We have made the mistake of seeking mathematical precision, which is not the same thing as engineering!

Engineering as Math

During the late 1980s and early 1990s there was a lot of talk about more programming-structural ideas. The thinking about the meaning of software engineering moved on to examine the ways in which we work to generate the code. Specifically, how could we work in ways that are more effective at identifying and eliminating problems in our designs and implementations?

Formal methods became a popular idea. Most university courses, at the time, would teach formal methods. A formal method is an approach to building software systems that has, built into it, a mathematical validation of the code written. The idea is that the code is proven to be correct.

The big problem with this is that while it is hard to write code for a complex system, it is even harder to write code that defines the behavior of a complex system and that also proves itself to be correct.

Formal methods are an appealing idea, but pragmatically they haven't gained widespread adoption in general software development practice because at the point of production, they make the code harder to produce, not less.

A more philosophical argument is a little different, though. Software is unusual stuff; it clearly appeals to people who often also enjoy mathematical thinking. So the appeal of taking a mathematical approach to software is obvious, but also somewhat limiting.

Consider a real-world analogy. Modern engineers will use all the tools at their disposal to develop a new system. They will create models and simulations and crunch the numbers to figure out if their system will work. Their work is heavily informed by mathematics, but then they will try it out for real.

In other engineering disciplines, math is certainly an important tool, but it doesn't replace the need to test and to learn empirically from real-world experience. There is too much variance in the real world to completely predict an outcome. If math alone was enough to design an airplane, then that is what aerospace companies would do, because it would be cheaper than building real prototypes, but they don't do that. Instead, they use math extensively to inform their thinking, and then they check their thinking by testing a real device. Software is not quite the same as an airplane or a space rocket.

Software is digital and runs on mostly deterministic devices called *computers*. So for some narrow contexts, if the problem is simple enough, constrained enough, deterministic enough, and the variability low enough, then formal methods can prove a case. The problem here is the degree to which the system as a whole is deterministic. If the system is concurrent anywhere, interacts with the "real world" (people) anywhere, or is just working in a sufficiently complex domain, then the "provability" quickly explodes to become impractical.

So, instead, we take the same course as our aerospace colleagues, apply mathematical thinking where we can, and take a data-driven, pragmatic, empirical, experimental approach to learning, allowing us to adapt our systems as we grow them incrementally.

As I write this book, SpaceX is busy blowing up rockets while it works to perfect Starship.[2] It has certainly built mathematical models of nearly every aspect of the design of its rockets, its engines, the fuel delivery systems, launch infrastructure, and everything else, but then it tests them.

Even something seemingly simple, like switching from 4mm stainless steel to 3mm stainless steel, may sound like a pretty controlled change. SpaceX has access to detailed data on the tensile strength of the metal. It has experience and data collected from tests that show exactly how strong pressure vessels constructed from the 4mm steel are.

Yet still, after SpaceX crunched the numbers, it built experimental prototypes to evaluate the difference. It pressurized these test pieces to destruction to see if the calculations were accurate and to gain deeper insight. SpaceX collected data and validated its models because these models will certainly be wrong in some esoteric, difficult-to-predict way.

The remarkable advantage that we have over all other engineering disciplines means that the models that we create in software are the executable result of our work, so when we test them, we are testing our products, not our best guess of the reality of our products.

If we work carefully to isolate the part of the system that we are interested in, we can evaluate it in exactly the same environment that it will be exposed to in production. So our experimental simulation can much more precisely and much more accurately represent the "real world" of our systems than in any other discipline.

---

2. At the time of writing, SpaceX is developing a new fully reusable spacecraft. SpaceX's intent is to create a system that will allow people to journey to and live on Mars as well as explore other parts of the solar system. It has adopted an intentionally fast, iterative style of engineering to rapidly create and evaluate a series of fast-to-produce prototypes. This is design engineering in extreme form at the limits of engineering knowledge and presents a fascinating example of what it takes to create something new.

In his excellent talk called "Real Software Engineering,"[3] Glenn Vanderburg says that in other disciplines "Engineering means stuff that works" and that almost the opposite has become true for software.

Vanderburg goes on to explore why this is the case. He describes an academic approach to software engineering that was so onerous that almost no one who had practiced it would recommend it for future projects.

It was heavyweight and added no significant value to the process of software development at all. In a telling phrase, Vanderburg says:

> *[Academic software engineering] only worked because sharp people, who cared, were willing to circumvent the process.*

That is not engineering by any sensible definition.

Vanderburg's description of "engineering as the stuff that works" is important. If the practices that we choose to identify as "engineering" don't allow us to make better software faster, then they don't qualify as engineering!

Software development, unlike all physical production processes, is wholly an exercise in discovery, learning, and design. Our problem is one of exploration, and so we, even more than the spaceship designers, should be applying the techniques of exploration rather than the techniques of production engineering. Ours is solely a discipline of design engineering.

So if our understanding of engineering is often confused, what is engineering really about?

The First Software Engineer

During the period when Margaret Hamilton was leading the development of the Apollo flight control systems, there were no "rules of the game" to follow. She said, "We evolved our 'software engineering' rules with each new relevant discovery, while top management rules from NASA went from "'complete freedom'" to "'bureaucratic overkill.'"

There was very little experience of such complex projects to call on at this time. So the team was often breaking new ground. The challenges facing Hamilton and her team were profound, and there was no looking up the answers on Stack Overflow in the 1960s.

Hamilton described some of the challenges:

> *The space mission software had to be man-rated. Not only did it have to work, it had to work the first time. Not only did the software itself have to be ultra-reliable, it needed to be able to perform error detection and recovery in real time. Our languages dared us to make the most subtle of errors. We were on our own to come up with rules for building software. What we learned from the errors was full of surprises.*

---

3. https://youtu.be/RhdlBHHimeM

At the same time, software in general was looked down on as a kind of "poor relation" compared to other, more "grown-up" forms of engineering. One of the reasons that Hamilton coined the term *software engineering* was to try to get people in other disciplines to take the software more seriously.

One of the driving forces behind Hamilton's approach was the focus on how things fail—the ways in which we get things wrong.

> *There was a fascination on my part with errors, a never ending pass-time of mine was what made a particular error, or class of errors, happen and how to prevent it in the future.*

This focus was grounded in a scientifically rational approach to problem-solving. The assumption was not that you could plan and get it right the first time, rather that you treated all ideas, solutions, and designs with skepticism until you ran out of ideas about how things could go wrong. Occasionally, reality is still going to surprise you, but this is engineering empiricism at work.

The other engineering principle that is embodied in Hamilton's early work is the idea of "failing safely." The assumption is that we can never code for every scenario, so how do we code in ways that allow our systems to cope with the unexpected and still make progress? Famously it was Hamilton's unasked-for implementation of this idea that saved the Apollo 11 mission and allowed the Lunar Module Eagle to successfully land on the moon, despite the computer becoming overloaded during the descent.

As Neil Armstrong and Buzz Aldrin descended in the Lunar Excursion Module (LEM) toward the moon, there was an exchange between the astronauts and mission control. As the LEM neared the surface of the moon, the computer reported 1201 and 1202 alarms. The astronauts asked whether they should proceed or abort the mission.

NASA hesitated until one of the engineers shouted "Go!" because he understood what had happened to the software.

> *On Apollo 11, each time a 1201 or 1202 alarm appeared, the computer rebooted, restarted the important stuff, like steering the descent engine and running the DSKY to let the crew know what was going on, but did not restart all the erroneously-scheduled rendezvous radar jobs. The NASA guys in the MOCR knew—because MIT had extensively tested the restart capability—that the mission could go forward.[4]*

This "fail safe" behavior was coded into the system, without any specific prediction of when or how it would be useful.

So Hamilton and her team introduced two key attributes of a more engineering-led style of thinking, with empirical learning and discovery and the habit of imagining how things could possibly go wrong.

---

4. Source: "Peter Adler" (https://go.nasa.gov/1AKbDei)

A Working Definition of Engineering

Most dictionary definitions of the word *engineering* include common words and phrases: "application of math," "empirical evidence," "scientific reasoning," "within economic constraints."

I propose the following working definition:

> *Engineering is the application of an empirical, scientific approach to finding efficient, economic solutions to practical problems.*

All of the words here matter. Engineering is applied science. It is practical. Using "empirical" means to learn and advance understanding and solutions toward the resolution of a problem.

The solutions that engineering creates are not abstract ivory-tower things; they are practical and applicable to the problem and the context.

They are efficient, and they are created with an understanding of, and constrained by, the economics of the situation.

Engineering != Code

Another common misperception of what *engineering* means when it comes to software development is that engineering is only the output—the code or perhaps its design.

This is too narrow an interpretation. What does engineering mean to SpaceX? It is not the rockets; they are the products of engineering. Engineering is the process of creating them. There is certainly engineering in the rockets, and they are certainly "engineered structures," but we don't see only the act of welding the metal as engineering unless we have a weirdly narrow view of the topic.

If my definition works, then engineering is about applying scientific rationalism to solving problems. It is the "solving of the problems" where the engineering really comes to play, not just the solutions themselves. It is the processes, tools, and techniques. It is the ideas, philosophy, and approach that together make up an engineering discipline.

I had an unusual experience while writing this book: I published a video about the failure of a game on my YouTube channel, which was dramatically more popular than most of my videos.

The most common negative feedback I got, in saying that this was a "failure of software engineering," was that I was blaming programmers and not their managers. I meant that it was a failure in the whole approach to producing software. The planning was bad, the culture was bad, the code was bad (lots of bugs apparently).

So, for this book, when I talk about engineering, unless I qualify it specifically, I mean **everything that it takes to make software**. Process, tools, culture—all are part of the whole.

The Evolution of Programming Languages

Early efforts in software engineering were focused primarily on creating better languages in which to program things. The first computers made little or no separation between hardware and software. They were programmed by plugging wires into patch boards or flipping switches.

Interestingly, this job was often given to "computers," often women, who had previously done the computation (math) before the computer (as a machine) arrived.

This underplays their role, though. The "program" at this point, specified by someone "more important" in the organization, was often of the form "we'd like to solve this mathematical problem." The organization of the work, and later the specifics of how to translate that into appropriate machine-settings, was left to these human "computers." These were the real pioneers of our discipline!

We would use a different language to describe these activities today. We would describe the description passed to the people doing the work as *requirements*, the act of forming a plan to solve the problem as *programming*, and the "computers" as the first real *programmers* of these early electronic computer systems.

The next big step was to move to "stored programs" and their encoding. This was the era of paper tape and punched cards. The first steps on the adoption of this storage media for programs was still pretty hardcore. Programs were written in machine code and stored on tape, or card, before being fed into the machines.

High-level languages that could capture ideas at a higher level of abstraction were the next major advance. This allowed programmers to make progress much more quickly.

By the early 1980s, nearly all the foundational concepts in language design had been covered. That doesn't mean there was no progress after this, but most of the big ideas had been covered. Nevertheless, software development's focus on language as a core idea in our discipline has continued.

There were several significant steps that certainly affected the productivity of programmers, but probably only one step gave, or came close to giving, Fred Brooks 10x improvement. That was the step from machine code to high-level languages.

Other steps along this evolutionary path were significant, such as procedural programming, object orientation, and functional programming, but all of these ideas have been around for a very long time.

Our industry's obsession with languages and tools has been damaging to our profession. This doesn't mean that there are no advances to be had in language design, but most work in language design seems to concentrate on the wrong kinds of things, such as syntactic advances rather that structural advances.

In the early days, certainly, we needed to learn and explore what is possible and what made sense. Since then, though, a lot of effort has been expended for relatively little progress. When Fred Brooks said there were no 10x improvements, the rest of his paper was focused on what we could do to overcome this limitation:

> The first step toward the management of disease was replacement of demon theories, and humors theories, by the germ theory. That very step, the beginning of hope, in itself dashed all hopes of magical solutions.

> ...the system should first be made to run, even though it does nothing useful except call the proper set of dummy subprograms. Then, bit-by-bit it is fleshed out, with the subprograms in turn being developed into actions or calls to empty stubs in the level below.

These ideas were based on deeper, more profound ideas than trivial details of language implementation.

These were issues more to do with the philosophy of our discipline and the application of some foundational principles that hold true whatever the nature of the technology.

Why Does Engineering Matter?

Another way to think of this is to consider how we go about the production of the things that help us. For the vast majority of human history, everything that we created was the product of craft. Craft is an effective approach to creating things, but it has its limits.

Craft is very good at creating "one-off" items. In a craft-based production system, each item will, inevitably, be unique. In its purest sense this is true of any production system, but in craft-based approaches this is more true because the precision, and so the repeatability, of the production process is generally low.

This means that the amount of variance between individually crafted artifacts is higher. Even the most masterful of craftspeople will create items with only human levels of precision and tolerance. This seriously impacts the ability of craft-based systems to reproduce things reliably. Grace Hopper said:

> To me programming is more than an important practical art. It is also a gigantic undertaking in the foundations of knowledge.

The Limits of "Craft"

We often have an emotional reaction to craft-based production. As human beings we like the variance; we like the feeling that our treasured, hand-crafted thing embodies the skill, love, and care of the craftsperson who created it.

However, at the root, craft-based production is fundamentally low-quality. A human being, however talented, is not as accurate as a machine.

We can build machines that can manipulate individual atoms, even subatomic particles, but a human being is extraordinarily talented if they can produce something, manually, with the accuracy of 1/10 of a millimeter.[5]

How does this precision matter in software? Let us think about what happens when our programs are executed. A human being can perceive change, any change, at the limit of approximately 13 milliseconds. To process an image or to react to something takes hundreds of milliseconds.[6]

At the time of writing, most modern consumer-level computers operate on a clock cycle of around 3GHz. That is 3 billion cycles per second. Modern computers are multicore and operate on instructions in parallel, so often they process more than one instruction per cycle, but let us ignore that and imagine, for simplicity, that each machine instruction that moves values between registers, adds them or references some in-cache piece of memory, takes a single clock cycle.

That is 3 billion operations per second. If we do the math and calculate how many instructions a modern computer can crunch through in the absolute minimum time that a human being could perceive any external event, that number is 39,000,000 instructions!

If we limit the quality of our work to human-scale perception and accuracy, we are, at the very best, sampling what is going on at a rate of 1:(39 million). So, what are our chances of us missing something?

Precision and Scalability

This difference between craft and engineering highlights two aspects of engineering that are important in the context of software: precision and scalability.

Precision is obvious: we can manipulate things at a much higher resolution of detail, through the application of engineering techniques, than by hand. Scalability is perhaps less immediately obvious but is even more important. An engineering approach is not limited in the same way that a craft-based approach is.

The limits of any approach that relies on human capability is, ultimately, limited by human capability. If I dedicate myself to achieving something extraordinary, I may learn to paint a line, file a piece of metal, or stitch leather car seats to within tiny fractions of a millimeter, but however hard I try, however gifted I may be, there are hard limits to how accurate human muscles and senses can be.

An engineer, though, can create a machine to make something smaller and more precise. We can build machines (tools) to make smaller machines.

This technique is scalable all the way down to the limits of quantum physics and all the way up to the limits of cosmology. There is nothing, at least in theory, to prevent us, via the application of

---

5. Atoms vary in size but are usually measured in tens of picometers (1 x 10^-12m). So, the best of human handcraft is 10 million times less accurate than a good machine.

6. "How Fast is Real-time? Human Perception and Technology," https://bit.ly/2Lb7pL1

engineering, to manipulate atoms and electrons (as we already do) or stars and blackholes (as we may do one day).

To put this more clearly into the context of software, if we are very skilled and train very hard, we could perhaps enter text and click buttons quickly enough to test our software at a rate where we could imagine being able to carry out a test of our software in a few minutes. Let's imagine for the sake of comparison that we can carry out one test of our software every minute (not a pace that I can imagine myself being able to sustain for very long).

If we can run a test per minute, we are under-testing compared to a computer by hundreds of thousands, probably millions, of times.

I have built systems that ran around 30,000 test cases in about 2 minutes. We could have scaled that up considerably further but had no reason to do so. Google claims to run 150 million test executions per day. That works out to 104,166 tests per minute.[7]

Not only can we use our computers to test hundreds of thousands of times more quickly than a human being, we can sustain that pace for as long as we have electricity for our computers. That is scalable!

Managing Complexity

There is another way in which engineering scales, where craft does not. Engineering thinking tends to lead us to compartmentalize problems. Before the American Civil War in the 1860s, if you wanted a gun, you went to a gunsmith. The gunsmith was a craftsman, and he was usually a man!

The gunsmith would create a whole gun for you. He would understand every aspect of that gun, and it would be unique to you. He would probably give you a mold for your bullets, because your bullets would be different from everyone else's and specific to your gun. If your gun had screws, each one was almost certainly different from all of the others, because it would have been hand-made.

The American Civil War was unique in its day. It was the first war where arms were mass-produced.

There is a story of the man who wanted to sell rifles to the northern states. He was an innovator and, it seems, a bit of a showman. He went to Congress to make his case to get the contract to make the rifles for the armies of the northern states.

He took with him a sack full of rifle components. As part of his presentation to the Congressmen, he emptied the bag of components onto the floor of Congress and asked the Congressmen to select components from the pile. From these components he assembled a rifle, won the contract, and invented mass production.

This was the first time that this kind of standardization was possible. A lot of things had to happen to make it possible; machines (tools) had to be engineered to make components that were

---

7. "The State of Continuous Integration Testing at Google," https://bit.ly/3eLbAgB

repeatably identical to one another, within some defined tolerance. The design had to be modular so that the components could be assembled, and so on.

The result was devastating. The American Civil War was, in essence, the first modern war. Hundreds of thousands of people were killed because of the mass production of armaments. These arms were cheaper, easier to maintain and repair, and more accurate than those that had gone before.

All this was because they were engineered with more precision, but also because there were lots more of them. The process of production could be de-skilled and scaled up. Instead of needing an expert master craftsperson for each weapon, the machinery in the factory could allow less-skilled people to create rifles of comparable precision to a master.

Later, as tooling, production techniques, and engineering understanding and discipline increased, these mass-produced weapons exceeded the quality, as well as the productivity, of even the greatest master craftsmen, and at a price that anyone could afford.

A simplistic view may interpret this as a "need to standardize," or a need to adopt "mass production for software," but this is, once again, confusing the fundamental nature our problem. This is not about production—it is about design.

If we design a gun that is modular and componentized in the way that the arms manufacturers of the American Civil War did, then we can design parts of that gun more independently. Viewing this from a design perspective rather than from a production engineering or manufacturing perspective, we have improved our management of the complexity of building guns.

Before this step, the gunsmith master-craftsmen would need to think of the whole gun if they wanted to change some aspect of its design. By componentizing the design, the Civil War manufacturers could explore changes incrementally to improve the quality of their products step-by-step. Edsger Dijkstra said:

> The art of programming is the art of organizing complexity.

Repeatability and Accuracy of Measurement

The other aspect of engineering that is commonly seen, and is sometimes used to reject engineering as an idea applicable to software, is that of repeatability.

If we can build a machine to reliably and accurately reproduce a nut and bolt, we can churn them out, and all of the copies of bolts will work with any of the copies of nuts that are produced.

This is a production problem and not really applicable to software. However, the more fundamental idea that underpins this kind of capability is applicable to software.

To make nuts and bolts, or anything else, that needs to reliably work together, we need to be able to measure things with a certain level of precision. Accuracy in measurement is an enabling aspect of engineering in any discipline.

Let us for a moment imagine a complex software system. After a few weeks of operation, let's say the system fails. The system is restarted, and two weeks later it fails again in much the same way; there is a pattern. How would a craft-focused team cope with this compared to an engineering-focused team?

The crafty team will probably decide that what they need is to test the software more thoroughly. Because they are thinking in craft terms, what they want is to clearly observe the failure.

This isn't stupid; it makes sense in this context, but how to do it? The commonest solution that I have seen to this kind of problem is to create something called a *soak test*. The soak test will run for a bit longer than the normal time between failure, let's say three weeks for our example. Sometimes people will try to speed up time so that the soak will simulate the problem period in a shorter time, but usually not.

The test runs, the system fails the test after two weeks, and the bug is, eventually, identified and fixed.

Is there any alternative to this strategy? Well, yes!

Soak tests detect resource leaks of one form or another. There are two ways to detect leaks; you can wait for the leak to become obvious, or you can increase the precision of your measurement so you catch the leak early before it becomes catastrophic.

I had a leak in my kitchen recently. It was in a pipe, buried in concrete. We detected the leak once it had soaked the concrete sufficiently for water to start to puddle on the surface. This is the "obvious" detection strategy.

We got a professional in to help us fix the leak. He brought a tool, an engineered solution. It was a highly sensitive microphone that "listened" for the sound of the leak underground.

Using this tool, he could detect the faint hiss of leaking water buried in concrete with sufficient, super-human precision to allow him to identify the location within a few inches and dig a small trench to get at the defective piece of pipe.

So back to our example: the engineering-focused team will use accurate measurement rather than waiting for something bad to happen. They will measure the performance of their software to detect leaks before they become a problem.

This approach has multiple benefits; it means that catastrophic failure, in production, is largely avoided, but it also means that they can get an indication of a problem and valuable feedback on the health of their system much, much sooner. Instead of running a soak test for weeks, the engineering-focused team can detect leaks during regular testing of the system and get a result in a matter of minutes. David Parnas said:

> *Software engineering is often treated as a branch of computer science. This is akin to regarding chemical engineering as a branch of chemistry. We need both chemists and chemical engineers, but they are different.*

Engineering, Creativity, and Craft

To think about engineering in general and software engineering specifically, I have been exploring some of these ideas for a few years. I have spoken on this topic at software conferences and occasionally written on this topic in blog posts.

I sometimes get feedback from people who are adherents to the ideas of software craftsmanship. This feedback is usually of the form "You are missing something important in dismissing craftsmanship."

The ideas of software craftsmanship were important. They represented an important step away from the big-ceremony, production-centered approaches to software development that preceded them. It is not my contention that software craftsmanship is wrong, but rather that it is not enough.

In part, these debates begin from an incorrect premise, one that I have already mentioned. Many of these software craftspeople make the common mistake of assuming that all engineering is about solving production problems. I have already covered that issue; if our problem is "design engineering," then this is a very different, much more exploratory, creative discipline compared to "production engineering."

In addition, though, my software craftspeople interlocutors are concerned about the dangers of throwing away the gains that software craftsmanship has brought—namely, a focus on the following:

- Skill

- Creativity

- Freedom to innovate

- Apprentice schemes

These things are important to any effective, professional approach to software development. However, they are not limited to craft-based approaches. Software craftsmanship movement was an important step in improving software development by refocusing on things that were important, with the things in the previous list being some of those important things.

These ideas had become lost, or at least subsumed, by attempts through the 1980s and 1990s to force-fit some kind of command-and-control, production-centered approach onto software development. This was a terrible idea because although waterfall-style processes and thinking have a place in problems where the steps are well understood, repeatable, and predictable, this bears little or no relationship to the reality of software development.

Software craftsmanship was a much better fit for the type of problem that software development really is.

The problem with craft-based solutions to problems is that they are not scalable in the way that engineering-based solutions are.

Craft can produce good things, but only within certain bounds.

Engineering discipline in virtually all human endeavors increases quality, reduces costs, and generally provides more robust, resilient, and flexible solutions.

It is a big mistake to associate ideas like skill, creativity, and innovation only with craft. Engineers in general, but certainly design engineers, exhibit all of these qualities in abundance all of the time. These attributes are central to the process of design engineering.

So taking an engineering approach to solving problems does not, in any way, reduce the importance of skill, creativity, and innovation. If anything, it amplifies the need for these attributes.

As for training, I wonder if my software crafty friends believe that a new graduate engineer leaving university is immediately given responsibility to design a new bridge or a space shuttle? Of course not!

An engineer at the beginning of their career will work alongside more experienced engineers. They will learn the practicalities of their discipline, their craft, maybe even more so than a craftsperson would.

I see no tension here between craft and engineering. If you take the reasonably formal view of craftsmanship, with guilds, apprentices, journeymen, and master craftsmen, then engineering really was the next step on from that. As scientific rationalism took hold, following on from the enlightenment thinking of the 17th and 18th centuries, engineering was really craft enhanced with a bit more accuracy and measurement. Engineering is the more scalable, more effective offspring of craft.

If you take the more colloquial definitions of craft—think craft fair here—then there are no real standards for quality or progress, so engineering is, perhaps, more of a jump.

Engineering, specifically the application of engineering thinking to design, is really the difference between our high-tech civilization and the agrarian civilizations that preceded us. Engineering is a discipline that allows us to undertake staggeringly complex problems and find elegant, efficient solutions to them.

When we apply the principles of engineering thinking to software development, we see measurable, dramatic improvements in quality, productivity, and the applicability of our solutions.[8]

Why What We Do Is Not Software Engineering

In 2019, Elon Musk's company SpaceX made a big decision; it was working on creating spacecraft that will one day allow humans to live and work on Mars and explore other parts of the solar system. In 2019, it switched from building its Starships out of carbon fiber to building them from stainless steel instead. Carbon fiber was a pretty radical idea; they had done a lot of work, including building prototype fuel tanks from the material. Stainless steel was also a radical choice; most rockets are built from aluminum because of its lightness and strength.

The SpaceX choice of stainless steel over carbon fiber was based on three things: the cost per kilogram was dramatically lower for steel; the high-temperature performance, to cope with re-entry temperatures, was better than aluminum; the low-temperature, cryogenic performance was dramatically better than both of the alternatives.

---

8. *Accelerate Book* describes how teams that take a more disciplined approach to development spend "44% more time on new work" than teams that don't. See https://amzn.to/2YYf5Z8.

Carbon fiber and aluminum are significantly weaker than steel at very low and high temperatures.

When was the last time you heard anyone make a justification for a decision associated with software creation that sounded even vaguely like that?

This is what engineering decisions look like. They are based on rational criteria, strength at a certain temperature, or economic impact. It is still experimental, it is still iterative, it is still empirical.

You make a decision based on the evidence before you and your theory of what that will mean, and then you test your ideas to see if they work. It is not some perfectly predictable process.

SpaceX built test structures and then pressurized them, first with water and then with liquid nitrogen, so that they could test the cryogenic performance of the materials (steel) and of their manufacturing process. Design engineering is a deeply exploratory approach to gaining knowledge.

Trade-Offs

All engineering is a game of optimization and trade-offs. We are trying to attempt to solve some problem, and, inevitably, we will be faced with choices. In building their rockets, one of the biggest trade-offs for SpaceX is between strength and weight. This is a common problem for flying machines, and actually for most vehicles.

Understanding the trade-offs that we face is a vital, fundamental aspect of engineering decision-making.

If we make our system more secure, it will be more difficult to use; if we make it more distributed, we will spend more time integrating the information that it gathers. If we add more people to speed up development, we will increase the communication overhead, coupling, and complexity, all of which will slow us down.

One of the key trade-offs that is vital to consider in the production of software, at every level of granularity from whole enterprise systems to single functions, is coupling. (We will explore that in much more detail in Chapter 13.)

The Illusion of Progress

The level of change in our industry is impressive, but my thesis is that much of this change is not really significant.

As I write this, I am at a conference on the topic of serverless computing.[9] The move to serverless systems is an interesting one; however, the difference between the toolkits provided by AWS, Azure, Google, or anyone else doesn't really matter.

---

9. Serverless computing is a cloud-based approach to providing "functions as a service." Functions form the only unit of computing, and the code to run them is started up on demand.

The decision to adopt a serverless approach is going to have some implications for the design of your system. Where do you store state? Where do you manipulate it? How do you divide up the functions of your system? How do you organize and navigate complex systems when the unit of design is a function?

These questions are much more interesting and much more important to the success of your endeavor, whatever it may be, than the detail of how you specify a function or how you use the storage or security features of the platform. Yet nearly all of the presentations that I see on this topic are about the tools, not the design of systems.

This is as if I was a carpenter and was being told the important differences between a slot-headed screw and a cross-headed screw, but I was not being told what screws are useful for, when to use them, and when to choose nails.

Serverless computing does represent a step forward as a computing model. I don't question that. This book is about the ideas that allow us to judge which ideas are important and which are not.

Serverless is important for several reasons, but principally because it encourages a more **modular approach** to design with a better **separation of concerns**, particularly with respect to data.

Serverless computing changes the economics of systems by moving the calculation from "cost per byte" to "cost per CPU cycle." This means, or should mean, that we need to consider very different kinds of optimizations.

Instead of optimizing our systems to minimize storage, by having normalized data stores, we should probably be accepting a more genuinely distributed model of computing using non-normalized stores and eventual-consistency patterns. These things matter because of their impact on the modularity of the systems that we create.

The tools matter only to the degree to which they "move the dial" on some more fundamental things.

The Journey from Craft to Engineering

It is important not to dismiss the value of craft. The care and attention to detail are necessary to create work of high quality. It is also important not to dismiss the importance of engineering to amplifying the quality and effectiveness of the products of craft.

The first people to build a controllable, heavier-than-air, powered flying machine were the Wright Brothers. They were excellent craftsmen and excellent engineers. Much of their work was based on empirical discovery, but they also did real research into the effectiveness of their designs. As well as being the first people to construct a flying machine, they were the first people to build a wind tunnel to allow them to measure the effectiveness of their wing designs.

An airplane wing is a remarkable structure. The Wright brothers construction is a beautiful, though by modern standards incredibly crude, device. It is built of wood and wire and covered in cloth taughtened and made wind-proof by banana oil.

It and the wind tunnel were used to evolve their understanding of the basics of a theory of aerodynamics, building on the work of earlier pioneers. However, primarily, the Wright Brothers' flying machine in general, and wing in particular, was built through a process of trial and error more than pure theoretical design.

To modern eyes it looks like the product of craft more than engineering. This is partly, though not wholly, true. Many people had tried craft-based approaches to building a "flying machine" and failed. One of the important reasons for the success of the Wright Brothers was that they employed engineering. They did the calculations and created and used the tools of measurement and research. They controlled the variables so that they could deepen their understanding and refine their model of flight. Then they created models and gliders and wind-tunnel pieces to test and then grow their understanding. The principles that they established weren't perfect, but they improved on not just the practicalities, but also the theory.

By the time the Wright Brothers had achieved heavier-than-air-controllable-flight, their aerodynamic research allowed them to build flying machines with an 8.3:1 glide ratio.[10]

To compare this with a modern airplane wing, say the wing of a modern sailplane: The wing of the Wright Flyer was under-cambered (a slow high-lift airfoil), and it was heavy by modern standards, though of light construction in its day. It used simple natural materials and achieved this 8.3:1.

Through engineering, empirical discovery, and experimentation, as well as materials science, refining of aerodynamic theory, computer modeling, and so on, a modern sailplane will have a carbon fiber, high-aspect-ratio wing. It is optimized to be light and strong to the degree that you can clearly see it bend and flex as it generates lift. It can achieve glide ratios of more than 70:1, nearly nine times better than the Wright Flyer.

Craft Is Not Enough

Craft is important, particularly so if by *craft* you really mean creativity. Our discipline is a deeply creative endeavor, but so is engineering. I believe that engineering is actually the height of human creativity and ingenuity. That is the kind of thinking that we need if we aim to create great works in software.

Time for a Rethink?

The evolution of **software engineering** as a discipline has not really achieved what many people hoped for. Software has changed, and is changing, the world. There have been some wonderful pieces of work and innovative, interesting, and exciting systems built, but for many teams, organizations, and individual developers, it is not always clear how to succeed, or even how to make progress.

---

10. The glide ratio is one measure of the efficiency of a flying machine. The ratio is between distance traveled and height lost. For example, for every foot (or meter) that the plane descends in a (unpowered) glide, it will move forward 8.3 feet (or meters). See https://en.wikipedia.org/wiki/Lift-to-drag_ratio.

Our industry is awash with philosophies, practices, processes, and technologies. There are religious wars among technologists over the best programming languages, architectural approaches, development processes, and tools. There often seems to be only a loose sense of what the objectives and strategies of our profession are or should be.

Modern teams fight with schedule pressure, quality, and maintainability of their designs. They often struggle to identify the ideas that really land with users, and they fail to allow themselves the time to learn about the problem domain, the technology, and the opportunities to get something great into production.

Organizations often struggle to get what they want out of software development. They often complain about the quality and efficiency of development teams. They often misunderstand the things that they can do to help overcome these difficulties.

Meanwhile, I perceive a fairly deep level of agreement among the experts, whose opinions I value, about some fundamental ideas that are not often, or at least not clearly enough, stated.

Perhaps it is time to think again about what some of those fundamentals are. What are the principles that are common to our discipline? What are the ideas that will be true for decades, not just for the current generation of technical tools?

Software development is not a simple task, and it is not a homogeneous task. However, there are some practices that are generic. There are ways of thinking about, managing, organizing, and practicing software development that have a significant, even dramatic, impact on all of these problematic aspects of the endeavor.

The rest of this book is intended to explore some of these generic ideas and to provide a list of foundational principles that should be common to all software development, whatever the problem domain, whatever the tools, whatever the commercial or quality demands.

The ideas in this book seem to me to represent something deep, something fundamental, about the nature of our endeavor.

When we get these things right, and many teams do, we see greater productivity, less stress and burnout in team members, higher quality in design, and more resilience in the systems that we create.

The systems that we build please their users more. We see dramatically fewer bugs in production, and teams that employ these ideas find it significantly easier to change almost any aspect of the systems that they work on as their learning evolves. The bottom-line result of this is usually greater commercial success for the organizations that practice in this way. These attributes are the hallmarks of **engineering**.

Engineering amplifies our ability to be creative, to make useful things, to proceed with confidence and quality. It allows us to explore ideas and ultimately to scale our ability to create things so that we can build ever bigger, more complex systems.

We are at the birth of a genuine engineering discipline for software. We could, if we grasp this opportunity, begin to change the way in which software development is practiced, organized, and taught.

This may well be a generational change, but it is of such enormous value to the organizations that employ us, and to the world in general, that we must try. What if we could build software more quickly and more cost-effectively? What if that software was also higher quality, easier to maintain, more adaptable, more resilient, and a better fit for the needs of its users?

Summary

In software we have somewhat redefined what *engineering* means. Certainly in some circles we have come to see engineering as an unnecessary, onerous, and burdensome thing that gets in the way of "real software development." Real engineering in other disciplines is none of these things. Engineers in other disciplines make progress more quickly, not less. They create work of higher quality, not lower.

When we begin to adopt a practical, rational, lightweight, scientific approach to software development, we see similar benefits. Software engineering will be specific to software, but it will also help us to build better software faster, not get in the way of us doing that.

3

Fundamentals of an Engineering Approach

Engineering in different disciplines varies. Bridge building is not the same as aerospace engineering, and neither is it the same as electrical engineering or chemical engineering, but all of these disciplines share some common ideas. They are all firmly grounded in scientific rationalism and take a pragmatic, empirical approach to making progress.

If we are to achieve our goal of trying to define a collection of long-lasting thoughts, ideas, practices, and behaviors that we could collectively group together under the name *software engineering*, these ideas must be fairly fundamental to the reality of software development and robust in the face of change.

An Industry of Change?

We talk a lot about change in our industry. We get excited about new technologies and new products, but do these changes really "move the dial" on software development? Many of the changes that exercise us don't seem to make as much difference as we sometimes seem to think that they will.

My favorite example of this was demonstrated in a lovely conference presentation by "Christin Gorman."[1] In it, Christin demonstrates that when using the then popular open source object relational mapping library Hibernate, it was actually more code to write than the equivalent behavior written in SQL, subjectively at least; the SQL was also easier to understand. Christin goes on to amusingly contrast software development with making cakes. Do you make your cake with a cake mix or choose fresh ingredients and make it from scratch?

---

1. Source: "Gordon Ramsay Doesn't Use Cake Mixes" by Christin Gorman, https://bit.ly/3g02cWO

Much of the change in our industry is ephemeral and does not improve things. Some, like in the Hibernate example, actually make things worse.

My impression is that our industry struggles to learn and struggles to make progress. This relative lack of advancement has been masked by the incredible progress that has been made in the hardware on which our code runs.

I don't mean to imply that there has been no progress in software—far from it—but I do believe that the pace of progress is much slower than many of us think. Consider, for a moment, what changes in your career have had a significant impact on the way in which you think about and practice software development. What ideas made a difference to the quality, scale, or complexity of the problems that you can solve?

The list is shorter than we usually assume.

For example, I have employed something like 15 or 20 different programming languages during my professional career. Although I have preferences, only two changes in language have radically changed how I think about software and design.

Those steps were the step from Assembler to C and the step from procedural to OO programming. The individual languages are less important than the programming paradigm to my mind. Those steps represented significant changes in the level of abstraction that I could deal with in writing code. Each represented a step-change in the complexity of the systems that we could build.

When Fred Brooks wrote that there were no order-of-magnitude gains, he missed something. There may not be any 10x gains, but there are certainly 10x losses.

I have seen organizations that were hamstrung by their approach to software development, sometimes by technology, more often by process. I once consulted in a large organization that hadn't released any software into production for more than five years.

We not only seem to find it difficult to learn new ideas; we seem to find it almost impossible to discard old ideas, however discredited they may have become.

The Importance of Measurement

One of the reasons that we find it difficult to discard bad ideas is that we don't really measure our performance in software development very effectively.

Most metrics applied to software development are either irrelevant (velocity) or sometimes positively harmful (lines of code or test coverage).

In agile development circles it has been a long-held view that measurement of software team, or project performance, is not possible. Martin Fowler wrote about one aspect of this in his widely read Bliki in 2003.[2]

---

2. Source: "Cannot Measure Productivity" by Martin Fowler, https://bit.ly/3mDO2fB

Fowler's point is correct; we don't have a defensible measure for productivity, but that is not the same as saying that we can't measure anything useful.

The valuable work carried out by Nicole Fosgren, Jez Humble, and Gene Kim in the "State of DevOps" reports[3] and in their book *Accelerate: The Science of Lean Software & DevOps*[4] represents an important step forward in being able to make stronger, more evidence-based decisions. They present an interesting and compelling model for the useful measurement of the performance of software teams.

Interestingly, they don't attempt to measure productivity; rather, they evaluate the effectiveness of software development teams based on two key attributes. The measures are then used as a part of a predictive model. They cannot prove that these measures have a causal relationship with the performance of software development teams, but they can demonstrate a statistical correlation.

The measures are **stability** and **throughput**. Teams with high stability and high throughput are classified as "high performers," while teams with low scores against these measures are "low performers."

The interesting part is that if you analyze the activities of these high- and low-performing groups, they are consistently correlated. High-performing teams share common behaviors. Equally, if we look at the activities and behaviors of a team, we can predict their score, against these measures, and it too is correlated. Some activities can be used to predict performance on this scale.

For example, if your team employs test automation, trunk-based development, deployment automation, and about ten other practices, their model predicts that you will be practicing **continuous delivery**. If you practice continuous delivery, the model predicts that you will be "high performing" in terms of software delivery performance and organizational performance.

Alternatively, if we look at organizations that are seen as high performers, then there are common behaviors, such as continuous delivery and being organized into small teams, that they share.

Measures of stability and throughput, then, give us a model that we can use to predict team outcomes.

Stability and throughput are each tracked by two measures.

Stability is tracked by the following:

- **Change Failure Rate**: The rate at which a change introduces a defect at a particular point in the process

- **Recovery Failure Time**: How long to recover from a failure at a particular point in the process

---

3. Source: Nicole Fosgren, Jez Humble, Gene Kim, https://bit.ly/2PWyjw7

4. The *Accelerate Book* describes how teams that take a more disciplined approach to development spend "44% more time on new work" than teams that don't. See https://amzn.to/2YYf5Z8.

Measuring stability is important because it is really a measure of the quality of work done. It doesn't say anything about whether the team is building the right things, but it does measure that their effectiveness in delivering software with measurable quality.

Throughput is tracked by the following:

- **Lead Time**: A measure of the efficiency of the development process. How long for a single-line change to go from "idea" to "working software"?

- **Frequency**: A measure of speed. How often are changes deployed into production?

Throughput is a measure of a team's efficiency at delivering ideas, in the form of working software.

How long does it take to get a change into the hands of users, and how often is that achieved? This is, among other things, an indication of a team's opportunities to learn. A team may not take those opportunities, but without a good score in throughput, any team's chance of learning is reduced.

These are technical measures of our development approach. They answer the questions "what is the quality of our work?" and "how efficiently can we produce work of that quality?"

These are meaningful ideas, but they leave some gaps. They don't say anything about whether we are building the right things, only if we are building them right, but just because they aren't perfect does not diminish their utility.

Interestingly, the correlative model that I described goes further than predicting team size and whether you are applying continuous delivery. The *Accelerate* authors have data that shows significant correlations with much more important things.

For example, organizations made up of high-performing teams, based on this model, make more money than orgs that don't. Here is data that says that there is a correlation between a development approach and the commercial outcome for the company that practices it.

It also goes on to dispel a commonly held belief that "you can have either speed or quality but not both." This is simply not true. Speed and quality are clearly correlated in the data from this research. The route to speed is high-quality software, the route to high-quality software is speed of feedback, and the route to both is great engineering.

Applying Stability and Throughput

The correlation of good scores in these measures with high-quality results is important. It offers us an opportunity to use them to evaluate changes to our process, organization, culture, or technology.

Imagine, for example, that we are concerned with the quality of our software. How could we improve it? We could decide to make a change to our process. Let us add a change approval board (CAB).

Clearly the addition of extra review and sign-offs are going to adversely impact on throughput, and such changes will inevitably slow down the process. However, do they increase stability?

For this particular example the data is in. Perhaps surprisingly, change approval boards don't improve stability. However, the slowing down of the process does impact stability adversely.

> We found that external approvals were negatively correlated with lead-time, deployment frequency, and restore-time, and had no correlation with change fail rate. In short, approval by an external body (such as a manager or CAB) simply doesn't work to increase the stability of production systems, measured by time to restore service and change fail rate. However, it certainly slows things down. It is, in fact, worse than having no change approval process at all.[5]

My real point here is not to poke fun at change approval boards, but rather to show the importance of making decisions based on evidence rather than guesswork.

It is not obvious that CABs are a bad idea. They sound sensible, and in reality that is how many, probably most, organizations try to manage quality. The trouble is that it doesn't work.

Without effective measurement, we can't tell that it doesn't work; we can only make guesses.

If we are to start applying a more evidence-based, scientifically rational approach to decision-making, you shouldn't take my word, or the word of Forsgren and her co-authors, on this or anything else.

Instead, you could make this measurement for yourself, in your team. Measure the throughput and stability of your existing approach, whatever that may be. Make a change, whatever that may be. Does the change move the dial on either of these measures?

You can read more about this correlative model in the excellent *Accelerate* book. It describes the approach to measurement and the model that is evolving as research continues. My point here is not to duplicate those ideas, but to point out the important, maybe even profound, impact that this should have on our industry. **We finally have a useful measuring stick.**

We can use this model of stability and throughput to measure the effect of any change.

We can see the impact of changes in organization, process, culture, and technology. "If I adopt this new language, does it increase my throughput or stability?"

We can also use these measures to evaluate different parts of our process. "If I have a significant amount of manual testing, it is certainly going to be slower than automated testing, but does it improve stability?"

We still have to think carefully. We need to consider the meaning of the results. What does it mean if something reduces throughput but increases stability?

Nevertheless, having meaningful measures that allow us to evaluate actions is important, even vital, to taking a more evidence-based approach to decision-making.

---

5. *Accelerate* by Nicole Forsgren, Jez Humble, and Gene Kim, 2018

The Foundations of a Software Engineering Discipline

So, what are some of these foundational ideas? What are the ideas that we could expect to be correct in 100 years' time and applicable whatever our problem and whatever our technology?

There are two categories: process, or maybe even philosophical approach, and technique or design.

More simply, our discipline should focus on two core competencies.

We should become **experts at learning**. We should recognize and accept that our discipline is a creative design discipline and has no meaningful relationship to production-engineering and instead focus on mastery of the skills of exploration, discovery, and learning. This is a practical application of a scientific style of reasoning.

We also need to focus on improving our skills in managing complexity. We build systems that don't fit into our heads. We build systems on a large scale with large groups of people working on them. We need to become **expert at managing complexity** to cope with this, both at the technical level and at the organizational level.

Experts at Learning

Science is humanity's best problem-solving technique. If we are to become experts at learning, we need to adopt and become skilled at the kind of practical science-informed approach to problem-solving that is the essence of other engineering disciplines.

It must be tailored to our problems. Software engineering will be different from other forms of engineering, specific to software, in the same way that aerospace engineering is different from chemical engineering. It needs to be practical, light weight, and pervasive in our approach to solving problems in software.

There is considerable consensus among people who many of us consider to be thought leaders in our industry on this topic. Despite being well known, these ideas are not currently universally or even widely practiced as the foundations of how we approach much of software development.

There are five linked behaviors in this category:

- Working iteratively
- Employing fast, high-quality feedback
- Working incrementally
- Being experimental
- Being empirical

If you have not thought about this before, these five practices may seem abstract and rather divorced from the day-to-day activities of software development, let alone software engineering.

Software development is an exercise in exploration and discovery. We are always trying to learn more about what our customers or users want from the system, how to better solve the problems presented to us, and how to better apply the tools and techniques at our disposal.

We learn that we have missed something and have to fix things. We learn how to organize ourselves to work better, and we learn to more deeply understand the problems that we are working on.

Learning is at the heart of everything that we do. These practices are the foundations of any effective approach to software development, but they also rule out some less effective approaches.

Waterfall development approaches don't exhibit these properties, for example. Nevertheless, these behaviors are all correlated with high performance in software development teams and have been the hallmarks of successful teams for decades.

Part II explores each of these ideas in more depth from a practical perspective: How do we become experts at learning, and how do we apply that to our daily work?

Experts at Managing Complexity

As a software developer, I see the world through the lens of software development. As a result, my perception of the failures in software development and the culture that surrounds it can largely be thought of in terms of two information science ideas: concurrency and coupling.

These are difficult in general, not just in software design. So, these ideas leak out from the design of our systems and affect the ways in which the organizations in which we work operate.

You can explain this with ideas like Conway's law,[6] but Conway's law is more like an emergent property of these deeper truths.

You can profitably think of this in more technical terms. A human organization is just as much an information system as any computer system. It is almost certainly more complex, but the same fundamental ideas apply. Things that are fundamentally difficult, like concurrency and coupling, are difficult in the real world of people, too.

If we want to build systems any more complex than the simplest of toy programming exercises, we need to take these ideas seriously. We need to manage the complexity of the systems that we create as we create them, and if we want to do this at any kind of scale beyond the scope of a single, small team, we need to manage the complexity of the organizational information systems as well as the more technical software information systems.

As an industry, it is my impression that we pay too little attention to these ideas, so much so that all of us who have spent any time around software are familiar with the results: big-ball-of-mud systems, out-of-control technical debt, crippling bug counts, and organizations afraid to make changes to the systems that they own.

---

6. In 1967, Mervin Conway observed that "Any organization that designs a system (defined broadly) will produce a design whose structure is a copy of the organization's communication structure." See https://bit.ly/3s2KZP2.

I perceive all of these as a symptom of teams that have lost control of the complexity of the systems that they are working on.

If you are working on a simple, throwaway software system, then the quality of its design matters little. If you want to build something more complex, then you must divide the problem up so that you can think about parts of it without becoming overwhelmed by the complexity.

Where you draw those lines depends on a lot of variables: the nature of the problem that you are solving, the technologies that you are employing, and probably even how smart you are, to some extent, but you must draw the lines if you want to solve harder problems.

Immediately as you buy in to this idea, we are talking about ideas that have a big impact in terms of the design and architecture of the systems that we create. I was a little wary, in the previous paragraph, of mentioning "smartness" as a parameter, but it is one. The problem that I was wary of is that most of us overestimate our abilities to solve a problem in code.

This is one of the many lessons that we can learn from an informal take on science. It's best to start off assuming that our ideas are wrong and work to that assumption. So we should be much more wary about the potential explosion of complexity in the systems that we create and work to manage it diligently and with care as we make progress.

There are five ideas in this category, too. These ideas are closely related to one another and linked to the ideas involved in becoming experts at learning. Nevertheless, these five ideas are worth thinking about if we are to manage complexity in a structured way for any information system:

- Modularity

- Cohesion

- Separation of concerns

- Information hiding/abstraction

- Coupling

We will explore each of these ideas in much more depth in Part III.

Summary

The tools of our trade are often not really what we think they are. The languages, tools, and frameworks that we use change over time and from project to project. The ideas that facilitate our learning and allow us to deal with the complexity of the systems that we create are the real tools of our trade. By focusing on these things, it will help us to better choose the languages, wield the tools, and apply the frameworks in ways that help us do a more effective job of solving problems with software.

Having a "yardstick" that allows us to evaluate these things is an enormous advantage if we want to make decisions based on evidence and data, rather than fashion or guesswork. When making a choice, we should ask ourselves, "does this increase the quality of the software that we create?" measured by the metrics of **stability**. Or "does this increase the efficiency with which we create software of that quality" measured by **throughput**. If it doesn't make either of these things worse, we can pick what we prefer; otherwise, why would we choose to do something that makes either of these things worse?

OPTIMIZE FOR LEARNING

4

Working Iteratively

Iteration is defined as "a procedure in which repetition of a sequence of operations yields results successively closer to a desired result."[1]

Fundamentally, iteration is a procedure that drives learning. Iteration allows us to learn, react, and adapt to what we have learned. Without iteration, and the closely related activity of collecting feedback, there is no opportunity to learn on an ongoing basis. Fundamentally, iteration allows us to make mistakes and to correct them, or make advances and enhance them.

This definition also reminds us that iteration allows us to progressively approach some goal. Its real power is that it allows us to do this even when we don't really know how to approach our goals. As long as we have some way of telling whether we are closer to, or further from, our goal, we could even iterate randomly and still achieve our goal. We can discard the steps that take us further away and prefer the steps that move us nearer. This is in essence how evolution works. It is also at the heart of how modern machine learning (ML) works.

---

1. Source: Merriam Webster Dictionary, https://www.merriam-webster.com/dictionary/iteration

The Agile Revolution

Teams were practicing more iterative, feedback-driven approaches to development from at least the 1960s. However, following a famous meeting of leading thinkers and practitioners, at a ski resort in Colorado, the Agile Manifesto outlined a shared philosophy that underpinned these more flexible, learning-centered strategies in contrast to the more heavyweight processes common at the time.

The Agile Manifesto[2] is a simple document. It is 9 lines of text and 12 principles, but it had a big impact.

Before this, the conventional wisdom, with a few quiet dissenters, was that if you were doing anything "serious" in software, then you needed the production-centered techniques of waterfall development.

Agile thinking took a while to break through, but now it, and not waterfall, is the predominant approach, at least in terms of thinking.

However, most organizations are still, at heat, culturally dominated by waterfall thinking at the organizational level, if not also at the technical level.

Nevertheless, agile thinking is built upon significantly more stable foundations than the ideas that went before it. At its heart, the phrase that best captures the ideas, maybe ideals, of the agile community is "inspect and adapt."

This change in perception is significant, but not enough. Why was this step significant? Because it represents a step in the direction of perceiving software development as a learning exercise rather than a production problem. Waterfall processes can be effective for some kinds of production problems, but they are an extremely poor fit for problems that involve exploration.

This step is important because although Fred Brooks' 10x step does not appear to be available in terms of technology, tooling, or process, there are some approaches that are so inefficient that improving them by an order of magnitude is perfectly possible. Waterfall, when applied to software development, is such a candidate.

Waterfall-style thinking starts from the assumption that "if we only think/work hard enough, we can get things right at the beginning."

Agile thinking inverts this. It starts from the assumption that we will inevitably get things wrong. "We won't understand what the users want," "we won't get the design right straight away," "we won't know if we have caught all the bugs in the code that we wrote," and so on and so on. Because they start off assuming that they will make mistakes, agile teams work in a way that, quite intentionally, mitigates the cost of mistakes.

---

2. The Agile Manifesto, https://agilemanifesto.org/

Agile thinking shares this idea with science. Approaching ideas from a skeptical perspective and looking to prove ideas wrong, rather than prove them right ("falsifiability"), are inherent to a more scientific mindset.

These two schools of thought, predictability versus exploration, promote quite radically different, incompatible approaches to project organization and team practice.

Based on the assumptions of agile thinking, we will approach the organization of our teams, processes, and technology to allow us to safely get things wrong, easily observe the mistake, make a change, and, ideally, do better next time.

Arguments over Scrum versus Extreme Programming or continuous integration versus feature branching or TDD versus skilled developers thinking hard, or anything else, are irrelevant. At its heart, any truly agile process is an exercise in "empirical process control."

This is a significantly better fit for software development, of any kind, than the production-centered, prediction-based waterfall approach that preceded it.

Working iteratively is different in some fundamental ways than working in a more planned, sequential approach. It is, though, a significantly more effective strategy.

To many readers, this may seem obvious, but it is not. Much of the history of software development was spent assuming that iteration was unnecessary and that a detailed plan of all the steps was the goal of the early stages of software development.

Iteration is at the heart of all exploratory learning and is fundamental to any real knowledge acquisition.

Practical Advantages of Working Iteratively

If we approach software engineering as an exercise in discovery and learning, iteration must be at its heart. However, a variety of other advantages to working iteratively may not be evident at first.

Perhaps the most important idea is that if we start to change our working practices to work more iteratively, it automatically narrows our focus and encourages us to think in smaller batches and to take modularity and separation of concerns more seriously. These ideas start out as a natural consequence of working more iteratively, but end up being part of a virtuous circle that enhances the quality of our work.

One of the common ideas from both Scrum and Extreme Programming (XP) was that we should work on small units of work to completion. The agile thought process was, "Progress in software development is hard to measure, but we can measure finished features, so let's work on smaller features so that we can see when they are finished."

This reduction in batch size was a big step forward. However, it gets complicated when you want to know how long it will take to "finish." This iterative approach to development is different from more traditional ways of thinking. For example, in continuous delivery we work so that every small change, multiple times per day, is releasable. It should be finished to the degree that we can safely and reliably release our software into production at any point. So what does "finished" really mean in that context?

Each change is finished because it is releasable, so the only sensible measure of "finished" is that it delivers some value to its users. That is a very subjective thing. How do we predict how many changes are needed to represent "value" to our users? What most organizations do is to guess at a collection of features that, in combination, represent "value," but if I can release at any point in the life of my software, this is a somewhat blurry concept.

There is a problem with guessing the set of changes that constitute "value," because it depends on the assumption that you know all of the features that you need when you start and can determine progress toward some idea of "completeness." This is an over-simplification of what the founders of the agile movement meant, but it is an assumption that most traditional organizations, making the transition to agile planning, have made.

One of the more subtle advantages of working iteratively is that we have a choice. We could iterate on the products that we create and steer them, based on good feedback from our customers and users, toward higher-value outcomes. This is one of the more valuable aspects of this way of working that is often missed by more traditional organizations that attempt to adopt it.

Nevertheless, whatever the intent or the outcome, this small batch–based approach did encourage us, as an industry, to reduce the size and complexity of the features that we would work on, and that is a really important step.

Agile planning depended, to a significant degree, on decomposing work into small enough pieces that we could complete our features within a single sprint, or iteration. Initially this was promoted as a way of measuring progress, but it had the much more profound impact of delivering definitive feedback on the quality and appropriateness of our work on a regular basis. This change increases the rate at which we can learn. Does this design work? Do our users like this feature? Is the system fast enough? Have I eliminated all of the bugs? Is my code nice to work in? and so on.

Working iteratively in small, definitive, and production-ready steps provides us with great feedback!

Iteration as a Defensive Design Strategy

Working iteratively encourages us to take a defensive approach to design. (We discuss the details of this in more depth in Part III.)

An interesting take on the foundations of agile thinking was first presented to me by my friend, Dan North. Dan described the difference between waterfall and agile thinking as, effectively, a problem in economics. Waterfall thinking is promulgated on the assumption that change gets more expensive as time goes on. It classically talks about the Cost of Change model, as represented in Figure 4.1.

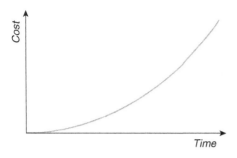

Figure 4.1
The classical cost of change

This worldview is problematic. It means that if this model is correct, the only sensible solution is to make the most important decisions early in the life of a project. The difficulty with this is that early in the life of a project, we know the least that we will ever know about it. So we are making crucial decisions in the life of a project based on ill-informed guesses, however hard we work at this point to inform them.

Software development never begins with "…every piece of work being completely understood," no matter how hard we analyze things before starting work. Given that we never begin with a "well-defined set of inputs," no matter how diligently we plan, the defined process model, or waterfall approach, falls at the first hurdle. It is impossible to make software development fit this inappropriate mold.

Surprises, misunderstandings, and mistakes are normal in software development because it is an exercise in exploration and discovery, so we need to focus on learning to protect ourselves from the missteps that we will inevitably make along the way.

Dan North's alternate view was this: given that the classic Cost of Change model clearly doesn't help us, what would? How much nicer would it be if we could flatten the Cost of Change curve? (See Figure 4.2.)

What if we could change our minds, discover new ideas, discover errors, and fix them, all at roughly the same cost whenever that happened? What if the Cost of Change curve was flat?

It would give us the freedom to discover new things and benefit from our discoveries. It would allow us to adopt an approach that would allow us to continuously improve our understanding, our code, and our user's experience of our products.

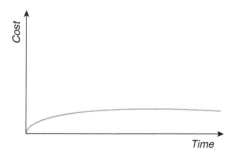

Figure 4.2
The agile cost of change

So, what would it take to achieve a flat Cost of Change curve?

We can't afford to spend lots of time in analysis and design without creating anything, because that means more time not learning what really works. So we need to compress things. We need to work iteratively. We need to do just enough analysis, design, coding, testing, and releasing to get our ideas out into the hands of our customers and users so that we can see what really works. We need to reflect on that and then, given that learning, adapt what we do next to take advantage of it.

This is one of the ideas at the heart of continuous delivery (see Figure 4.3).

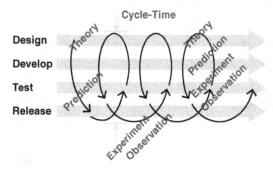

Figure 4.3
Iteration in continuous delivery

The Lure of the Plan

The people who promoted waterfall thinking were well intentioned. They thought that it was the best way forward. Our industry has spent decades trying to make this approach work, and it doesn't.

The difficulty here is that a waterfall approach sounds very sensible: "Think carefully before you start," and "Plan carefully what you are going to do and then execute the plan diligently." Based on our industrial-age experience, these ideas make a lot of sense. If you have a well-defined process, this defined process control approach works extremely well.

When making physical things, the problems of production engineering and the problems of scaling up often outweigh the problems of design. However, this is changing now even in the manufacture of physical things. As manufacturing gets more flexible and some manufacturing plants can change direction, then even in manufacturing this kind of rigid process has been challenged and overturned. This kind of "production-line" thinking dominated most organizations for at least a century, though, and we are somewhat programmed to think about problems this way.

It takes a difficult intellectual leap to recognize that the paradigm in which you are operating is fundamentally the wrong one. This is even more true when the whole world assumes that paradigm to be correct.

Process Wars

If there is no 10x improvement available from language, formalism, or diagramming, where else can we look?

The way in which we organize ourselves and our approach to the skills and techniques of learning and discovery that seem so inherent to our discipline seem like a fruitful avenue to explore.

In the early days of software development, the early programmers were usually highly educated in mathematics, science, or engineering. They worked as individuals or in small groups to develop systems. These people were explorers in a new domain, and like most explorers, they brought their experience and prejudices along with them. Early approaches to software development were often very mathematical.

As the computer revolution kicked in and software development became more ubiquitous, demand rapidly outstripped supply. We needed to produce more, better software faster! So we started looking at other industries to try to copy how they coped with working efficiently at scale.

This is where we made the horrible mistake of misunderstanding the fundamental nature of software development and misapplied techniques from manufacturing and production. We recruited armies of developers and tried to create the software equivalent of mass-production lines.

The people who did this were not stupid, but they did make a big mistake. The problem is multifaceted. Software is complex stuff, and the process of its creation bears no real relationship to a traditional "production problem," which is how most people seem to have thought about it.

Initial attempts at industrializing our discipline were painful, pervasive, and very damaging. It resulted in the creation of a lot of software, but much of it was problematic. It was slow, inefficient, late, did not deliver what our users wanted, and was extremely difficult to maintain. Through the 1980s and 1990s software development exploded as a discipline, and so did the complexity of the processes applied to it in many large organizations.

These failings were despite the fact that many aspects of this problem were well understood by leading thinkers in the discipline.

The Mythical Man Month by Fred Brooks, again, described these problems and how to avoid them in some detail in 1970. If you have never read this seminal work in our discipline, you would probably be surprised at how accurately it describes the problems that you, most likely, face nearly every day in your work as a software developer. This despite the fact that it is based on Brooks's experience of developing the operating system for the IBM 360 mainframe computer in the late 1960s using the comparatively crude technology and tools of the day. Brooks was, yet again, touching on something more important and more fundamental than language, tools, or technology.

During this period many teams produced great software, often completely ignoring the then current "wisdom" of how projects should be planned and managed. There were some common themes in these teams. They tended to be small. The developers were close to the users of their software. They tried ideas quickly and changed tack when things didn't work as they expected. This was revolutionary stuff during this period—so revolutionary in fact that many of these teams essentially operated in stealth mode, where the organization where they worked applied heavy-weight processes that slowed them down.

By the late 1990s, in reaction to these heavyweight processes, some people began to try to define strategies that were more effective. Several different competing approaches to software development were gaining in popularity. Crystal, Scrum, Extreme Programming, and several others tried to capture this very different approach. These viewpoints were formalized into the Agile Manifesto.

In software, it took the agile revolution to overthrow that norm, but even today many, perhaps even most, organizations at heart remain plan/waterfall-driven.

In addition to the difficulty of recognizing the problem, there remains a fair bit of wishful thinking in organizations that cling to waterfall-style planning. It would be lovely if an organization could:

- Correctly identify its users' needs
- Accurately assess the value to the organization if those needs were met
- Accurately estimate how much it would cost to fulfill those needs
- Make a rational decision on whether the benefit outweighed the cost
- Make an accurate plan
- Execute the plan without deviation
- Count the money at the end

The trouble is that this is not credible either at the business level or at a technical level. The real world, and software development within it, just doesn't work like this.

Industry data says that for the best software companies in the world, two-thirds of their ideas produce zero or negative value.[3] We are terrible at guessing what our users want. Even when we ask our users, they don't know what they want either. The most effective approach is to iterate. It is accepting that some, maybe even many, of our ideas will be wrong and work in a way that allows us to try them out as quickly, cheaply, and efficiently as possible.

Assessing the business value of an idea is notoriously difficult, too. There is a famous quote from IBM president Thomas J. Watson, who once predicted that the world demand for computers would one day get as high as five!

This is not a technology problem; this is a human-limitation problem. To make progress we must take a chance, make a guess, be willing to take a risk. We are very bad at guessing, though. So to make progress most efficiently, we must organize ourselves so that our guesses won't destroy us. We need to work more carefully, more defensively. We need to proceed in small steps and limit the scope, or blast radius, of our guesses and learn from them. We need to work iteratively!

Once we have an idea that we would like to execute on, we need to find a way to decide when to stop. How do we call a halt on a bad idea? Once we have decided that the idea is worth the risk of attempting it, how do we limit that blast radius in a way that means that we don't lose everything on a terrible idea? We need to be able to spot the bad ideas as soon as we can. If we can eliminate the bad ideas just by thinking about it, great. However, many ideas aren't that obviously bad. Success is a slippery concept. An idea may even be a good idea, but may be let down by bad timing or poor execution.

We need to find a way to try our ideas with minimum cost, so that if it is bad, we can find that out quickly and at relatively low cost. A 2012 survey of software projects carried out by the McKinsey Group in association with Oxford University found that 17% of large projects (budgets over $15M) went so badly that they threatened the existence of the company that undertook them. How can we identify these bad ideas? If we work in small steps, get real reaction to the progress or otherwise, and constantly validate and review our ideas, we can see soonest, with lowest investment, when things start to work differently to our hopes and plans. If we work iteratively in small steps, the cost of any single step going wrong is inevitably lower; therefore, the level of this risk is reduced.

In "The Beginning of Infinity," David Deutsch describes the profound difference between ideas that are limited in scope and ideas that are not. The comparison of a planned, waterfall, defined-process approach and an iterative, exploratory, experimental approach is a comparison between two such fundamentally different ideas. Defined process control models[4] require a "defined process." By definition this is finite in scope. At the limit of such an approach, there is, at some level, the capacity of a human brain to hold the detail of the entire process. We can be smart and use ideas like abstraction

---

3. Source: "Online Controlled Experiments at Large Scale," https://stanford.io/2LdjvmC

4. Ken Schwaber described waterfall as a "defined process control model" that he defined as: "The defined process control model requires that every piece of work be completely understood. Given a well-defined set of inputs, the same outputs are generated every time. A defined process can be started and allowed to run until completion, with the same results every time." Schwaber compares this to the "empirical process control model" represented by an agile approach. See https://bit.ly/2UiaZdS.

and concepts like modularity to hide some of the detail, but ultimately defining the process end to end in some kind of plan requires us to have covered everything that will happen. This is an inherently limited approach to solving problems. We can only solve the problems that we can understand up front.

An iterative approach is very different. We can begin when we know almost nothing and yet still make useful progress. We can start with some simple, understandable facet of the system. Use this to explore how our team should work on it, try out our first thoughts on the architecture of our system, try out some technologies that we think might be promising, and so on. None of these things is necessarily fixed. We have still made progress even if we found that the tech was a bad idea and our first concept of the architecture was wrong. We now know better than we did before. This is an inherently open-ended, infinite process. As long as we have some kind of "fitness function," a way of telling if we are heading toward our goal or away from it, we can continue in this vein forever, refining, enhancing, and improving our understanding, our ideas, our skills, and our products. We can even decide to change our "fitness function" along the way if we decide that there are better goals to aim for.

A Beginning of Infinity

In his mind-expanding book *The Beginning of Infinity*, physicist David Deutsch describes science and the enlightenment as the quest for "good explanations" and explains how various ideas in human history represent a "beginning of infinity" that allow us to cope with any conceivable relevant application of these good explanations.

A good example of this is the difference between an alphabet and a pictographic form of writing.

Humans began with the pictographic forms of writing, and Chinese and Japanese writing still take this form (for some writing styles). These are beautiful to look at, but they have a serious flaw. If you come across a word that is new to you, you hear it spoken; you can't write it down until you get someone else to tell you how. Pictographic forms of writing are not really incremental; you have to know the correct symbol for each word. (There are approximately 50,000 characters in Chinese writing.)

An alphabet works in a profoundly different way. Alphabets encode sounds, not words. You can spell any word, maybe incorrectly, in a way that anyone can, at least phonetically, understand what you wrote.

This is true even if you have never heard the word spoken or seen it written before.

Equally you can read a word that you don't know. You can even read words that you don't understand or don't know how to pronounce. You can't do either of these things with pictographic writing. This means that the range of an alphabetic approach to writing is infinite, and a pictographic one is not. One is a scalable approach to representing ideas; the other is not.

This idea of infinite reach or scope is true of an agile approach to development and not true of a waterfall-based approach.

A waterfall approach is sequential. You must answer the questions of the stage that you are in before proceeding to the next stage. This means that however clever we are, there must, at some point, be a limit at which the complexity of the system as a whole goes beyond human understanding.

Human mental capacity is finite, but our capacity to understand is not necessarily so. We can address the physiological limits of our brains by using techniques that we have evolved and developed. We can abstract things, and we can compartmentalize (modularize) our thinking and so scale our understanding to a remarkable degree.

An agile approach to software development actively encourages us to start work on solving problems in smaller pieces. It encourages us to begin work before we know the answer to everything. This approach allows us to make progress, maybe sometimes in suboptimal or even bad directions, but nevertheless, after each step, we learn something new.

This allows us to refine our thinking, identify the next small step, and then take that step. Agile development is an unbounded, infinite approach because we work on small pieces of the problem before moving forward from a known and understood position. This is a profoundly more organic, evolutionary, unbounded approach to problem-solving.

This is a profound difference and explains why agile thinking represents an important and significant step forward in our ability to make progress in solving, ideally, harder and harder problems.

This doesn't mean that agile thinking is perfect or the final answer. Rather, it is an important, significant, enabling step in the direction of better performance.

The lure of the plan is a false one. This is not a more diligent, more controlled, more professional approach. Rather, it is more limited and more based on hunch and guesswork and can, realistically, work only for small, simple, well-understood, well-defined systems.

The implications of this are significant. It means that we must, as Kent Beck famously said in the subtitle to his seminal work *Extreme Programming Explained*, "Embrace change"!

We must learn to have the confidence to begin work precisely when we don't yet know the answers and when we don't know how much work will be involved. This is disquieting for some people and for some organizations, but it is only the same as the reality of much of the human experience. When a business starts out on a new venture, they don't really know when, or even whether, it will be a success. They don't know how many people will like their ideas and whether they will be willing to pay for them.

Even for something as mundane as a trip in your car, you can't be certain how long it will take or if the route that you pick will still be the best route once you have begun. These days we have wonderful tools like satellite navigation systems with radio connections that not only can plan our route at the start but can iteratively update the picture with traffic information, allowing us to "inspect and adapt" to the changing circumstances of our journey.

An iterative approach to planning and execution allows us to always have the most up-to-date picture of the situation that we are really in, rather than some predictive, theoretical, always-inaccurate version of that situation. It allows us to learn, react, and adapt as changes happen along the way. Working iteratively is the only effective strategy for a changing situation.

Practicalities of Working Iteratively

So, what can we do to work this way? The first thing is to work in smaller batches. We need to reduce the scope of each change and make change in smaller steps; in general, the smaller the better. This allows us to try out our techniques, ideas, and technology more frequently.

Working in small batches also means that we limit the time-horizon over which our assumptions need to hold. The universe has a smaller window of time within which it can intrude on our work, so things are less likely to change in damaging ways. Finally, if we make small steps, even if a small step is invalidated by changing circumstance or just misunderstanding on our part, there is less work lost. So, small steps really matter.

The obvious incarnation of this idea in agile teams is the idea of iterations or sprints. Agile disciplines promote the idea of working to completed, production-ready code, within a small, fixed period of time. This has multiple, beneficial effects, the effects described in this chapter. However, this is only one, coarse-grained incarnation of working more iteratively.

At a completely different scale, you can think of the practices of continuous integration (CI) and test-driven development (TDD) as being inherently iterative processes.

In CI we are going to commit our changes frequently, multiple times per day. This means that each change needs to be atomic, even if the feature that it contributes to is not yet complete. This changes how we approach our work but gives us more opportunities to learn and to understand if our code still works alongside everyone else's.

TDD is often described by the practices that contribute to it: Red, Green, Refactor.

- Red: Write a test, run it, and see it fail.

- Green: Write just enough code to make the test pass, run it, and see it pass.

- Refactor: Modify the code and the test to make it clear, expressive, elegant, and more general. Run the test after every tiny change and see it pass.

This is a deeply fine-grained, iterative approach. It encourages a substantially more iterative approach to the fundamental technicalities of writing code.

For example, in my own coding, I nearly always introduce new classes, variables, functions, and parameters via a multistage series of tiny refactoring steps, frequently checking that my code continues to work, by running my test, as I go.

This is iterative working at a very fine resolution. It means that my code is correct and working for more of the time, and that means that each step is safer.

At each point in the process, I can re-evaluate and change my mind and the direction of my design and code easily. I keep my options open!

These properties are why working iteratively is so valuable and such a foundationally important practice for an engineering discipline for software development.

Summary

Iteration is an important idea and a foundation of our ability to move toward a more controlled approach to learning, discovery, and better software and software products. However, as ever, there is no free lunch. If we want to work iteratively, we must change the way that we work in many ways to facilitate it.

Working iteratively has an impact on the design of the systems that we build, how we organize our work, and how we structure the organizations in which we work. The idea of iteration is woven deeply into the thinking behind this book and the model for software engineering that I present here. All the ideas are deeply interlinked, and sometimes, it may be tricky to figure out where iteration ends and feedback begins.

5

Feedback

Feedback is defined as "The transmission of evaluative or corrective information about an action, event, or process to the original, or controlling, source."[1]

Without feedback, there is no opportunity to learn. We can only guess, rather than make decisions based on reality. Despite this, it is surprising how little attention many people and organizations pay to it.

For example, many organizations create a "business case" for new software. How many of those organizations go on to track the cost of development and evaluate it, along with the real benefits delivered to customers to validate that their "business case" was met?

Unless we can know and understand the results of our choices and actions, we cannot tell if we are making progress.

This seems so obvious to be not really worth stating, but in practice guesswork, hierarchy, and tradition are the much more widely used arbiters for decision-making in most organizations.

Feedback allows us to establish a source of evidence for our decisions. Once we have such a source, the quality of our decisions is, inevitably, improved. It allows us to begin to separate myth from reality.

---

1. Source: Merriam Webster Dictionary. https://www.merriam-webster.com/dictionary/feedback

A Practical Example of the Importance of Feedback

It can be difficult to understand abstract ideas. Let's imagine a simple, practical example of how important speed and quality in feedback really are.

Imagine being faced with the problem of balancing a broom.

We could decide to carefully analyze the structure of the broom, work out its center of gravity, closely examine the structure of the handle, and calculate exactly the point at which the broom will be perfectly balanced. We could then very carefully maneuver the broom into the precise position that we had planned and, through perfect execution, ensure that we had left no residual impulse that left the broom accelerating out of balance.

This first approach is analogous to a waterfall development model. It is possible to imagine it working but incredibly unlikely that it will. The result is extremely unstable. It relies on our predictions being perfect, and given the least perturbation, or inaccuracy in our predictions, the broom falls.

Alternatively, we could put the broom on our hand and move our hand in response to how it tipped.

The second approach is based on feedback. It is quicker to set up, and the speed and quality of the feedback will drive its success. If we are too slow moving our hand, we will have to make big corrections. If we are too slow sensing the direction of tilt of the broom, we will have to make big corrections or the broom will fall. If our feedback is fast and effective, we can make tiny corrections and the broom will be stable. In fact, even if something comes along and disturbs the broom, or us, we can react quickly and correct the problem.

This second approach is so successful that this is how space rockets "balance" on the thrust of their engines. It is so stable that if I am any good at it, even if you unexpectedly shoved me and forced me to stagger, I could probably keep the broom in balance.

This second approach feels more ad hoc; it feels, in some sense, less rigorous, but it is profoundly more effective.

I can imagine you thinking, at this point, "what has our author been drinking? What do brooms have to do with software?" My point here is that there is something deep and important about how processes work.

The first example is of a planned, predictive approach. This approach works well as long as you completely understand all of the variables and as long as nothing comes along to change your understanding or your plan. This is really the basis of any detailed, planned approach. If you have a detailed plan, there is only one correct solution, so either the problem has to be so simple to make that possible or you have to be omniscient in your abilities to predict the future.

The second, alternative approach still involves a plan "I am going to balance the broom," but the plan is all about outcomes and says nothing about the mechanism through which you will achieve it. Instead, you are just going to start work and do whatever it takes to achieve the desired outcome. If that means responding to feedback and moving your hand a few millimeters very quickly, good. If it means taking a few staggering steps forward and sideways while moving your hand a meter or more because something unexpected happened, that is fine too, as long as the outcome is achieved.

The second approach, although it may seem more ad hoc, more like "winging it," is actually profoundly more effective and more stable in terms of outcome. In the first approach there is only one correct solution. In the second there are many, so we are more likely to achieve one of them.

Feedback is an essential component of any system that operates in a changing environment. Software development is always an exercise in learning, and the environment in which it takes place is always changing; therefore, feedback is an essential aspect of any effective software development process.

The NATO Conference[2]

By the late 1960s, it had become obvious that computer programming was a difficult thing to do well. The systems being built were increasing in size, complexity, and importance. The number of people programming them was growing quickly. As this increase in difficulty dawned on people, they began thinking about what they could do to make the process of creating software more efficient and less error-prone.

One outcome of this thinking was to hold a famous conference to try to define what software engineering was. The conference was held in 1968 and was intended to explore the meaning and practice of software engineering in broad terms.

The conference was an "invitation-only" event, recruiting global experts, of the time, in the field to discuss a wide range of ideas in the context of software engineering. Given the remarkable growth in capacity in computer hardware over the past 50 years, it is inevitable that some ideas are extremely dated:

> **Dr. H J Helms**: *In Europe alone, there are about 10,000 installed computers—this number is increasing at a rate of anywhere from 25 percent to 50 percent per year. The quality of software provided for these computers will soon affect more than a quarter of a million analysts and programmers.*

Other ideas seem more durable:

> **A J Perlis**: *Selig's picture requires a feedback loop, for monitoring of the system. One must collect data on system performance, for use in future improvements.*

While Perlis's language sounds dated, the idea could be describing a modern DevOps approach to development rather than the creation of something written in Algol![2]

---

2. Source: "NATO Conference on Software Engineering 1968," https://bit.ly/2rOtYvM

Many other contributions were similarly prescient:

F Selig: *External specifications, at any level, describe the software product in terms of the items controlled by and available to the user. The internal design describes the software product in terms of the program structures which realize the external specifications. It has to be understood that feedback between the design of the external and internal specifications is an essential part of a realistic and effective implementation process.*

This description sounds remarkably like the stories[3] of agile development to modern ears, describing the importance of separating "what" from "how" in the requirements process.

There are cores of universal truth in which, with the benefit of 21st century hindsight, we recognize the problems and practice of our trade:

d'Agapeyeff: *Programming is still too much of an artistic endeavor. We need a more substantial basis to be taught and monitored in practice on the:*

(i)   structure of programs and the flow of their execution;

(ii) shaping of modules and an environment for their testing;

(iii) simulation of run time conditions.

With the benefit of that hindsight, ideas like "shaping modules and environments [to facilitate] testing" and "simulating run time conditions" sound completely modern and correct and form much of the basis of a continuous delivery approach to software development.

Reading these proceeds today, there are many ideas that are clearly durable. They have stood the test of time and are as true today as they were in 1968.

There is something different, something more profound, in saying "Establish feedback loops" or "Assume that you will get things wrong" compared to "Use language X" or "Prove your designs with diagramming technique Y."

Feedback in Coding

In practice, how does this need for fast, high-quality feedback impact how we should work?

If we take feedback seriously, we want lots of it. Writing code and relying on the testing team to report on it six weeks later is not going to suffice.

My own approach to writing code has evolved significantly over the course of my career. I now employ feedback at multiple levels all the time. I make changes in tiny steps.

---

3. A *user story* is an informal description of a feature of the system, written from the perspective of a user of the system. It was one of the ideas introduced in Extreme Programming.

I generally take a test-driven approach to the way that I write code. If I want to add some new behavior to my system, I will first write a test.

As I begin writing the test, I want to know if my test is correct. I would like some feedback to indicate the correctness of my test. So I write the test and run it in order to see it fail. The nature of the failure gives me feedback that helps me understand if my test is correct.

If the test passed, before I have written any code to make it pass, there is something wrong with my test, and I need to correct it before proceeding. All of this describes the application of fine-grained feedback techniques focused on learning quickly.

As I described in the previous chapter, I make changes to my code as a series of tiny steps. There are, at least, two levels of feedback at play here. For example, I use the refactoring tools in my IDE a lot to help me with the first, but I also get feedback at every step on whether my code is working and, more subjectively, if I like what I see as my design evolves. As a result, my ability to spot mistakes, or missteps, is greatly enhanced.

This second level of feedback is provided by the fact that every time I make a change, I can rerun the test that I am currently working with. This gives me very fast confirmation that my code continues to work after the change.

These feedback cycles are incredibly short, or should be. Most of the feedback cycles I have mentioned here take a handful of seconds at most. Some, like running your unit test to validate that everything is still working, is probably, more likely, measured in milliseconds.

This short, fast, feedback cycle is incredibly valuable because of its speed and the immediacy of its relevance to what you are working on.

Organizing our work into a series of tiny steps gives us more opportunities to reflect on our progress and steer our designs toward better outcomes.

Feedback in Integration

When I commit my code, it will trigger my continuous integration system and evaluate my change in the context of everyone else's. I get a new level of feedback at this point. I gain deeper understanding. In this case, I can now learn if something in my code has "leaked out" and caused some other part of the system to fail.

If all the tests pass at this stage, I get feedback that I am safe to proceed to work on the next thing.

This is the vitally important level of feedback that underpins the idea of continuous integration.

Sadly, continuous integration is still widely misunderstood and poorly practiced. If we are trying to establish an intellectually rigorous approach to software development, an engineering approach then is important to evaluate the pros and cons of ideas dispassionately. This often seems to be difficult for our industry. Many ideas are widely adopted because they feel better rather than because they are better.

A good example of this is the debate between practitioners of **continuous integration** (CI) and **feature branching** (FB).

Let's pick apart the pros and cons of these approaches rationally.

Continuous integration is about evaluating every change to the system along with every other change to the system as frequently as possible, as close to "continuously" as we can practically get.

The definition for CI states:

> (CI) is the practice of merging all developers' working copies to a shared mainline several times a day.[4]

Most CI experts will relax "several times a day" to "at least once per day" as an acceptable, though not desirable, compromise.

So, by definition, CI is about exposing changes in small increments to evaluation at least once per day.

Branching, of any kind, also by definition, is about isolating change:

> Branches allow contributors to isolate changes.[5]

In basic, definitional terms, CI and FB then are not really compatible with each other. One aims to expose change as early as possible; the other works to defer that exposure.

FB looks simple, and its practitioners enjoy it because it appears to make life simpler. "I can code independently of my teammates." The problem comes at the point when changes are merged. CI was invented to get over the problem of "merge-hell."

In the bad old days, and in some recalcitrant organizations to this day, teams and individuals would work on sections of code until they were deemed "complete" before merging them into the whole.

What happened was that at this point all sorts of unexpected problems were identified, so the merge became complex and took a long, and unpredictable, time to accomplish.

Two approaches were adopted to try to resolve the problem; CI was one. The other approach was to improve the quality of the merge tools.

A common argument from FB practitioners is that the merge tools are now so good that merging is rarely a problem. However, it is always possible to write code that merge tools will miss; merging code is not necessarily the same as merging behavior.

Say you and I are working in the same codebase, and we have a function that does several things to transform a value. We both independently decide that this function needs to increment the value by one, but we each implement that in a different part of the function. It is entirely possible that the merge will miss that these two changes are related because they are in different parts of the code, and we get both. Now our value is incremented by two instead of one.

---

4. A definition for continuous integration may be found here: https://bit.ly/2JVRGiv.

5. A definition for branching in version control can be found here: https://bit.ly/2NIAlI8.

Continuous integration, when practiced as it is defined, means that we get regular, frequent drips of feedback. It gives us powerful insight into the state of our code and the behavior of our system throughout the working day, but it comes at a cost.

For CI to work, we have to commit our changes frequently enough to gain that feedback and that insight. This means working very differently.

Instead of working on a feature until it is "finished," or "ready for production" continuous integration and its big brother continuous delivery demand of us to make changes in small steps and have something ready for use after every small step. This changes how we think about the design of our system in some important ways.

This approach means that the process to design our code is more like one of guided evolution, with each small step giving us feedback, but not necessarily yet adding up to a whole feature. This is a very challenging change of perspective for many people, but it is a liberating step when embraced and is one that has a positive impact on the quality of our designs.

Not only does this approach mean that our software is always releasable and that we are getting frequent, fine-grained feedback on the quality and applicability of our work, but it also encourages us to design our work in a way that sustains this approach.

Feedback in Design

One of the reasons that I value TDD so highly, as a practice, is the feedback that it gives me on the quality of my design. If my tests are hard to write, that tells me something important about the quality of my code.

My ability to create a simple, effective test, and the effectiveness of my design, is related through the attributes of quality that we consider important in "good" code. We can argue about an exhaustive definition of what "good quality" in code means for a long time, but I don't think that I need to do that to make my point. I suggest that the following attributes are pretty much agreed to be hallmarks of quality in code; they may not be the only attributes of quality, but I am sure that you will agree with me that they are important:

- Modularity

- Separation of concerns

- High cohesion

- Information hiding (abstraction)

- Appropriate coupling

I expect that by now this list sounds familiar. As well as being "hallmarks of quality" in code, they are also the tools that allow us to manage complexity. This is not a coincidence!

So how do you put "quality," on the basis of these attributes, into code? In the absence of TDD, it is solely down to the experience, commitment, and skills of a developer.

With TDD, we write the test first, by definition. If we don't write the test first, then it isn't test-*driven* development.

If we are going to write the test first, we have to be a strange, dumb kind of person to make our own lives more difficult. So we are going to try to do that in a way that makes life easier.

For example, we are extremely unlikely to write a test in a way that means we can't get the results back from the code that we are testing. Since we are writing the test first, before we have written any non-test code, that means that we are, at the moment we create the test, also designing the interface to our code. We are defining how external users of our code will interact with it.

Since we need the results for the test, we will design the code in a way that makes it easy for us to get at the results that we are interested in. This means that, in TDD, there is a pressure applied to write code that is more testable. What does testable code look like?

It is all of the following:

- Is modular
- Has a good separation of concerns
- Exhibits high cohesion
- Uses information hiding (abstraction)
- Is appropriately coupled

The Fundamental Role of Testing

In classic approaches to development, testing was sometimes left as an exercise for the end of a project, sometimes left to the customer, and sometimes so squeezed by time pressures as to almost disappear completely.

This kind of approach made the feedback loop so extended that it was essentially useless. Errors introduced in coding or design were often not discovered until after the development team had rolled off the project and handed maintenance on to some production support team.

Extreme Programming (XP) and its application of TDD and CI spun this on its head, placing testing front and center in the development process. This reduced the feedback loop to seconds, giving almost instant feedback on mistakes that, in turn, could, when done well, eliminate whole classes of bugs that, in the absence of TDD, often made it into production.

In this school of thought, testing drove the development process and, even more importantly, the design of the software itself. Software written using TDD looked different from software that was written without. To make the software testable, it was important to make sure that expected behaviors could be evaluated.

This pushed designs in particular directions. Software that was "testable" was modular, was loosely coupled, exhibited high-cohesion, had a good separation of concerns, and implemented information hiding. These also happen to be properties that are widely regarded as markers of quality in software. So TDD not only evaluated the behavior of software, but increased the quality of its design.

Testing in software is extremely important. Software is fragile in a way that few other things in human experience are. The tiniest defect—a comma out of place—can result in catastrophic failure.

Software is also much more complex than most human creations. A modern passenger plane consists of around 4 million parts. The software in a modern Volvo Truck is around 80 million lines of code, each one composed of multiple instructions and variables.

TDD was not a new idea when Kent Beck described it in his book in the late 1990s. Alan Perlis had described something similar at the NATO Software Engineering Conference in 1968, but Beck introduced the concept and described it in significantly more depth, so it was more widely adopted.

TDD remains a controversial idea in many quarters, but the data is pretty good. This approach can dramatically reduce the bug count in a system, and it has a positive impact on the quality of the design of a system.

TDD applies a pressure to create code that is objectively "higher quality." This is irrespective of the talent or experience of the software developer. It doesn't make bad software developers great, but it does make "bad software developers" better and "great software developers" greater.

TDD, and other aspects of a test-driven approach to development, has an important impact on the quality of the code that we create. This is the effect of optimizing for better feedback, but this effect doesn't stop there.

Feedback in Architecture

A more subtle effect of the application of a feedback-driven approach is seen on the broad software architecture of the systems that we build, as well as the detailed, code-level, design decisions that we make.

Continuous delivery is a high-performance, feedback-driven approach to development. One of its cornerstones is the idea that we should produce software that is always ready for release into production. This is a high standard and demands a very high frequency and quality of feedback.

Achieving this requires organizations to change many different aspects of their development approach. Two aspects that come to the fore may be considered architectural qualities of the systems that we build. We need to take the **testability** and **deployability** of our systems seriously.

I advise the companies that I work with to aim for creating "releasable software" at least once per hour. This means that we must be able to run probably tens, maybe hundreds of thousands of tests every hour.

Assuming infinite money and compute capacity, we can run our tests in parallel to optimize for fast feedback, but there is a limit. We can imagine running each test independently and in parallel with all of the others.

Some tests will need to test the deployment and configuration of the system, so the limiting case for time to feedback is based on the time to deploy the system and get it up and running, and the time to run the slowest test case.

If any single test takes longer than an hour to run or if your software takes longer than an hour to deploy, it won't be possible to run your tests this quickly, however much money you spend on hardware.

So the testability and deployability of our system add constraints to our ability to gather feedback. We can choose to design our systems to be more easily testable and more easily deployable, allowing us to gather feedback more efficiently and over shorter time periods.

We'd prefer tests that take seconds or milliseconds to run and deployment to complete in a handful of minutes or, even better, a few seconds.

Achieving these levels of performance in deployability and testability takes work and focus by the team, and a commitment to the ideas of continuous delivery by the development organization, but it also often requires some careful architectural thinking.

There are two effective routes: either you can work to build monolithic systems and optimize them for deployability and testability, or you can modularize them into separate, individually "deployable units." This second approach is one of the driving ideas behind the popularity of microservices.

The microservice architectural approach allows teams to develop, test, and deploy their services independently of one another; it also decouples them organizationally, enabling firms to grow more effectively and efficiently.

The independence of microservices is a significant benefit, but also a significant complication. Microservices are, by definition, independently deployable units of code. That means that we don't get to test them together.

Applying continuous delivery to monolithic systems is effective, but it still demands of us that we can make small changes and evaluate them multiple times per day. For larger systems, we are still going to need to be able to work alongside many other people in a codebase, so we need the protections that good design and continuous integration will bring.

Whether we choose to decompose our systems into smaller, more independent modules (microservices) or develop more efficient but more tightly coupled codebases (monoliths), both of these approaches have significant impacts on the architecture of the software systems that we create.

The adoption of continuous delivery in both approaches, monolith and microservice, promotes more modular, better abstracted, more loosely coupled designs, because only then can you deploy them and test them efficiently enough to practice continuous delivery.

This means that valuing and prioritizing feedback in our development approach promotes more sensible, more effective architectural decision-making.

This is a profound and important idea. It means that through the adoption of some generic principles we can gain a significant, measurable impact on the quality of the systems that we create. By focusing process, technology, practice, and culture on the efficient delivery of high-quality feedback, we can create better-quality software and do that with greater efficiency.

Prefer Early Feedback

In general, it is an effective practice to try to get definitive feedback as early as possible. When I am coding, I can use my development tools to highlight errors in my code as I type. This is the fastest, cheapest feedback loop, and one of the most valuable. I can take advantage of this by using techniques like type systems to give me fast definitive feedback on the quality of my work.

I can run the test (or tests) in the area of the code that I am working on in my development environment and get feedback very quickly—usually in less than a few seconds.

My automated unit tests, created as the output of my TDD approach, give me my second level of feedback as I work and regularly run them in my local development environment.

My full suite of unit and other commit tests will be run once I have committed my code. This gives me a more thorough, but more costly in terms of time, validation that my code works along with other people's code.

Acceptance tests, performance tests, security tests, and anything else that we consider important to understanding the validity of our changes give us further confidence in the quality and applicability of our work, but at the cost of taking longer to return results.

So working to prefer to identify defects, first in compile-ability (identified in our development environment) and then in unit tests and, only after those validations have succeeded, in other forms of higher-level tests, means that we can fail soonest and get the highest quality, most effective feedback.

Continuous delivery and DevOps practitioners sometimes refer to this process of preferring early failures as *shift-left*, though I prefer the less obscure "Fail fast!"

Feedback in Product Design

The impact of taking feedback on the quality of the systems that we create seriously is important and profound, but ultimately, software developers are not paid to make nicely designed, easily testable software. We are paid to create value of some kind for the organizations that employ us.

This is one of the tensions that is often at the heart of the relationship between the more business-focused people and the more technically focused people in most traditional organizations.

This is a problem that is addressed by a focus on enabling the *continuous delivery of useful ideas into production*.

How do we know that the ideas that we have, the products that we create, are good ones?

The real answer is that we don't know until we get feedback from the consumers of our ideas (our users or customers).

Closing the feedback loop around the creation of product ideas and delivering value into production is the real value of continuous delivery. It is the reason that it has become so popular in organizations around the world, not the narrower (though still important) technical advantages.

Applying the principles of employing and optimizing for fast, high-quality feedback enables organizations to learn faster; to discover what ideas work, or don't, for their customers; and to adapt their products to better meet customer needs.

The most effective software development organizations in the world take this aspect very seriously indeed.

Adding telemetry to our systems that allows us to gather data about which features of our systems are used, and how they are used, is now the norm. Gathering information (feedback) from production systems to not only diagnose problems, but also to help us to more effectively design the next generation of products and services, moves organizations from being "business and IT" to being "digital businesses." This has become so sophisticated in many areas that the information that is gathered is often more valuable than the services provided and can provide insights into customer wants, needs, and behavior that even the customers themselves are not conscious of.

Feedback in Organization and Culture

The measurability of software development has long been a problem. How do we measure success, and how do we measure improvement? How can we tell if the changes that we make are effective or not?

For most of the history of software development, this was based on either measuring the things that were easy to measure (e.g., "lines of code" or "developer days" or "test coverage") or guessing and making subjective decisions on the basis of intuition. The problem is that none of these things is really correlated in any realistic way with success, whatever that means.

More lines of code doesn't mean better code; it probably means worse code. Test coverage is meaningless unless the tests are testing something useful. The amount of effort that we put into software is not related to its value. So guesswork and subjectivity may well be as good as these measures.

So how can we do better? How can we establish useful feedback without some kind of measure of success?

There are two approaches to this problem. The first has been established for some time in agile development circles. We accept that the judgments are somewhat subjective, but we try to adopt some reasonable discipline to mitigate the subjectivity. The success of this approach is, inevitably, inexorably tied to the individuals involved. It is "individuals and interactions over processes and tools."[6]

This strategy was important historically in moving us away from more formulaic, big-ceremony approaches to software development and remains important as a foundational principle.

Agile approaches to development brought the team, the people *in the work*, into the feedback loop so that they could observe the results of their actions, reflect on them, and refine their choices over time to improve their situation. This subjective, feedback-driven approach was fundamental to that most fundamental agile idea of "inspect and adapt."

A small refinement that I would add to this subjective approach to feedback to improve the quality of the feedback is to be specific about its nature.

For example, if your team has an idea to improve its approach to something, take a leaf from the scientist's book and be clear about where you think you are now (current state) and where you would prefer to be (target state). Describe a step that you think will take you in the correct direction. Decide how you will decide whether you are closer to, or further away from, your target state. Make the step and check to see if you are closer to, or further from, the target and repeat until you are at the target.[7]

This is a simple, light weight application of the scientific method. This should be obvious. This should be "motherhood and apple pie," but it is not what most people in most organizations do. When people apply this kind of approach, they get much better results. For example, this is the idea that underpins Lean thinking[8] and, specifically, the "Toyota Way," the Lean approach to production that revolutionized the car industry and many others.

For many years I have believed that this is all we could really do to apply still subjective but better organized approaches to problem-solving. In recent years, my mind has been changed by the excellent work of the Google DORA group.[9] I now believe that their work has identified some more

---

6. "Individuals and interactions over processes and tools" is a statement from the Agile Manifesto; see https://agilemanifesto.org/.

7. Mike Rother described this approach in more detail in his book *Toyota Kata*; see https://amzn.to/2Fvsl74. It is, though, really just a refinement of the Scientific Method.

8. Lean thinking is a catchall term for ideas aligned with and associated with Lean Production and Lean Process.

9. The DORA group designed the scientifically defensible approach to data collection and analysis at the heart of the "State of DevOps Report," which was produced annually from 2014. Their approach and findings are described in more detail in the book *Accelerate: The Science of Lean Software and DevOps*.

specific, less subjective measures that we can usefully apply to evaluating changes in organization and culture, as well as more technically focused changes.

This does not imply that the previous approach is redundant. Human creativity must be applied, data-driven decision making can be dumb too, but we can inform, and reinforce, subjective evaluation with data and be a little more quantitative in our evaluations of success.

The stability and throughput measures described in Chapter 3 are important. They are not ideal, and the model that they operate within is a correlative model, not a causative one. We don't have the evidence to say "X causes Y"; it is more complex than that. There are also lots of questions that we would like to be able to answer more quantitatively but don't know how. **Stability** and **throughput** are important because they are the best that we currently understand, not because they are perfect.

Nevertheless, this is an enormous step forward. Now we can use these measures of efficiency and quality, which are measures of sensible, useful outcomes, to evaluate almost any kind of change. If my team decides to reorganize where they sit to improve communications, we can monitor stability and throughput to see if they change. If we want to try some new technology, does it make us produce software more quickly, improve our throughput numbers, or improve our quality to improve our stability numbers?

This feedback is invaluable as a "fitness function" for guiding our efforts toward the better outcomes predicted by the DORA model. By tracking our scores in terms of stability and throughput as we evolve our process, technology, organization, and culture, we can be sure that the changes that we make are in fact beneficial. We move from being victims of fashion or guesswork to being more like engineers.

These changes are still proxies for the real value of the software that we produce. That value is shown in the impact our changes have on users. However, these changes measure important properties of our work and are not open to manipulation. If your stability and throughput numbers are good, your technical delivery is good. So if you are not successful with good stability and throughput, your product ideas or business strategy is at fault.

Summary

Feedback is essential to our ability to learn. Without fast, effective feedback, we are guessing. Both the speed and the quality of feedback matter. If the feedback is too late, it is useless. If it is misleading or wrong, the decisions that we make on its basis will be wrong, too. We often don't think about what feedback we need to inform our choices and how important the timelines of feedback that we gather really are.

Both continuous delivery and continuous integration are ideas that are fundamentally grounded in the idea of optimizing our development process to maximize the quality and the speed of the feedback that we collect.

6

Incrementalism

Incrementalism is defined as follows: "Incremental design is directly related to any modular design application, in which components can be freely substituted if improved to ensure better performance."[1]

Working incrementally is about building value progressively. Put simply, this is about taking advantage of the modularity or componentization of our systems.

If working iteratively is about refining and improving something over a series of iterations, then working incrementally is about building a system, and ideally releasing it, piece by piece. This is captured beautifully in Figure 6.1, taken from *User Story Mapping* [Patton].[2]

Iterative

Incremental

Figure 6.1
Iterative versus incremental

---

1. Source: Wikipedia, https://en.wikipedia.org/wiki/Continuous_design

2. I first saw this comparison between the "iterative" and "incremental" approaches in the book *User Story Mapping* by Jeff Patton. See https://bit.ly/3s9jvY6.

To create complex systems, we need both approaches. An incremental approach allows us to decompose work and to deliver value step-by-step (*incrementally*), getting to value sooner and delivering value in smaller, simpler steps.

Importance of Modularity

Modularity is an important idea. It is important in the development of technology but is not specific to information technology. When stone-age craftspeople made flint axes with a wooden handle, this was a modular system. If you broke the handle, you could keep the ax-head and make a new handle. If you broke the ax-head, you could lash a new one to your old, trusty handle.

As machines got more complex, the importance and value of modularity grew along with them. Through all but the last few years of the twentieth century, when an airplane designer wanted to do something new, they divided their work into two major modules: the power plant (engine) and airframe. A large proportion of aviation advancement was carried out as a kind of technical relay race. If you wanted to try a new engine, you tried it first in a proven airframe. If you wanted to try a new airframe, you used a proven power plant.

When the Apollo program started in the 1960s, with the goal of sending men to the moon, one of the early leaps forward was creating a mission profile called a *lunar orbit rendezvous* (LOR). LOR meant that the spacecraft would be divided into a series of modules, each focused on a specific part of the challenge. There was the Saturn V whose job was to get everything else into Earth's orbit, and then the final stage was to have another task-specific module propel the rest of the components of the spacecraft from Earth to the moon.

The rest of the Apollo spacecraft was composed of four main modules:

- The Service Module's job was to get everything else from Earth to the moon and back again.

- The Command Module was the main habitat for the astronauts; its main job though was to return the astronauts from Earth's orbit to the surface.

- The *lunar excursion module* (LEM) was made up of the other two modules: the Descent and Ascent modules. The Descent Module got the astronauts from lunar orbit to the surface of the moon.

- The Ascent Module returned the astronauts to lunar orbit where they rendezvoused, docked, with the Command and Service Modules before heading back to Earth.

This modularity had lots of advantages. It meant that each component could be built to focus on one part of the problem and would need to compromise less in its design. It allowed different groups—in this case completely different companies—to work on each module largely independent of the others. As long as the different groups agreed on how the modules would interface with each other, they could work to solve the problems of their module without constraint. Each module could be lighter because, for example, the Lunar Module didn't need to carry the means of returning to Earth all the way to the surface of the moon.

Although it is a stretch to call any Apollo spacecraft simple, each module could be simpler than if they were designed to cope with a larger part of the whole problem.

I hope that this diversion is making you think about how this relates to software. Although none of these complex machines was simple, they were minimalist in terms of meeting their needs.

This is really the philosophy of component-based approaches to design, like microservices, or actually any service-oriented design.

Divide the problem into pieces aimed at solving a single part of a problem. This approach has many advantages. Each component of the system is simpler, more focused on the task at hand. Each component is easier to test, is faster to deploy, and sometimes may even be deployed independently of the others. Once you reach that point, and not before, you are really in the realm of microservices.

However, microservices are not the only approach where we can achieve and benefit from modularity in any software system. It is really a matter of taking design seriously.

Taking a modular approach forces you to consider the boundaries between the modules of the system and take them seriously. These boundaries are important; they represent one of the key points of coupling in the system, and focusing on the protocols of information exchange between them can make a significant difference to how easy it is to isolate work and increase flexibility. I explore these ideas in more detail in later chapters.

Organizational Incrementalism

One of the huge benefits that modularity brings is isolation; the internal details of one module are hidden from, and irrelevant to, other modules. This is important for technical reasons, but it is even more important for organizational reasons.

A modular approach frees teams to work more independently. They can each make small incremental steps forward without needing to coordinate, or at least with minimal coordination, between teams. This freedom allows organizations that embrace it fully to move forward and innovate at unprecedented pace.

Beyond the value of the ability to make technical changes incrementally, this approach also frees organizations to adopt an incremental approach to cultural and organizational change.

Many organizations struggle to achieve effective changes in their working practices. Such "transformations" are notoriously difficult. The main barrier to making such a change is always how you spread a solution across an organization. There are two barriers that make this spread of changes difficult. The first is explaining and motivating people to make the change, and the second is overcoming the organizational or procedural barriers that limit its adoption.

The most common approach to implementing change seems to be to try to standardize processes across an organization. "Process mapping" and "business transformation" are big business for management consultancies. The problem is that all organizations, certainly those involved in creative work, are dependent on human creativity. If we could "standardize" the process into a series of steps, we could automate it and eliminate the costly, error-prone people. How many times have you used an automated telephone filtering system and gotten to some menu that doesn't have an option that matches your inquiry or simply dumps the call? This is because some things aren't simple to break into simple steps, as anyone who has ever written a computer program will attest.

When we are discussing software development, we are nowhere close to being able to eliminate human creativity from this endeavor. So to enable human creativity, we need to leave room in the process and policies that structure our work for creative freedom. One of the defining characteristics of high-performing teams in software development is their ability to make progress and to change their minds, without asking for permission from any person or group outside of their small team.[3]

Let's pick this apart a little. Let us start with "small teams." Although we now have more data to back up the assertion,[4] it has long been known that small teams outperform large ones. In his book *The Mythical Man Month,* Fred Brooks wrote:

> *The conclusion is simple: If a 200-man project has 25 managers who are the most competent and experienced programmers, fire the 175 troops and put the managers back to programming.*

These days, most agile practitioners would consider a team of 25 to be a large team. Current thinking is that the optimum team size is eight or fewer people.

Small teams are important for a variety of reasons, but their ability to make progress in small, incremental steps is an important one. To carry out organizational change, the most effective strategy is to create many small, independent teams and allow them the freedom to make their own changes. This progress can, and should still, be structured. It should be constrained to some degree to allow separate, independent teams to head in a roughly similar direction, targeted at fulfilling a larger-scale organizational vision, but still this is a fundamentally more distributed approach to organizational structure than has been traditional for most big firms.

The key transformation then that most organizations need to make is toward greater autonomy for people and teams to deliver high-quality, creative work. Distributed, incremental change is the key.

Modular organizations are more flexible, more scalable, and more efficient than more traditional organizational structures for software development.

Tools of Incrementalism

My five principles for learning and my five principles for managing complexity are deeply interlinked. It is hard to talk about any of them without referring to the others.

---

3. The *Accelerate Book* describes how teams that take a more disciplined approach to development spend "44% more time on new work" than teams that don't. See https://amzn.to/2YYf5Z8.

4. In their book *Accelerate: The Science of Lean Software & DevOps*, Nicole Forsgren, Jez Humble, and Gene Kim describe the characteristics of high-performing teams. See https://amzn.to/3g0Lvup.

The most profound tools to enable incrementalism are **feedback** and **experimentation**, but we also need to focus on **modularity** and **separation of concerns**.

Beyond those deeper principles, though, what are the less abstract ideas that can help us achieve a more incremental approach to change? What is it that we need to do that will allow us to work incrementally?

Incrementalism and modularity are closely linked. If we want to make a change incrementally, we must be able to make that change while limiting its impact in other areas. Working to improve the modularity of our system is a good idea, so how do we do that?

If my code is a big spaghetti ball-of-mud and I make a change in one place, I may inadvertently affect another part of the code. There are three important techniques that will allow me to make such a change more safely.

I can architect my system to limit the scope of the change. By designing systems that are modular and have a good separation of concerns, I can limit the impact of my changes beyond the area of the code that is my immediate focus.

I can adopt practices and techniques that allow me to change the code with lower risk. Chief among these safer practices is **refactoring**. That is the ability to make changes in small, simple, controlled steps that allow me to improve or at least modify my code safely.

Refactoring skills are often undervalued by developers who seem to miss their import. If we can make changes in often tiny increments, we can be much more confident in the stability of that change.

If I use the refactoring tools within my development environment to, say, "extract a method" or "introduce a parameter," then I can be confident that the change will be done safely, or I can buy better development tools.

Such tiny changes are also easy to back away from if I decide that I don't like the results; I can work iteratively as well as incrementally. If I combine my fine-grained incrementalism with strong **version control**, I am always only a small number of steps away from a "safe place." I can always withdraw to a position of stability.

Finally, there is testing. **Testing**, and specifically automated testing, gives us protection to move forward incrementally with significantly more confidence.

There are subtleties to working effectively with high levels of automated testing that we will explore in later chapters, but automated testing is an important component of our ability to make change quickly, with assurance.

There is one more aspect to automated testing that is often missed by people who have not really adopted it as a pervasive part of their daily working practice. That is the impact that testing has on design and specifically the modularity and separation of concerns in our designs.

A test-driven approach to automated testing demands that we create mini executable specifications for the changes that we make to our systems. Each of these little specifications describes the necessary conditions to begin the test, executes the behavior under test, and then evaluates the results.

To manage the amount of work necessary to achieve all of this, we are crazy if we don't try to make our lives easier by keeping the tests as simple as we can and by designing our system as testable code.

Since *testable code* is modular with a good separation of concerns, automated testing creates a positive feedback loop that enhances our ability to design better systems, limit the blast radius of mistakes, and make changes more safely. Ultimately, the combination of these three techniques provides a massive step forward in our ability to make changes incrementally.

Limiting the Impact of Change

Our aim is to manage complexity with these techniques, so we allow ourselves to develop systems more incrementally. We will always prefer to make progress in many small steps, rather than a few larger, riskier steps.

As we have already explored, if we have an organization of more than one small team of people creating software, then we can do that most efficiently if those different groups of people are able to make progress independently of one another.

There are only two strategies that make sense, and both are incremental in nature.

We can decompose our systems into more independent pieces, as we have already described in this chapter, or we can improve the speed and quality of feedback that we gather when we integrate our changes through continuous integration.

To make the pieces of our system more independent, we can use the powerful technique of the **Ports & Adapters** pattern.[5]

At any interface point between two components of the system that we want to decouple, a **port**, we define a separate piece of code to translate inputs and outputs, the **adapter**. This allows us more freedom to change the code behind the adapters without forcing change on other components that interact with it through this port.

This code is the core of our logic, so being able to change this without coordinating with other teams or people is a big win. As a result, we can safely make incremental progress in this part of the code and then deal with the significantly trickier and costly changes in the agreed-upon protocols of information exchange between components. These changes should, ideally, happen a lot less often, so teams will break one another's code significantly less often, too.

We should always treat these integration points, these ports, with a little more care than other parts of our systems because they cause more pain when things need to change here. The Ports & Adapters approach gives us a strategy to embody that "more care" in our code.

---

5. Ports & Adapters is an architectural pattern aimed at producing more loosely coupled application components; it is also known as Hexagonal Architecture. See https://bit.ly/3cwH3Sd.

Note, this has nothing to do with the technology in use. Ports & Adapters is just as useful—probably more useful—for binary information sent through a socket than it is for structured text sent via a REST API call.

The other important, and often overlooked, tool in managing the impact of change is speed of feedback. If I write some code that breaks your code, then how much that matters is very different depending on when we find out that I broke it.

If we only discover that I broke something months later, then the implications may be serious. If our code is already in production when we find the problem, the implications could be very serious.

If, on the other hand, we find out within a few minutes of my making the change, then it is no big deal. I can resolve the problem that I created, maybe before you even notice. This is the problem that **continuous integration** and **continuous delivery** solve.

This means that we can use either, or both, of these strategies to limit the impact of change. We can design our systems to enhance our ability to make changes, without forcing the need to change on others, and we can optimize our working practices to make changes in small, incremental steps. Committing those small changes to some shared evaluation system and then optimizing that evaluation system give us feedback quickly enough to allow us to react to it and to manage any problems that our changes may cause.

Incremental Design

I have been a long-time advocate for agile approaches to software development. In part this is because I see agile as an important step, a "beginning of infinity" step, as I described in an earlier chapter. This matters because it means that we can begin work before we have all the answers. We learn as we incrementally make progress, which is an idea at the heart of this book.

This challenges many software developers preconceptions. Many people that I talk to struggle with the idea of being able to write code before they have a detailed idea of the design they want to create.

Even more find the idea of incrementally architecting a complex system almost inconceivable, but both of these ideas are at the heart of any high-quality engineering approach.

Complex systems don't spring fully formed from the mind of some genius creator; they are the fruits of working through problems, deepening our understanding, and exploring ideas and potential solutions through sometimes hard work.

In part, this is challenging because it requires that we flip some kind of mental switch, and it demands a certain level of self-confidence that we will be able to solve problems that we don't yet know anything about when they eventually surface.

My arguments in this book about what engineering really is and what software development really is are intended to give you some help in flipping that mental switch, if you haven't already.

The confidence to make progress in the face of ignorance of the future is a different kind of problem. In some ways it's one that has some more practical solutions.

First, we need to accept that change, missteps, and the impact of the unexpected, as our knowledge deepens, are all simply inevitable, whether you acknowledge them or not. It is simply the reality of all complex creation of any kind, and in the context of software development specifically, it is the nature of the beast.

Complaints that "they" always get the requirements wrong are one symptom of this. Yes, no one knows what to build at the start. If they tell you that they do, they really don't understand the problem.

Accepting that we don't know, doubting what we do know, and working to learn fast is a step from dogma toward engineering.

We use facts about what we know and have discovered incrementally and, at every stage, look to extrapolate our next step forward into the unknown, based on all of the stuff that we currently believe that we know. This is a more scientifically rational worldview. As physicist Richard Feynman once said, science is "a satisfactory philosophy of ignorance." He also said:

> The scientist has a lot of experience with ignorance and doubt and uncertainty, and this experience is of very great importance, I think.

The techniques of managing complexity are important for several reasons, but in this context of software development, as an act of discovery it is a vital one because they allow us to limit the "blast radius" when our "step forward" turns out to be a misstep. You can think of this as defensive design or defensive coding, but a better way to think of it is as **incremental design**.

We can choose to write code in ways that are merely a sequence of steps organized, or rather not organized, as a big ball of mud, poorly compartmentalized. Alternatively, we can write code in ways that effectively acknowledge and manage its complexity as it evolves.

If we do the former, then the more tightly coupled, less modular, less cohesive the code, the more difficult it is to change. That is why the properties that allow us to manage the complexity in our code that I keep repeating are important. If we adopt these ideas at every level of granularity perva-sively in our work, then we close fewer doors on change, and we leave more options open to make change—even unexpected change—in the future. This is different from over-engineering and writ-ing code that copes with every eventuality. This is code that is **organized to make change easier**, not code that does everything that you can think of right now.

If I begin writing a system that does something useful and requires that I store results somewhere, then I could do what many developers do and mix the code that does the useful things with the code that does the storage. If I do this and then find out that the storage solution I picked is too expensive, too buggy, or too slow, my only option is to go and rewrite all of my code.

If I separated the concerns of "something useful" from "storage," then I may factionally increase my line count in code. I may have to think a tiny bit harder about how to establish that separation, but I have opened the door to incremental working and incremental decision-making.

I don't believe that I am being immodest when I tell you that I think that I am regarded by people who have worked with me as a good programmer. Occasionally, people have called me a 10x programmer. If these things are true, they are not true because I am cleverer than other people or type faster or have access to better programming languages. They are true because I work incrementally. I do what I describe here.

I am wary of over-engineering my solutions. I never aim to add code for things that I don't know are needed now. However, I do always try to separate the concerns in my design, break out different parts of the system, design interfaces that abstract the ideas in the code that they represent, and hide the detail of what happens on the other side of the interface. I strive for simple, obvious solutions in my code, but I also have some kind of internal warning system that sounds off when my code starts to feel too complex, too coupled, or just insufficiently modular.

I could name a few rules of thumb, such as that I don't like functions longer than about ten lines of code or with more than about four parameters, but these are only guides. My aim is not small, simple code, but rather code that I can change when I learn new things. My goal is code that I can grow incrementally to fulfill its function as that function becomes clearer to me over time.

Working in ways that allow us the freedom to change our code and change our minds as our understanding deepens is fundamental to good engineering and is what incrementalism is built upon. Striving to be able to work incrementally then is also striving for higher-quality systems. If your code is hard to change, it is low quality, whatever it does.

Summary

Working incrementally is fundamental from building any complex system. It is an illusion to imagine that such systems spring "fully formed" from the minds of some expert or experts; they don't. They are the result of work and the gradual accretion of knowledge and understanding as we make progress. Organizing our work to facilitate and validate this learning allows us to take, as yet unseen, routes in the direction of progress. These ideas are at the core of what allows us to make progress effectively.

7

Empiricism

Empiricism, in the philosophy of science, is defined as "emphasizing evidence, especially as discovered in experiments. It is a fundamental part of the scientific method that all hypotheses and theories must be tested against observations of the natural world rather than resting solely on a priori reasoning, intuition, or revelation."[1]

By this definition, empiricism is closely related to experiment. However, I keep both concepts in my list of five because experiments can be carried out in such controlled circumstances that we could easily be experimenting with ideas that don't translate into meaningful reality, in an engineering sense.

Even in modern physical engineering, with all of our computer models and simulations, we still see engineers test the things that they create, often to destruction, to learn how accurate or not their simulations are. Empiricism is a vital aspect of *engineering*.

For readers who are not so interested in counting angels on the head of some semantic pin, why does this matter?

Unlike pure science, engineering is firmly rooted in the application of ideas to solving real-world problems. I could easily decide that I needed to achieve some goal of architectural purity or some performance target that required me to invent and explore new techniques in software, but unless these ideas are realized in some tangible value and unless my software can do more things that matter or deliver new value, they are irrelevant, however much I experimented with them.

---

1. Source: Wikipedia, https://en.wikipedia.org/wiki/Empiricism

Grounded in Reality

The other dimension to this is that our production systems will always surprise us, and they should! Ideally they will not surprise us too often in very bad ways, but any software system is really only the best guess, so far, of its developers. When we publish our software into production, this is, or should be, an opportunity to learn.

This is an important lesson that we can learn from science and engineering in other disciplines. One of the deeply important aspects of a scientific, rational approach to solving problems is the idea of skepticism. It doesn't matter who has an idea, how much we would like the idea to be true, or how much work we have put into an idea; if the idea is bad, it is bad.

Evidence from looking at the impact of choices in software products suggests that, for the best companies, only a fraction of their ideas produce the effects that they predicted.

> Features are built because teams believe they are useful, yet in many domains most ideas fail to improve key metrics. Only one third of the ideas tested at Microsoft improved the metric(s) they were designed to improve.[2]

Empiricism, making decisions based on evidence and observations of reality, is vital to making sensible progress. Without that analysis and reflection, organizations will continue to proceed on the basis of only guesswork and will continue to invest in ideas that lose them money or reputation.

Separating Empirical from Experimental

We can be empirical by using the information that we gather as part of our experiments to make decisions. We explore that aspect in the next chapter. We can also be empirical by observing the outcome of our ideas less formally. This is not a replacement for being experimental, but rather a way in which we can improve the quality of our characterization of the current situation at the point when we are thinking of our next experiments.

I am aware that in exploring the ideas of empiricism and experimentation separately, I am in danger of descending into the arcana of philosophy and etymology. This is not my intent, so let me illustrate why it is worth considering these two closely related ideas independently with practical examples.

"I Know That Bug!"

A few years ago, I had the fantastic experience of building one of the world's highest-performance financial exchanges from scratch. It was during this period of my career that I started to take engineering thinking and discipline seriously in my approach to software development.

---

2. In a paper titled "Online Experiments at Large Scale" (https://stanford.io/2LdjvmC), the authors describe how two- to three-thirds of ideas for changes to software produced zero or negative value for the organization that implemented them.

We were about to make a release into production when we found a serious bug. This was a relatively unusual occurrence for us. This team employed the disciplines described in this book, including continuous delivery, so we had constant feedback on the continual flow of small changes. We rarely found big problems this late in the day.

Our release candidate was undergoing final checks before release. Earlier in the day, one of our colleagues, Darren, told us at stand-up that he had seen a weird messaging failure on his development workstation when running our suite of API acceptance tests. He had apparently seen a thread that was blocked in our underlying third-party pub-sub messaging code. He tried to reproduce it, and could, but he could do so on only one particular pairing station. That was weird, because the configuration of our environments was wholly automated and version controlled using a fairly sophisticated infrastructure-as-code approach.

Later that afternoon, we had started work on the next set of changes. Almost immediately, our build grid showed a dramatic change with lots of acceptance tests failing. We started exploring what was happening and noticed that one of our services was showing a very high CPU load. This was unusual because our software was generally extremely efficient. On further investigation, we noticed that our new messaging code was apparently stuck. This must be what Darren had seen. Clearly, we had a problem with our new messaging code!

We reacted immediately. We told everyone that the release candidate may not be ready for release. We started thinking that we may have to take a branch, something that we generally tried to avoid, and back out our messaging changes.

We did all this before we stopped and thought about it. "Hang on, this doesn't make any sense; we have been running this code for more than a week, and we have now seen this failure three times in a couple of hours."

We stopped and talked through what we knew; we collected our facts. We had upgraded the messaging at the start of the iteration, and we had a thread dump that showed the messaging stalled; so had Darren, but his dump looked stalled in a different place. We had been running all of these tests in our deployment pipeline repeatedly and successfully for more than a week, with the messaging changes.

At this point we were stuck. Our hypothesis, failing messaging, didn't fit the facts. We needed more facts so that we could build a new hypothesis. We started again, where we would usually start solving a problem but had omitted to on this occasion because the conclusion had looked so obvious. We characterized our problem, so we started gathering data to tell the story. We looked at the log files and found, as you may have guessed, an exception that clearly pointed the finger at some brand new code.

Long story short: the messaging was fine. The apparent "messaging problem" was a symptom, not a cause. We were actually looking at a thread dump that was in a normal waiting state and working as it should. What had happened was that we had been hit by a threading bug in some new code, unrelated to messaging. It was an obvious, simple fix, and we would have found it in five minutes with no fuss if we hadn't jumped to the conclusion that it was a messaging problem; in fact, we did fix it in five minutes once we stopped to think and built our hypothesis based on the facts that we had, rather than jumping to some wrong but apparently "obvious" conclusion.

It was only when we stopped and listed the facts of what we were seeing that we realized the conclusions we had jumped to really didn't fit those facts. It was this and this alone that prompted us to go and gather more facts—enough to solve the problem we had, rather than the problem we imagined we had.

We had a sophisticated automated test system, and yet we ignored the obvious. It was obvious we must have committed something that broke the build. Instead, we joined together various facts and jumped to the wrong conclusion because there was a sequence of events that led us down the wrong path. We built a theory on sand, not validating as we went, but building new guesses on top of old. It created an initially plausible, seemingly "obvious" cause, except that it was completely wrong.

Science works! Make a hypothesis. Figure out how to prove or disprove it. Carry out the experiment. Observe the results and see they match your hypothesis. Repeat!

The lesson here is that being empirical is more complex than it looks and takes more discipline to achieve. You could imagine that when we correlated the problem Darren had seen with the failing tests we were being empirical and reacting to the messages reality was sending us. However, we weren't. We were jumping to conclusions and skewing the facts to fit our preferred guess at what was going wrong. If at that point we had simply walked through "what we knew" in a more organized way, it would have been completely obvious that this wasn't a "messaging problem" because our messaging changes had been working all week and hadn't changed since they had been working.

Avoiding Self-Deception

Being **empirical** requires us to be more organized in how we assemble the signals we gather from reality and assemble them into theories that we can test through experimentation.

Human beings are remarkable, but being as smart as we are takes an enormous amount of processing. Our perception of reality is not "reality," and we have a series of biological tricks to make our perception of reality appear to be seamless. For example, our visual sampling rate is surprisingly slow. The smoothness of your perception of reality, as gathered through your eyes, is an illusion created by your brain. In reality, your eyes sample a small patch of your visual field, scanning at a rate of roughly once every couple of seconds, and your brain creates a "virtual reality" impression of what is really going on.

Most of what you see is a guess made up by your brain. This matters because we have evolved to fool ourselves. We jump to conclusions, now because if we had taken the time to do a detailed accurate analysis of our visual field back in the days when we were fighting for survival, we would have been eaten by a predator before we had finished.

We have all sorts of cognitive shortcuts and biases that we have evolved over millions of years to allow us to survive in the real world. However, in the world that we have created, our modern high-tech civilization has taken the place of the dangerous savanna populated by predators, and we have developed a more effective way to solve problems. It is slower than jumping to often wrong conclusions, but it is dramatically more effective at solving problems—sometimes even staggeringly hard problems. Richard Feynman famously characterized science as follows:

The first principle is that you must not fool yourself – and you are the easiest person to fool.[3]

Science is not what most people think it is. It is not about large hadron colliders or modern medicine or even physics. Science is a problem-solving technique. We create a model of the problem before us, and we check to see if *everything that we currently know* fits the model. We then try to think of ways in which we can prove the model is wrong. David Deutsch says that the model is composed of "good explanations."[4]

Inventing a Reality to Suit Our Argument

Let's look at another example of how easily we can fool ourselves.

While we were building our super-fast exchange,[5] we did a lot of experimentation with the creation of *very* fast software. We discovered, through experiment, lots of interesting things. Most notable was an approach to software design that we dubbed **mechanical sympathy**.

In this approach, we designed our code based on a fairly deep understanding of how the underlying hardware worked so that we could take advantage of it. One of several important lessons we learned, through experimentation, was that once you had eliminated dumb mistakes,[6] the most significant impact on the raw performance of a piece of code in a modern computer was a cache-miss.

Avoiding cache-misses came to dominate our approach to design for the seriously high-performance parts of our code.

One of the most common causes of a cache-miss for most systems that we found by measurement was concurrency.

When we were building our exchange, a common idea in the software industry, the received wisdom at the time ran something like this: "Hardware is approaching physical limits that mean that CPU speed is no longer increasing. So our designs will have to 'go parallel' to keep them performing well."

There were academic papers on this topic and languages specifically designed to make parallel programing easier and more pervasive in solving everyday programming problems. In reality, there

---

3. Nobel prize–winning physicist, Richard Feynman (1918–1988), https://bit.ly/2PLfEU3

4. The Beginning of Infinity" by David Deutsch, https://amzn.to/2IyY553

5. Read more about the innovative architecture of our exchange here: https://bit.ly/3a48mS3.

6. The most common performance mistake is to use the wrong kind of data structure to store something. Many developers do not consider the time of retrieval of different kinds of collections.
   For small collection sizes, a simple array (O(n) on retrieval) may be faster than something like a hash table (with O(1) semantics). For larger collections, the O(1) solution will be best for random access. After that, the implementation of the collections can start to have a cost.

is a lot wrong with this model, as we demonstrated, but for the purpose of this story I will look at only one aspect. There was an academic language being talked about at the time that aimed to automatically parallelize solutions.[7]

A demonstration of the power of this language was shown by processing the text of a book to parse out words from the stream of characters. Given our experience and our belief in the large costs of concurrency, at least when the problem demands that we combine the results from the different concurrent threads of execution, we were skeptical.

We didn't have access to the academic language, but one of my colleagues, Mike Barker, did a simple experiment. He implemented the same algorithm that the language academics were describing in Scala and a simple, brute-force approach in Java and then measured the results by processing the text of Lewis Carol's *Alice in Wonderland* over a series of runs.

The concurrent Scala algorithm was implemented in 61 lines of code; the Java version took 33. The Scala version could process an impressive-sounding 400 copies of the book per second. That's impressive until you compare it to the simpler, easier to read, single-threaded code in Java that could process 1,600 copies per second.

The language researchers had started with a theory—that parallelism was the answer—but they had gotten so caught up in an implementation that they never thought to test their starting premise, which was that this would result in a faster outcome. It resulted in a slower outcome and more complex code.

Separating Myth from Reality: Example

It is understood that CPU development has reached a limit and that ever-increasing clock-cycle speedups have paused. Clock cycles have not increased since around 2005! There are good reasons for this, based on the physics of making transistors out of silicon. There is a relationship between the density of the transistors and the heat that they generate in operation. Building a chip that goes much faster than 3GHz means that overheating becomes a serious problem.

So if we can't get speed gains by increasing the rate at which we process instructions linearly in our CPUs, we can parallelize, and the processor manufacturers have. This is good: modern processors are marvelous devices, but how do we use all that power? We can do work in parallel!

This is fine for running unconnected, independent processes, but what if you want to build a fast algorithm? The obvious conclusion (guess) is that it is inevitable that the solution to this problem is to parallelize our algorithms. In essence, the idea here is that we can speed things up by throwing more threads of execution at the problems that we tackle.

There have been several general-purpose programming languages built upon this assumption to help us to more effectively write parallel solutions to problems.

---

7. Presentation outlining automatic parallelization: https://bit.ly/35JPqVs

Unfortunately, this is a much more complex problem than it looks. For some unusual tasks, parallel execution is the answer. However, as soon as there is any need to bring the information from those different threads of execution back together again, the picture changes.

Let us gather some feedback. Instead of jumping to the conclusion that parallelizing things is the answer, let us gather some data.

We could try something simple. For example, let's write a trivially simple algorithm to increment a simple integer 500 million times.

Without any feedback, it seems obvious that we could throw lots of threads at this problem. However, when you carry out this experiment and gather the data (feedback), the results may surprise you:

Method	Time (ms)
Single thread	300
Single thread with lock	10,000
Two threads with lock	224,000
Single thread with CAS	5,700
Two threads with CAS	30,000

The table shows the result of this experiment carried out using different approaches. First, the baseline test. Write the code on a single thread and increment a long value. It takes 300 ms to get to 500 million.

As soon as we introduce the code to synchronize things, we start to see some costs that we hadn't anticipated (unless we are low-level concurrency experts). If we still do all the work on a single thread but add a lock to allow the results to be used from a different thread, it adds 9,700 ms to the cost. Locks are extremely expensive!

If we decide to divide up the work between only two threads and synchronize their results, it is 746 times slower than doing the work on a single thread!

So locks are extremely expensive. There are more difficult to use, but more efficient, ways to coordinate the work between threads. The most efficient way to do this is a low-level concurrency approach called *compare-and-swap* (CAS). Sadly, even this approach is 100 times slower than work on a single thread.

Based on this feedback, we can make more informed, evidence-based decisions. If we want to maximize the rate at which an algorithm makes progress, we should try to keep as much work as possible on a single thread, unless we can make progress and never join the results back together again.

(This experiment was first carried out by Mike Barker when we worked together a few years ago.)

The example in the preceding sidebar is a demonstration of several of the concepts at the heart of this book. It demonstrates the importance of feedback, experimentation, and empiricism.

Guided by Reality

The researchers in this scenario were acting with good intent, but they had fallen into the trap that is pervasive, outside of the realms of science and engineering: they had come up with a guess to solve the problem and then rushed ahead to implement their guess without checking first to see if their guess was right or wrong.

It took Mike a few hours of coding, using the researcher's own sample problem, to show that their assumed solution didn't make sense. Being skeptical and checking our ideas is work, but it is the only way to make real progress rather than proceeding on guesswork, supposition, and hubris.

The best way to start is to **assume that what you know, and what you think, is probably wrong** and then figure out how you could find out *how it is wrong*.

The programming-language academics in this story had bought into a myth that was not grounded in reality. They had built their model for parallelizing programming languages, because it was a cool problem to solve if you were a language academic.

Unfortunately, this did not take into account the costs of parallelism; they had ignored the reality of modern computer hardware and computer science. It has long been understood that parallelism costs when you need to "join results back together." Amdahl's law shows that there is a harsh limit to the number of concurrent operations that make sense, unless they are wholly independent of one another.

The academics assumed that "more parallelism is good," but that is an idea that is based on some kind of imaginary, theoretical machine, where the costs of concurrency were low; such machines don't exist.

These academics were not being empirical, though they were being experimental. This lack of empiricism meant that their experiments were the wrong experiments, so the model that they built did not match real-world experience.

Empiricism is the mechanism through which we can sense-check the validity of our experiments. It helps us to place them into context and, in effect, test the validity of the simulations of reality at the heart of our experiments.

Summary

Engineering rather than pure science demands of us some consideration of the practicality of our solutions. This is really where **empiricism** comes into play. It is not enough to look only at the world, make guesses based on what we see, and then assume that our guesses must be correct because we got the information that informed them from the real world. That is poor science and poor engineering. However, engineering is a practical discipline. So we must, continually, be skeptical about our guesses, and the experiments that we create to test them, and check them against our experience of reality.

8

Being Experimental

Experimentation is defined as "a procedure carried out to support, refute, or validate a hypothesis. Experiments provide insight into cause-and-effect by demonstrating what outcome occurs when a particular factor is manipulated."[1]

Taking an experimental approach to solving problems is profoundly important. I would argue that science, and the experimental practice at its heart, is what differentiates our modern, high-tech society from the agrarian societies that preceded us, more than anything else. Human beings have existed as a distinct species for hundreds of thousands of years, and yet the rate of progress that we have made in the last 300 or 400 years since Newton or Galileo, periods that most people would mark as the beginning of modern science, has outstripped everything that went before by many orders of magnitude. There are estimates that the whole of human knowledge doubles every 13 months in our civilization.[2]

In large part this is because of the application of humanity's best problem-solving technique.

Most software development, though, does not really work this way. Most software development is consciously carried out as an exercise in craft where someone guesses what users may like. They guess about a design and/or technology that could achieve their product goals. Developers then guess about whether the code that they write does what they mean it to, and they guess about whether there are any bugs in it. Many organizations guess about whether their software is useful or made more money than it cost to build it.

We can do better. We can use guesses where they are appropriate, but then we can design experiments to test the guesses.

---

1. Source: Wikipedia, https://en.wikipedia.org/wiki/Experiment

2. Buckminster Fuller created the knowledge doubling curve: https://bit.ly/2WiyUbE.

This sounds slow, expensive, and complex, but it is not. This is really only a shift in approach and mindset. This is not about "working harder"; this is about "working smarter." The teams that I have seen that have worked this way and taken these ideas to heart are not slow or overly academic. They are, though, more disciplined in the way that they approach problem-solving, and as a result, they find better, cheaper solutions to problems more quickly and produce software with greater quality that pleases their users more.

What Does "Being Experimental" Mean?

One of the key ideas that is at the root of scientific thinking is to move away from decisions made by authority. Richard Feynman, as ever, has a great quote on this topic:

Science is the belief in the ignorance of experts.

He also said:

Have no respect whatsoever for authority; forget who said it and instead look what he starts with, where he ends up, and ask yourself, 'Is it reasonable?'

Despite the somewhat sexist language of his time, the sentiment is correct.

We must move away from making decisions based on what the most important, charismatic, or famous people say, even if it is Richard Feynman, and instead make decisions and choices based on evidence.

This is a big change for our industry and not how it usually works. Sadly, this is also true of society at large, not just software development, so if we are to succeed as engineers, we must do better than society at large.

What made you pick the programming language that you use or the framework or the editor in which you write your code? Do you have conversations in which you argue about the relative merits of Java versus Python? Do you think everyone who uses VI as their editor is smart or a fool? Do you think that functional programming is the one true way, or do you believe that object orientation is the best thing ever invented? Yes, me too!

I am not proposing for every such decision that we should create an exhaustive, controlled experiment, but we should stop having religious wars about these things.

If we want to make the argument that Clojure is better than C#, why not do a little trial and measure the stability and throughput of the result? At least then we could decide on some basis of evidence, even if not perfect, rather than make decisions like this on the basis of who was most persuasive in the argument. If you disagree with the results, do a better experiment and show your reasoning.

Being experimental does not mean basing every decision on hard physics. All sciences are based on experiment, but the degree of control varies. In engineering, experimentation remains at its heart, but is a pragmatic, practical form of experimentation.

Four characteristics define "being experimental" as an approach:

- **Feedback**: We need to take feedback seriously, and we need to understand how we will collect results that will provide us with a clear signal and deliver them efficiently back to the point at which we are thinking. We need to close the loop.

- **Hypothesis**: We need to have an idea in mind that we are aiming to evaluate. We are not wandering around willy-nilly, randomly collecting data. That is not good enough.

- **Measurement**: We need a clear idea of how we will evaluate the predictions that we are testing in our hypothesis. What does "success" or "failure" mean in this context?

- **Control the variables**: We need to eliminate as many variables as we can so that we can understand the signals that our experiment is sending to us.

Feedback

It is important, from an engineering perspective, to recognize the effect that speeding the efficiency and quality of feedback can give.

The Need for Speed

I once worked at a company that produced complex, financial trading software. The developers were very good, and the company successful, but still they knew that they could do better, and my job was to help to improve their software development practices.

When I joined, they had adopted a reasonably effective approach to automated testing. They had lots of tests. They operated an overnight build, and the bulk of their offering consisted of a large C++ build, which took nine-and-a-half hours to complete, including running all the tests. So they ran the build every night.

One of the developers told me that in the three years that they had been working this way, there had been only three occasions when all the tests passed.

So, each morning they would pick the modules where all the tests had passed and release those, while holding back modules that had produced a test failure.

This was fine, as long as one of the passing modules didn't rely on changes in one of the failing modules, and sometimes they did.

There were lots of things that I wanted to change, but as a first step, we worked to improve the efficiency of the feedback, with no other changes.

After a lot of experimentation and hard work, we managed to get a fast-stage, commit build to run in 12 minutes and the rest of the tests to run in 40 minutes. This was doing the same work as the nine-and-a-half-hour build, only faster! There were no other changes in organization, process, or tooling, beyond speeding up the build and getting the results more efficiently to developers.

In the first two-week period following the release of this change, there were two builds where all tests passed. In the two weeks after that, and for as long as I worked there, there was at least one build per day where all tests passed and all the code was releasable.

Making no other change than improving the speed of the feedback gave the teams the tools that they needed to fix the underlying instability.

The "war story" in the box "The Need for Speed" is a good demonstration of the effectiveness of applying the techniques of experimentation to our work, as well as optimizing for good feedback. In this case, we experimented to improve the efficiency and quality of the feedback to developers. During the course of this work we established better measures of build performance, controlled the variables with improved version control and infrastructure as code, and A/B tested several different technical solutions and build systems.

It was only through taking a fairly disciplined approach to applying this kind of experimental thinking to this problem—a problem that various attempts had tried to improve on before—that we were able to make progress. Several of our ideas didn't pan out. Our experiments showed us that it was no good investing lots of time and effort on certain tools or techniques, because they wouldn't give us the speedups that we needed.

Hypothesis

When talking about science and engineering, people often talk about "eliminating guesswork." I am guilty of using that phrase in the past, too. It is wrong, though. In one important sense, science is built on guesswork; it is just that a scientific approach to problem-solving institutionalizes the guesswork and calls it a *hypothesis*. As Richard Feynman so eloquently put it in his wonderful lecture on the scientific method[3]:

We look for a new law by the following process, **first we guess it!**

Guesses or hypotheses are the starting point. The difference between science and engineering, compared with other less effective approaches, is that the others stop there.

To be scientific, once we have a guess, in the form of a hypothesis, we start making some predictions, and then we can try to find ways to check those predictions.

---

3. Nobel Prize–winning physicist Richard Feynman on the scientific method: https://bit.ly/2RiEivq

Feynman goes on, in that great presentation, to say this:

If your guess disagrees with experiment, then it (your guess) is wrong!

That is the heart of it! That is where we need to get to in order to be able to claim that what we do is engineering rather than guesswork.

We need to be able to test our hypotheses. Our tests can take a variety of forms. We can observe reality (production), or we can carry out some more controlled experiment, perhaps in the form of an automated test of some kind.

We can focus on getting good feedback from production to inform our learning, or we can try our ideas in more controlled circumstances.

Organizing our thinking, and our work, to proceed as a series of experiments to validate our hypotheses is an important improvement in the quality of our work.

Measurement

Whether we are collecting data to interpret from reality (production) or carrying out a more controlled experiment, we need to take measurement seriously. We need to think about what the data that we collect means and be critical of it.

It is too easy to fool ourselves by trying to "fit the facts to the data." We can achieve some level of protection from such mistakes by thinking carefully, as part of the design of our experiment, what measurements we think will make sense. We need to make a prediction, based on our hypothesis, and then figure out how we can measure the results of our prediction.

I can think of lots of examples of measuring the wrong things. At one of my clients, they decided that they could improve the quality of their code by increasing the level of test coverage. So, they began a project to institute the measurement, collected the data, and adopted a policy to encourage improved test coverage. They set a target of "80 percent test coverage." Then they used that measurement to incentivize their development teams, bonuses were tied to hitting targets in test coverage.

Guess what? They achieved their goal!

Some time later, they analyzed the tests that they had and found that more than 25 percent of their tests had no assertions in them at all. So they had paid people on development teams, via their bonuses, to write tests that tested nothing at all.

In this case, a much better measure would have been stability. What this organization really wanted was not more tests but better quality code, so measuring that more directly worked better.

This difficulty in measuring the wrong things does not only apply to "metrics" and human beings' cleverness at gaming the system.

I spent more than ten years of my career working in low-latency finance systems. When we started out, we were very focused on measuring latency and throughput, so we worked hard to capture measurements, setting ourselves targets like "The system should be able to process 100,000 messages per second with no more than 2ms latency." Our first attempts were based on averages, which we later found out were meaningless. We needed to be more specific; there were times in the subsequent trading cycle when our peak load far exceeded the equivalent rate of 100,000 msg/sec, peaking in numbers that were equivalent to millions of msg/sec. Average latency didn't matter if there were outliers beyond certain limits. In the real world of high-frequency trading, 2ms wasn't an average—that was the limit!

In this second example, we started out being experimental, but, in part due to the accuracy of our measurement, even though we were measuring some of the wrong things, we quickly started to learn and improve the quality and accuracy of our measurements and to better target our experiments. **It's all about learning!**

Not everyone cares to this degree of precision in measurement, but the principles remain the same, whatever kind of software you are building. Being experimental demands that we pay more attention to the measurement of our system, whatever that means in our context.

Controlling the Variables

To gather feedback and make useful measurements, we need to control the variables, as far as we practically can. When Jez Humble and I wrote our book *Continuous Delivery*, we subtitled it *Reliable Software Releases Through Build, Test, and Deployment Automation*. I don't think that I thought of it like this at the time, but what this is really saying is "control the variables to make your releases reliable."

Version control allows us to be more precise about the changes that we release into production. Automated testing allows us to be more precise about the behavior, speed, robustness, and general quality of the software that we produce. Deployment automation and ideas like **infrastructure as code** allow us to be more precise about the environments in which our software operates.

All these techniques allow us to be much more sure that when we put our software into production, it will do what we intend.

My take on **continuous delivery** as a generalized approach to software development is that it allows us to proceed with much more surety. It eliminates, to a large extent, the variables around the quality of our work so that we can concentrate on whether our product ideas are good. We can get a much clearer picture of "are we building the right things" because we have taken control of "are we building the things right."

By controlling many of the technical variables in software development, continuous delivery allows us to make progress with significantly more confidence than before. This allows software development teams to take real advantage of the techniques of optimizing for learning that are at the heart of this book.

For example, a continuous delivery deployment pipeline is an ideal experimental platform for learning about the changes that we want to make to our production systems.

Working so that our software is always in a releasable state, the idea at the heart of CD is an idea that maximizes the feedback that we can get on the quality of our work and one that strongly encourages us to work in smaller steps. This, in turn, means that we are pretty much forced to work iteratively and incrementally.

Having software that is always in a releasable state, well, it would be foolish of us not to take advantage of that! It means that organizations can release more frequently and gather a lot more feedback, a lot sooner, on the quality of their ideas and build better products.

Automated Testing as Experiments

Experiments can take many forms, but in software we have an enormous advantage over every other discipline in that we have this fantastic experimental platform: a computer!

We can run literally millions of experiments every second if we want. These experiments too, may take a variety of different forms; we can think of the compilation step as a form of experiment: "I predict that my code will compile without any warnings" or "I predict that none of my UI code accesses a database library." By far the most flexible form of experiment, though, in the context of software, is an automated test.

Any automated test to validate our software could be considered an experiment if you try hard enough. However, if you write your automated tests after you have written the code, the value of the experiment is reduced. An experiment should be based on some kind of hypothesis, and deciding if your code works or not is a pretty lame hypothesis.

What I am thinking of is organizing our development around a series of iterative experiments that make tiny predictions about the expected behavior of our code, and that will allow us to incrementally increase the function of our software.

The clearest form of such an experiment is software development guided by tests, or **test-driven development** (TDD).

TDD is an effective strategy where we use tests as executable specifications for the behavior of our system. Precisely defining the change in behavior that we are aiming to achieve is our hypothesis: "given this specific context, when this thing happens, then we expect this outcome." We create this prediction, in the form of a small, simple test, and then confirm that the predictions of our test case were met when we complete the code and carry out the experiment.

We can operate this TDD approach at different levels of granularity. We can begin by creating user-centered specifications, using the techniques of **acceptance test–driven development** (ATDD), sometimes also referred to as **behavior-driven development** (BDD). We use these high-level executable specifications to guide the more fine-grained, more technical unit testing.

Software developed using these techniques has significantly and measurably fewer bugs than software developed more conventionally.[4]

This is a welcome improvement in quality, but we don't really see the value until we also factor in the impact that such reductions have on productivity. Presumably, as a result of this reduction in defects, development teams spend significantly less time on other activities, such as bug detection, triage, and analysis.

The result is that high-performing teams that employ techniques like TDD, continuous integration, and continuous delivery spend 44 percent more time on useful work.[5] These teams are much more productive than the norm while, at the same time, producing a higher-quality outcome. You can have your cake and eat it!

The practices of extreme programming in the context of continuous delivery, specifically continuous integration and TDD, provide a wonderful, scalable, experimental platform in which we can evaluate and refine our ideas in design and implementation. These techniques have an important, significant impact on the quality of our work and the rate at which we can produce good software. These are the kinds of outcomes that in other disciplines we would ascribe to engineering.

Putting the Experimental Results of Testing into Context

Forgive me for being a little philosophical for a moment, but then I expect you are getting used to that by now.

Let's think about what a body of tests, like those I just described, really means.

I am making a claim for scientific rationality as a guiding principle of the approach that I am attempting to describe here. A common mistake of software developers, and maybe people in general, is that as soon as we mention "science" we almost always think "physics."

I am an amateur physics nerd. I love physics and the mental models it allows me to construct to understand the things around me. I sometimes joke about physics being the one true science, but I don't mean it.

Science is much broader than only physics, but outside the realms of the simplified abstractions that we use at the heart of physics, other sciences are often messier and less precise. That does not diminish the value of scientific-style reasoning. Biology, chemistry, psychology, and sociology are all sciences, too. They don't make predictions with the same accuracy as physics because they can't control the variables quite as rigorously in experiment, but they still provide deeper insight and

---

4. There are several studies, academic and informal, on the impact of TDD on defect reduction. Most studies agree that defect reduction is in a range from 40 percent to well over 250 percent. Source: https://bit.ly/2LFixzS, https://bit.ly/2LDh3q3, https://bit.ly/3MurTgF

5. Source: "State of DevOps" reports (various years) and *Accelerate: The science of Lean and DevOps* by Fosgren, Humble, and Kim. See https://amzn.to/369r73m.

better results than the alternatives. I am not for a moment expecting us to be as thorough or as precise as physics.

Nevertheless, in software we have some profound advantages over nearly every other form of engineering, and several of the sciences, where experiments are often difficult for ethical or practical reasons. We can completely create and control the "universe" that our software inhabits. We can exercise delicate, precise control if we choose to do so. We can create millions of experiments, at low cost, allowing us to use the power of statistics to our advantage. Simplistically, this is what modern machine learning really is.

Computers give us the opportunity to take control of our software and carry out experiments on it at scales that would be unimaginable in any other context.

Finally, there is one more, quite profound ability that software gives to us.

So we aren't going to be physicists, but let's imagine for a moment that we are. If you and I come up with a new idea in physics, how do we know if it is a good one? Well, we need to be sufficiently well read to understand that it fits with the facts as physics currently understands them. It is no good suggesting that "Einstein was wrong" if we don't know what Einstein said. Physics is a vast subject, so however well read we are, we will need to get the idea clearly enough described that it is reproducible by others so that they can test it, too. If any test of the idea fails, after checking that it wasn't a mistake in the testing, we can reject the idea.

In software, we can do all of that with our tests, and instead of it taking months or years for our ideas to bear fruit, we can get results in minutes. This is our super-power!

If we think of our software existing in a tiny universe that we create, however big or complex the software, then we can control that universe precisely and evaluate our software's role in it. If we work to be able to "control the variables" to the extent that we can reliably and repeatably re-create that universe—infrastructure as code as a part of a continuous delivery deployment pipeline, for example—then we have a good starting point for our experiments.

The full set of all the tests that we have written, including the collection of experiments asserting our understanding of the behavior of our system in that controlled universe, is our body of knowledge of the system.

We can give the definition of the "universe" and the "body of knowledge" to anyone, and they can confirm that they are, as a whole, internally consistent—the tests all pass.

If we want to "create new knowledge" in the system, we can create a new experiment, a test, that defines the new knowledge that we expect to observe, and then we can add that knowledge in the form of working code that meets the needs of the experiment. If the new ideas are not consistent with previous ideas, meaning the "body of knowledge" in our mini, controlled universe, then experiments will fail, and we will know that this idea is wrong, or at least inconsistent with the recorded statement of the knowledge in the system.

Now, I recognize that this is a somewhat idealistic representation of a software system and its associated tests, but I have worked on several systems that got very close to this ideal. However, even if you got only 80 percent of the way there, think of what this means. You have an indication, within minutes, of the validity and consistency of your ideas, system-wide.

As I said earlier, this is our super-power. This is what we can do with software if we treat it as an engineering process, rather than one based on craft alone.

Scope of an Experiment

Experiments come in all sizes. We can do something tiny, almost trivial, or we can do something big and complicated. Sometimes we need both of these things, but the idea of "working in a series of experiments" sounds daunting to some people.

Let me describe one common type of experiment that I regularly perform in my own software development to put your mind to rest.

When practicing TDD, I begin an intended change to my code with a test. The aim is to create a failing test. We want to run the test and see it fail to check that the test is actually testing something. So I begin by writing the test. Once I have the test as I want it, I will predict the *exact error message* that I expect the test to fail with: "I expect this test to fail with a message saying 'expected x but was 0'" or something similar. This is an experiment; this is a tiny application of the scientific method.

- I thought about and characterized the problem: "I have decided on the behavior that I want of my system and captured it as a test case."

- I formed a hypothesis: "I expect my test to fail!"

- I made a prediction: "When it fails, it will fail with this error message…."

- I carried out my experiment: "I ran the test."

This is a tiny change from how I worked before, but it has had a significant, positive impact on the quality of my work.

Applying a more disciplined, experimental approach to our work need not be complex or onerous. If we are to become software engineers, we need to adopt disciplines like this and apply them consistently to our work.

Summary

A key attribute of working in a more experimental way is the degree to which we exert control over the variables involved. Part of the definition of "experimentation" at the start of this chapter is "demonstrating what happens when a particular factor is manipulated." To work more experimentally, we need our approach to our work to be a little more controlled. We'd like the results of our "experiments" to be reliable. In the technical context of the systems that we build, working experimentally and taking control of what variables that we can, through effective automated testing and continuous delivery techniques like infrastructure as code, make our experiments more reliable and repeatable. More profoundly, though, they also make our software more deterministic, and so higher quality, more predictable, and reliable in use.

Any software engineering approach worth its name must result in better software for the same amount of work. Organizing our work as a sequence of many small, usually simple, experiments does this.

OPTIMIZE FOR MANAGING COMPLEXITY

9

Modularity

Modularity is defined as "the degree to which a system's components may be separated and recombined, often with the benefit of flexibility and variety in use."[1]

I have been writing code for a long time, and from the beginning of my learning, even when writing simple video games in assembly language, modularity was lauded as important in the design of our code.

Yet, much of the code that I have seen—in fact most of the code that I have seen and maybe even some of the code that I have written—has been far from modular. At some point this changed for me. My code is always modular now; it has become an ingrained part of my style.

Modularity is of vital importance in managing the complexity of the systems that we create. Modern software systems are vast, complicated, and often genuinely complex things. Most modern systems exceed the capacity of any human being to hold all of the details in their heads.

To cope with this complexity, we must divide the systems that we build into smaller, more under-standable pieces—pieces that we can focus on without worrying too much about what is going on elsewhere in the system.

This is always true, and again this is a kind of fractal idea that operates at different granularities.

As an industry, we have made progress. When I began my career, computers, and their software, were simpler, but we had to work harder to get things done. Operating systems did little beyond providing access to files and allowing us to show text on the screen. Anything else we needed to do

---

1. Source: Dictionary definition from Merriam-Webster. Used with Permission. Wikipedia, https://en.wikipedia .org/wiki/Modularity.

had to be written from scratch for every program. Want to print something out? You need to understand and write the low-level interactions with your specific printer.

We have certainly moved on by improving the abstraction and modularity of our operating systems and other software.

Yet, lots of systems don't look modular themselves. That is because it is hard work to design modular systems. If software development is about learning, then, as we learn, our understanding evolves and changes. So it is possible, probable even, that our views on which modules make sense and which don't will change over time, too.

For me, this is the real skill of software development. This is the property that most differentiates the code written by experts, masters of their craft, from that written by neophytes. While it takes skill to achieve good modularity in our designs, what I perceive in a lot of the code that I see is that people don't just "do modularity badly," but, rather, they "don't attempt it at all." A lot of code is written as though it is a recipe, meaning a linear sequence of steps collected together in methods and functions spanning hundreds or even thousands of lines of code.

Imagine for a moment if we turned on a feature, in your codebase, that rejected any code that contained a method longer than 30 lines of code or 50 or 100? Would your code pass such a test? I know that most of the code that I have seen in the wild would not.

These days when I begin a software project, I will establish a check in the continuous delivery deployment pipeline, in the "commit stage," that does exactly this kind of test and rejects any commit that contains a method longer that 20 or 30 lines of code. I also reject method signatures with more than five or six parameters. These are arbitrary values, based on my experience and preferences with the teams that I have worked on. My point is not to recommend these specific values; rather, it is that "guiderails" like these are important to keep us honest in our design. Whatever the time pressure, writing bad code is never a time-saver!

Hallmarks of Modularity

How can you tell if your system is modular? There is a simplistic level in the sense that a module is a collection of instructions and data that can be included in a program. That captures the "physical" representation of the bits and bytes that form the module.

More practically, though, what we are looking for is something that divides our code into little compartments. Each compartment can be reused multiple times, perhaps in a variety of contexts.

The code in a module is short enough to be readily understood as a stand-alone thing, outside the context of other parts of the system, even if it needs other parts of the system to be in place to do useful work.

There is some control over the scope of variables and functions that limit access to them so that there is a notion in some sense of there being an "outside" and an "inside" to the module. There is an interface of some kind that controls access, manages communication with other code, and deals with other modules.

Undervaluing the Importance of Good Design

There are a few reasons why many software developers don't pay attention to ideas like these. As an industry, we have undervalued the importance of software design. We obsess over languages and frameworks. We have arguments over IDEs versus text editors or object-oriented programming versus functional programming. Yet none of these things comes close to being as important, as foundational, as ideas like modularity or separation of concerns to the quality of our output.

If you have code with good modularity and good separation of concerns, whatever the programming paradigm, language, or tools, it will be better, easier to work on, easier to test, and easier to modify as you learn more about the problem that you are trying to solve. It will also be more flexible in use than code that does not have these properties.

My impression is that either we don't teach these skills at all or there is something inherent in programming (or programmers) that makes us dismiss their importance.

Clearly, designing for modularity is a different kind of skill to knowing the syntax of a programming language. It is a skill that we need to work on if we hope to develop some degree of mastery, and we can spend a lifetime and probably never perfect it.

This, though, is to me what software development is really about. How can we create code and systems that will grow and evolve over time but that are appropriately compartmentalized to limit damage if we make a mistake? How do we create systems that are appropriately abstracted so that we can treat the boundaries between our modules as opportunities to enhance our systems rather than liabilities that prevent us from changing them?

This is an important point in the thesis of this book.

I once taught a class on test-driven development (TDD). I was attempting to demonstrate how TDD could help us reduce the complexity in our designs when one of the course attendees (I won't call them a *programmer*) asked why it mattered if the code was less complex. I confess that I was shocked. If this person didn't see the differences in impact and value between obtuse, complex code and clear, simple code, then they have a different view of our job than I do. I did my best to answer his question, talking about the importance of maintainability and the advantages in terms of efficiency, but I am not convinced that my arguments made much impression.

Fundamentally, complexity increases the cost of ownership for software. This has a direct economic impact as well as a more subjective one: complex code isn't as nice to work on!

The real issue here, though, is that complex code is, kind of by definition, more difficult to change. That means you have one chance to get it right when you write it the first time. Also, if my code is complex, then I probably don't really understand it as well as I think that I do; there are more places for mistakes to hide.

If we work to limit the complexity of the code that we write, we can make mistakes and have a better chance of correcting them. So either we can bet on our own genius and assume that we will get everything perfectly correct at the start, or we can proceed more cautiously. We start by assuming that there will be things that we didn't think of, misunderstandings, and changes in the world that mean that we will likely need to revisit our code one day. Complexity costs!

It is important that we are open to new ideas. It is important that we continually question our assumptions. However, that doesn't mean that all ideas have equal merit. There are dumb ideas, and they should be dismissed; there are great ideas, and they should be valued.

Knowing the syntax of a language is not enough to be a "programmer," let alone to be a good programmer. Being "idiomatic in language X" is less valuable and less important than high—quality in design. Knowing the abstruse details of "API Y" does not make you a better software developer; you can always look up the answer to that kind of question!

The real skills—the things that really differentiate great programmers from poor programmers—are not language-specific or framework-specific. They lie elsewhere.

Any programming language is only a tool. I have been privileged to work with a few world-class programmers. These people will write good code in a programming language that they have never used before. They will write nice code in HTML and CSS or Unix shell scripts or YAML. One of my friends even writes readable Perl!

There are ideas that are deeper and more profound than the language used to express them. Modularity is one of these ideas; if your code is not modular, it is almost certainly not as good as code that is!

The Importance of Testability

I was an early adopter of TDD, taking my first tentative steps in that direction in response to Kent Beck's book *Extreme Programming Explained* published in 1999. My team experimented with Kent's intriguing ideas and got them wrong that same year. Nevertheless, we got great benefit from the approach.

TDD is one of the most significant steps that software development practice has taken during my career. The confusing thing is that the reason I value it so highly has little to do with "testing" as we would usually conceive it. In fact, I now think that Kent Beck made a mistake including "test" in the name of the practice, at least from a marketing perspective. And no, I don't know what he should have called it instead!

Chapter 5 described how we can get fast, accurate feedback on the quality of our designs from our tests and how making our code testable enhances its quality. This is an enormously important idea.

There are a few things, beyond the good taste of an experienced, skilled programmer, that can give us early feedback on the quality of our design. We may learn weeks, months, or years later that our design is good or bad when we attempt to change it, but short of that, there are no objective measures that indicate quality, unless, that is, we attempt to drive our design from tests.

If our tests are difficult to write, it means that our design is poor. We get a signal, immediately. We get feedback on the quality of our design as we attempt to refine it for the next increment in behavior. These lessons are delivered automatically to us if we follow the **Red, Green, Refactor** discipline of TDD. When our tests are hard to write, our design is worse than it should be. If our tests are easy to write our code, the stuff that we are testing inevitably exhibits the properties that we value as hallmarks of high quality in code.

Now, this does not imply that a test-driven approach to design will automatically create great design. It is not a magic wand. It still relies upon the skill and experience of the designer. A great software developer will still create a better outcome than a poor one. What driving our designs from tests does is encourage us to create testable code and systems and so, given the limits of our experience and talent, enhances the outcome.

We don't have any other techniques I can think of that really do that to a similar extent! This **talent amplifier** then is an important tool if we are to move from craft to engineering.

If we aspire to be engineers, advising people to "do better" is not enough. We need tools that will guide us and help us achieve a better outcome. Striving for testability in our systems is one such tool.

Designing for Testability Improves Modularity

Let's get back on topic and think about this specifically in the context of modularity. How does designing to achieve testability encourage greater modularity?

If I want to test the effectiveness of the airfoil of a wing on an airplane, I can build the airplane and go flying. This is a terrible idea that even the Wright Brothers, who built the first powered, controlled airplane, realized wouldn't work.

If you take this rather naive approach, then you have to do all of the work first before you learn anything. When you try to learn this way, how will you measure the effectiveness of this airfoil versus another? Build another airplane?

Even then, how do you compare the results? Maybe the wind was gustier when you flew the first prototype versus the second. Maybe your pilot had a bigger breakfast on the first flight than the second. Perhaps the air pressure or the temperature varied, so the wings delivered different amounts of lift because of that. Maybe the fuel batch was different between the two, so the engine was producing different power levels. How can you manage all these variables?

If you take this whole-system, waterfall approach to solving this problem, the complexity of the system is now expanded to encompass the entire environment in which the airfoil operates.

The way to scientifically measure an airfoil is to take control of these variables and standardize them across your experiments. How can we reduce the complexity so that the signals that we get back from our experiment are clear? Well, we could put the two airplanes into a more controlled environment, maybe something like a big wind tunnel. That would allow more precise control of the airflow over the wings and the wind. Maybe we could do this in a temperature and pressure-controlled environment. Only with this sort of control can we expect to get to more repeatable results.

If we are going to start down this road, we don't really need an engine or flight controls or the rest of the airplane for that matter. Why not just make two models of the wings with the airfoils that we would like to test and try those in our temperature- and pressure-controlled wind tunnel?

That would certainly be a more accurate experiment than just going flying, but this still requires us to build the whole wing twice. Why not make a small model of each airfoil? Make each model as precisely as possible, using exactly the same materials and techniques, and compare the two. If we are going to go that far, we could do this on a smaller scale, and we'd need a simpler wind tunnel.

These small pieces of airplane are modules. They are parts that certainly add to the behavior of the whole plane, but they are focused on a specific part of the problem. It is true that such experiments will give you only a partially true picture. The aerodynamics of airplanes are more complex than only the wings, but modularity means that we can measure things that we couldn't measure without it, so the part, the module, is certainly more testable than the whole.

In the real world, this is how you conduct experiments to determine how the shape of wings, and other things, affect lift.

Modularity gives us greater control and greater precision in the things that we can measure. Let's move this example into the software world. Imagine that you are working on System B, which is downstream from System A and upstream from System C (see Figure 9.1).

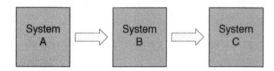

Figure 9.1
Coupled systems

This is typical of working on big systems in complex organizations. This presents a problem: how do we test our work? Many, maybe even most, organizations faced with this problem jump to the assumption that it is essential to test everything together to be sure that the system is safe to use.

There are many problems with this approach. First, if we measure only at this scale, we face the "test the whole airplane" problem. The whole system is so complex that we lack precision, reproducibility, control, and clear visibility of what any results that we do collect really mean.

We can't evaluate our part of the system with any degree of precision, because the upstream and downstream parts, System A and System C, get in our way. There are many types of tests that are simply impossible as a result of this decision. What happens to System B if System A sends it malformed messages?

That case is impossible to measure, while the real System A is in place sending well-formed messages. How should System B respond when the communications channel to System C is broken?

Again, we can't test that scenario while a real System C, with working comms, is in place, getting in the way of us faking a comms error.

The results that we do collect don't tell us much. If a test fails, is that because there is a problem with our system, or is it one of the others? Maybe the failure means that we have the wrong versions of the upstream or downstream systems. If everything works, is that because we are ready to release? Or is it because the cases we are trying to evaluate are so simplistic, due to this mega-system not being testable that they aren't really finding the bugs that are really there?

If we are measuring the whole, composite system (see Figure 9.2), then our results are vague and confusing. The rather cartoony diagram in Figure 9.2 illustrates an important problem: we need to be clear what it is that we are measuring, and we need to be clear of the value of our measurements. If we are doing the kind of end-to-end tests in this diagram, then what is the objective of our test? What do we hope to demonstrate? If our aim is to demonstrate that all of the pieces work together, well, that may be useful in some contexts, but this style of testing is insufficient to tell us if System B, the one that we are truly responsible for in this scenario, really works. These sorts of tests make sense only as a supplement, a small supplement, to a better, more thorough, more modular testing strategy. They certainly do not replace that more detailed testing is necessary to demonstrate the correct working of our system, System B!

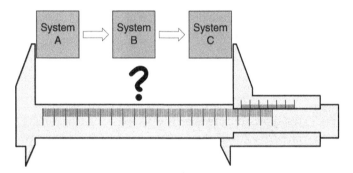

Figure 9.2
Testing coupled systems

So what would it take to achieve that more detailed testing? Well, we would need a **point of measurement**, which is a place in our whole system where we can insert probes of some kind that will allow us to reliably gather our measurements. I have represented these "points of measurement" in this series of diagrams as fictional calipers. In reality, we are talking about being able to inject test data into our **system under test** (SUT), invoke behaviors within it, and collect the outputs so that we can interpret the results. I know that the calipers are a bit cheesy, but that is the mental model I have when I think about testing a system. I am going to insert my system into a **test rig** of some kind so that I can evaluate it. I need a measuring device (my test cases and test infrastructure) that allows me to attach probes to my SUT so that I can see how it behaves.

My calipers in Figure 9.2 are not very helpful for the reasons that we have already explored, but also because the bigger and more complex the system, the more variable the results. We have not controlled the variables enough to get a clear, repeatable result.

If you have a suite of even automated tests that you run to evaluate your software to determine if it is ready to release and those tests don't produce the same result every time, what do those results really mean?

If our aim is to apply some engineering thinking, we need to take our measurements seriously. We need to be able to depend upon them, which means that we need them to be deterministic. For any given test or evaluation, I should expect, given the same version of the software under test, to see the same results every time I run it, however many times I run it, and whatever else is going on when I run it.

There is enough value in that statement that it is worth doing extra work, if necessary, to achieve that repeatable outcome. It will have an impact on not only the tests that we write and how we write them but also, importantly, the design of our software, and that is where the real value of this engineering approach begins to show.

When we built our financial exchange, the system was completely deterministic to the extent that we could record the production inputs and replay them some time later to get the system into **precisely the same state** in a test environment. We did not set out with that goal. That was a side effect of the degree of testability, and so determinism, that we achieved.

Complexity and Determinism

As the complexity of the system under test grows, the precision with which we can measure things reduces. For example, if I have a piece of software that is performance critical, I can isolate it and put it into a test rig of some kind that allows me to create a series of controlled test runs. I can do things like discard the early runs to eliminate any of the effects of runtime optimization, and I can run through enough executions to apply statistical techniques to the data that I collect. If I take all of these things seriously enough, my measurements can be accurate and reproducible down to certainly microseconds and sometimes even nanoseconds.

Doing the same things in a whole-system performance test, for a system of any significant size, is practically impossible. If I measure performance for a whole system, the variables will have exploded. What other tasks are underway at the same time on the computers running my code? What about the network? Is that being used for anything else while my measurements are underway?

Even if I control for these things, locking down the network and access to my performance test environment, modern operating systems are complex things. What if the OS decides to do some housekeeping while my test is running? That will surely skew the results, won't it?

Determinism is more difficult to achieve as the complexity and scope of the system grow.

The real root cause of a lack of determinism in computer systems is concurrency. This can take various forms. The clock ticking away incrementing the system time is one form of concurrency; the OS re-organizing your disk when it thinks it has some spare time is another. In the absence of concurrency, though, digital systems are deterministic. For the same sequence of bytes and instructions, we get the same result every time.

One useful driver of modularity is to isolate the concurrency so that each module is deterministic and reliably testable. Architect systems so that entry into a module is sequenced and its outcomes are more predictable. Systems written this way are *very* nice to work on.

This may seem a fairly esoteric point, but in a system in which every behavior that its users observe is deterministic, in the way that I have described, it would be eminently predictable and testable with no unexpected side effects, at least to the limits of our testing.

Most systems are not built like this, but if we take an engineering-led approach to their design, they can be.

If, instead, we could apply our calipers to measure only our component (see Figure 9.3), we could measure with much greater accuracy and precision and with much more reliability. Stretching my analogy to breaking point, we could measure other dimensions of the problem, too.

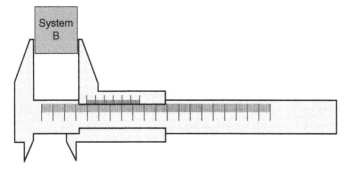

Figure 9.3
Testing modules

So, what would it take to measure with this increased precision and specificity? Well, we would like our measuring points to be stable so that we get the same result from our measurement every time, all other things being equal. We would like our evaluations to be deterministic.

We would also like to not have to re-create our measurement points from scratch each time that the system changes.

To be clear, what I am describing here is a stable, modular interface to the part of the system that we would like to test. We compose larger systems of smaller modules, modules with clearly defined interfaces, for inputs and outputs. This architectural approach allows us to measure the system at those interfaces.

Reading this here, I hope that this seems obvious. The problem is that few real-world computer systems look like this.

If we make it a fundamental part of our job to test, with automated testing, the systems that we create, then we are very strongly encouraged by the extra work that we are forced to do if we get it wrong to create more modular systems. This is fractal. This is true at all levels of granularity, from entire enterprise systems down to individual methods, functions, and classes.

It is simply not possible to test a system, in the way that this book assumes, that is not, in some way, modular. We need those "points of measurement." Our ability to test is supported and enhanced by modularity, and modularity is encouraged by being guided in our designs by tests.

This does not necessarily imply a collection of tiny, independent components. This can equally work for large complex systems. The key here is to understand the scope of measurement that makes sense and work to make those measurements easy to achieve and stable in terms of the results that they generate.

When I was involved in creating a financial exchange, we treated the whole enterprise system as a single system, but we established clear, well-defined integration points for every external interaction and faked those external systems. Now we had control; now we could inject new account registrations and collect data that, in real operation, would have been sent to banks or clearinghouses and so on.

This allowed us, for some of our testing, to treat the whole system as a black box, inject data to get the system into an appropriate state for a test, and collect its outputs to evaluate the system's response. We treated every point at which our system interacted with a third-party system and every integration point as a point of measurement where we could plug in to our test infrastructure. This was possible only because our entire enterprise system was designed with testability in mind from day one.

Our system was also extremely modular and loosely coupled. So, as well as evaluating the system as a whole, we could do more detailed testing for single, service-level components, too. Inevitably all of the behavior within a service was also developed using fine-grained TDD techniques for pretty much every line of code. We could also test tiny pieces of the behavior of the system in isolation from everything else. As I said, modularity and testability are fractal.

Testability deeply informed the architectural choices that we made and, over time, had a profound impact not just on the obvious measures of quality, like how many, or how few bugs we could find, but more subtly, and perhaps more importantly, on the architectural compartmentalization of our system.

Historically, we have, as an industry, undervalued or even missed the importance of *testability* and specifically test-first development as a tool to drive good design and to give us early, clear feedback on the quality of our designs.

Services and Modularity

The idea of a service in software terms is rather slippery. There are no mainstream languages, for example, that directly support the idea of services, yet still the idea is pretty pervasive. Software developers will argue about what makes a good service or a bad one and architect their systems to support the concept.

From a purely practical perspective, we can think of a service as code that delivers some "service" to other code and hides the detail of how it delivers that "service." This is just the idea of "information hiding" and is extremely important if we want to manage the complexity of our systems as they grow (see Chapter 12). Identifying "seams" in the design of our systems where the rest of the system doesn't need to know, and shouldn't care about, the detail of what is happening on the other side of those "seams" is a very good idea. This is really the essence of design.

Services, then, provide us with an organizing idea of little compartments in our systems that hide detail. This is a useful idea. So a service can certainly, sensibly, be thought of as a module of our system. If that is the case, what about these "seams," these points where a service or module touches something outside of its boundary? The thing that provides any meaning at all to the concept of a "service" in software terms is that it represents a boundary. There is a difference between what is known and what is exposed, on either side of these boundaries.

One of the commonest problems that I see in larger codebases is a result of ignoring this difference. Often the code that represents these boundaries is indistinguishable from the code on either side. We use the same kinds of method calls, and we even pass the same data structures across such boundaries. There is no validation of inputs at these points or assembly and abstraction of outputs. Such codebases quickly become tangled messes that are difficult to change.

There has been an advance in this respect, but it is a small step, and to some degree, we took that step by accident. That is the move to REST APIs.

My background is, in part, in high-performance computing, so the idea of using text, XML, or HTML as a way of encoding the information that flows between services leaves me a bit cold; it's way *too slow*! However, it does rather strongly encourage the idea of having a translation point at the edges of your service or API. You translate the incoming message into some more tractable form for consumption by your service, and you translate the outputs of your service into some horrible, big, slow, text-based message for output. (Sorry, I let my biases creep in there.)

Software developers still get this wrong, though. Even in systems built along these lines, I still see code that passes the HTML straight through, and the whole service interacts with that HTML—yuck!

The seams or boundaries should be treated with more care. They should be translation and validation points for information. The entry point to a service should be a little defensive barrier that limits the worst abuses of consumers of that service. What I am describing here is a Ports & Adapters kind of model at the level of an individual service. This approach should be just as true for a service that communicates via standard method or function calls as one that uses HTML, XML, or any other form of messaging.

The base idea here is one of modularity! A system is not modular if the internal workings of adjacent modules are exposed. Communication between modules (and services) should be a little more guarded than communication within them.

Deployability and Modularity

In my book *Continuous Delivery*, Jez Humble and I described a way to organize our work so that our software was always releasable. We advised (and continue to advise) that you work so that your software is always in a releasable state. Part of achieving this repeatable, reliable ability to release software is ensuring that it is easily and simply deployable.

Since writing the *Continuous Delivery* book, I now believe, even more profoundly, that working so that our software is both testable and deployable has a deep impact on the quality of our work.

One of the core ideas in my earlier book is the idea of the **deployment pipeline**, a mechanism that takes commits in at one end and produces a "releasable outcome" at the other. This is a key idea. A deployment pipeline is not simply a little workflow of build or test steps; it is a mechanized route from commit to production.

This interpretation has some implications. This means that everything that constitutes "releasability" is within the scope of your deployment pipeline. If the pipeline says everything is good, there should be no more work to do to make you comfortable to release—nothing...no more integration checks, sign-offs, or staging tests. If the pipeline says it is "good," then it is "good to go!"

This, in turn, has some implications for the sensible scope of a deployment pipeline. If its output is "releasable," it must also be "independently deployable." The scope of an effective deployment pipeline is always an "independently deployable unit of software."

Now this has an impact on modularity. If the output of the deployment pipeline is deployable, it means that the pipeline constitutes a definitive evaluation of our software. It's definitive at least to the degree that we care, and consider safe and sensible, to establish its readiness for release.

There are only two strategies that make sense if we are to take that idea to its logical conclusion. We can build, test, and deploy everything that constitutes our system together, or we can build, test, and deploy parts of that system separately. There is no halfway solution. If we don't trust the output of our deployment pipeline sufficiently and feel it necessary to test the results it generates with the output of other deployment pipelines, then that presents problems; the messages that our deployment pipeline is sending to us are now unclear, and since we are trying to be engineers, that isn't good enough!

Now the scope of our evaluation is compromised. When are we done? Are we finished when our pipeline completes or when every other pipeline that is needed to verify the output for our pipeline has been run? If the latter, then the "cycle time"[2] for our changes includes the cycle times of everyone else's changes too, so we have a monolithic evaluation system.

The most scalable approach to software development is to distribute it. Reduce the coupling and dependencies between teams and their products to the degree that each team can, independently, create, test, and deploy their work with no reference to another team. This is the approach that has allowed Amazon, with its famous "two-pizza teams,"[3] to grow at an unprecedented rate.

Technically, one way to accomplish this independence is to take the modularity of the system so seriously that each module is, in terms of build, test, and deployment, independent from every other module. This is what microservices are. They are so modular that we don't need to test them with other services prior to release. If you are testing your microservices together, they aren't really microservices. Part of the definition of a microservice is that they are "independently deployable."

Deployability can up the stakes on modularity. As we have seen, deployability defines the effective scope of a deployment pipeline. Our choices of what really works, if we value high-quality work based on fast, efficient feedback, are really quite limited.

We can make the choice to build, test, and deploy everything that constitutes our system together and eliminate dependency-management problems altogether (everything lives in a single repository), but then we must take on the responsibility to create fast enough feedback to allow developers to do a good job, which may take a big investment in engineering to get the feedback that drives any high-quality process quickly enough.

Alternatively, we can work so that each module is, essentially, independent of every other module. We can build, test, and deploy each of these things separately, without the need to test them together.

This means that the scope of our builds, tests, and deployment is small. Each of them is simpler, so it is easier to achieve fast, high-quality results.

However, this comes at the sometimes very significant cost of a more complex, more distributed architecture in our systems. We are forced, now, to take modularity very seriously indeed.

We must design for it; we must be skilled at the techniques of protocol design so that the interactions between modules, the protocol of information exchange between them, is stable and is not allowed to change in a way that forces change on other modules. We probably need to consider and apply ideas like runtime version management for APIs and so on.

Nearly everyone would like some ideal middle ground between these two extremes, but in reality, it doesn't exist. The middle ground is a fudge and is often slower and more complex than the monolithic approach that everyone strives, so assiduously, to avoid. The more organizationally distributed approach that is microservices is the best way that we know to scale up software development, but it is not a simple approach and comes at a cost.

---

2. Cycle time is a measure of the efficiency of your development process. How long does it take to go "from idea to useful software in the hands of users"? In continuous delivery, we use the optimization of cycle time as a tool to direct us toward more efficient approaches to development.

3. Amazon famously reorganized following a memo from CEO Jeff Bezos. In his memo Bezos stated that "…no team should be bigger than can be fed by two pizzas."

Modularity at Different Scales

Modularity is important at every scale. Deployability is a useful tool when thinking of system-level modules, but this, alone, is not enough to create high-quality code. There is a modern pre-occupation with services.

This is a useful architectural tool and one that has been at the heart of my approach to system design for at least the last three decades. However, if the modularity of your design stops there, you may still have poor, hard-to-work-with systems.

If, as I argue, the importance of modularity is a tool to help us manage complexity, then we need to take that to the point of readable code. Each class, method, or function should be simple and readable and, where appropriate, composed of smaller, independently understandable submodules.

Again, TDD helps to encourage such fine-grained code. For the code to be testable at this resolution, techniques like dependency injection encourage code with a bigger surface area. This heavily influences the modularity of our designs.

At smaller scales, dependency injection is the most effective tool to provide pressure on our code that encourages us to create systems composed of many small pieces. The dependencies are the calipers, the points of measurement, that we can inject into our system to achieve a more thoroughly testable outcome. Again, ensuring that our code is testable encourages designs that are genuinely modular and as a result code that is easier to read.

Some people criticize this style of design. This criticism generally takes the form that it is harder to understand code that has a bigger surface area in this way. It is harder to follow the flow of control through the system. This criticism misses the point. The problem here is that if it is necessary to expose that surface area in order to test that code, then that is the surface area of the code. How much harder is it to understand if it is obscured by poor interface design and a lack of tests? The root of this criticism is really about what constitutes "good design." I propose that focusing our design on the management of complexity is a valuable benchmark to define what we mean by "high quality" in code.

Testing, when done well, exposes something important and true about the nature of our code, the nature of our designs, and the nature of the problem that we are solving that is not otherwise easily accessible. As a result, it is one of the most important tools in our arsenal to create better, more modular systems and code.

Modularity in Human Systems

I discuss the impact of this engineering thinking in detail in Chapter 15, but it's useful to call out the particular importance of modularity in this respect. Much of my professional career has been spent working on large computer systems. In this kind of world, the constant refrain has been "how do we scale?" Sometimes, rarely, that is about the software, but mostly when people in big organizations ask that question, what they really mean is "how can we add more people so that we can produce software faster?"

The real answer is that for any given computer system there are very serious limits to that. As Fred Brooks famously said:

> You can't make a baby in a month with 9 women.[4]

However, there are other options; you can make nine babies in nine months with nine women, which averages out at a baby per month. At this point my, or Fred's, analogy breaks down!

In software terms, if not with babies, the problem is about coupling. As long as the pieces are truly independent of one another, truly decoupled, then we can parallelize all we want. As soon as there is coupling, there are constraints on the degree to which we can parallelize. The cost of integration is the killer!

How do we integrate the work from separate streams of development? If you are as nerdy as I am, this may be ringing bells; this is about something deeply fundamental. This is about information and concurrency. When you have independent streams of information, the cost of bringing them together to form a coherent whole can be extremely high if there is any overlap. The best way to parallelize things is to do it in a way where there is no need to re-integrate (nine babies). Essentially, this is the microservice approach. Microservices are an organizational scalability play; they don't really have any other advantage, but let's be clear, this is a *big* advantage if scalability is your problem!

We know that just adding more people to a team does not make that team go faster. In a lovely metadata study of more than 4,000 software projects that compared the relative performance (time to create 100,000 lines of code) in teams of 5 or fewer and teams of 20 or more, the teams of 5 took only one week longer than the teams of 20 people over a 9-month period. So small teams are nearly 4 times as productive, per person, as larger teams.[5]

If we need small teams to efficiently create good, high-quality work, then we need to find ways to seriously limit the coupling between those small teams. This is at least as much an organizational strategy problem as it is a technical one. We need **modular organizations** as well as **modular software**.

So if we want our organizations to be able to scale up, the secret is to build teams and systems that need to coordinate to the minimum possible degree, we need to decouple them. Working hard to maintain this organizational modularity is important and one of the real hallmarks of genuinely high-performing, scalable organizations.

---

4. A quote from Fred Brooks' influential, and still true, book from the 1970s, *The Mythical Man Month*

5. In a study Quantitative Software Management (QSM) also found that the larger teams produced 5x more defects in their code. See https://bit.ly/3ll93oe.

Summary

Modularity is a cornerstone of our ability to make progress when we don't have an omniscient view of how our software should work in the future. In the absence of modularity, we can certainly create naive software that will solve a problem in front of us now. Without working in ways that provide some layers of insulation between the parts of software, though, our ability to continue to add new ideas and to grow our software will rapidly diminish to the point where, in some real-world cases, there is no forward progress at all. This is the first in our collection of tools needed to defend against complexity.

Modularity as a design idea is fractal. It is more than only the "modules," whatever their form, supported in our programming languages. It is more complex and more useful than that. It is, at its heart, the idea that we must retain our ability to change code and systems in one place, without worrying about the impact of those changes elsewhere.

This starts us thinking about other aspects of this problem, so modularity is intimately connected to the other ideas that we need to consider in managing the complexity of our systems—ideas like abstraction, separation of concerns, coupling, and cohesion.

10

Cohesion

Cohesion (in computer science) is defined as "the degree to which the elements inside a module belong together."[1]

Modularity and Cohesion: Fundamentals of Design

My favorite way to describe good software design is based on this Kent Beck quote:

Pull the things that are unrelated further apart, and put the things that are related closer together.

This simple, slightly jokey phrase has some real truth in it. Good design in software is really about the way in which we organize the code in the systems that we create. All my recommended principles to help us manage complexity are really about compartmentalizing our systems. We need to be able to build our systems out of smaller, more easily understandable, more easily testable, discrete pieces. To achieve this, we certainly need techniques that will allow us to "Pull the unrelated things further apart," but we also need to take seriously the need to "put the related things closer together." That is where cohesion comes in.

Cohesion is one of the more slippery concepts here. I can do something naive, like support the idea of modules in my programming language and claim, as a result, that my code is modular. This is wrong; simply throwing a collection of unrelated stuff into a file does not make the code modular in any but the most trivial sense.

---

1. Source: Wikipedia https://en.wikipedia.org/wiki/Cohesion_(computer_science)

When I speak of modularity, I really mean components of the system that genuinely hide information from other components (modules). If the code within the module is not cohesive, then this doesn't work.

The trouble is that this is open to overly simplistic interpretations. This is probably the point at which the art, skill, and experience of the practitioner really come into play. This balance point between genuinely modular systems and cohesion often seems to confuse people.

A Basic Reduction in Cohesion

How often have you seen a piece of code that will retrieve some data, parse it, and then store it somewhere else? Surely the "store" step is related to the "change" step? Isn't that good cohesion? They are all the steps that we need together, aren't they?

Well, not really—let's look at an example. First my caveats: it is going to be hard to tease apart several ideas here. This code is inevitably going to demonstrate a bit of each of the ideas in this section, so I rely on you to focus on where it touches on cohesion and smile knowingly when I also touch on separation of concerns, modularity, and so on.

Listing 10.1 shows rather unpleasant code as a demonstration. However, it serves my purpose to give us something concrete to explore. This code reads a small file containing a list of words, sorts them alphabetically, and then writes a new file with the resulting sorted list—load, process, and store!

This is a fairly common pattern for lots of different problems: read some data, process it, and then store the results somewhere else.

Listing 10.1   Really Bad Code, Naively Cohesive

```
public class ReallyBadCohesion
{
    public boolean loadProcessAndStore() throws IOException
    {
        String[] words;
        List<String> sorted;

        try (FileReader reader =
                new FileReader("./resources/words.txt"))
        {
            char[] chars = new char[1024];
            reader.read(chars);
            words = new String(chars).split(" |\0");

        }
```

```
        sorted = Arrays.asList(words);
        sorted.sort(null);

        try (FileWriter writer =
                    new FileWriter("./resources/test/sorted.txt"))
        {
            for (String word : sorted)
            {
                writer.write(word);
                writer.write("\n");
            }
            return true;
        }
    }
}
}
```

I find this code extremely unpleasant, and I had to force myself to write it like this. This code is screaming "poor separation of concerns," "poor modularity," "tight coupling," and almost "zero abstraction," but what about cohesion?

Here we have everything that it does in a single function. I see lots of production code that looks like this, only usually much longer and much more complex, so even worse!

A naive view of cohesion is that everything is together and so easy to see. So ignoring the other techniques of managing complexity for a moment, is this easier to understand? How long would it take you to understand what this code does? How long if I hadn't helped with a descriptive method name?

Now look at Listing 10.2, which is a slight improvement.

Listing 10.2   Bad Code, Mildly Better Cohesion

```
public class BadCohesion
{
    public boolean loadProcessAndStore() throws IOException
    {
        String[] words = readWords();
        List<String> sorted = sortWords(words);
        return storeWords(sorted);
    }

    private String[] readWords() throws IOException
    {
        try (FileReader reader =
                    new FileReader("./resources/words.txt"))
```

```
        {
            char[] chars = new char[1024];
            reader.read(chars);
            return new String(chars).split(" |\0");
        }
    }

    private List<String> sortWords(String[] words)
    {
        List<String> sorted = Arrays.asList(words);
        sorted.sort(null);
        return sorted;
    }

    private boolean storeWords(List<String> sorted) throws IOException
    {
        try (FileWriter writer =
                    new FileWriter("./resources/test/sorted.txt"))
        {
            for (String word : sorted)
            {
                writer.write(word);
                writer.write("\n");
            }
            return true;
        }
    }
}
```

Listing 10.2 is still not good, but it is more cohesive; the parts of the code that are closely related are more clearly delineated and literally closer together. Simplistically, everything that you need to know about readWords is named and contained in a single method. The overall flow of the method loadProcessAndStore is plain to see now, even if I had chosen a less descriptive name. The information in this version is more cohesive than the information in Listing 10.1. It is now significantly clearer which parts of the code are more closely related to one another, even though the code is functionally identical. All of this makes this version significantly easier to read and, as a result, makes it much easier to modify.

Note that there are more lines of code in Listing 10.2. This example is written in Java, which is a rather verbose language, and the boilerplate costs are quite high, but even without that there is a small overhead to improving the readability. This is not necessarily a bad thing!

There is a common desire among programmers to reduce the amount of typing that they do. Clear concision is valuable. If we can express ideas simply, then that is of significant value, but you don't measure simplicity in terms of the fewest characters typed. `ICanWriteASentenceOmittingSpaces` is shorter, but it is also much less pleasant to read!

It is a mistake to optimize code to reduce typing. We are optimizing for the wrong things. Code is a communication tool; we should use it to communicate. Sure, it needs to be machine-readable and executable too, but that is not really its primary goal. If it was, then we would still be programming systems by flipping switches on the front of our computers or writing machine code.

The primary goal of code is to communicate ideas to humans. We write code to express ideas as clearly and simply as we can—at least that is how it should work. We should never choose brevity at the cost of obscurity. Making our code readable is, to my mind, both a professional duty of care and one of the most important guiding principles in managing complexity. So I prefer to optimize to reduce thinking rather than to reduce typing.

Back to the code: this second example is clearly more readable. It is much easier to see its intent, it is still pretty horrible, it is not modular, there is not much separation of concerns, it is inflexible with hard-coded strings for filenames, and it is not testable other than running the whole thing and dealing with the file system. But we have improved the cohesion. Each part of the code is now focused on one part of the task. Each part has access only to what it needs to accomplish that task. We will return to this example in later chapters to see how we can improve on it further.

Context Matters

I asked a friend, whose code I admire, if he had any recommendations to demonstrate the importance of cohesion, and he recommended the *Sesame Street* YouTube video,[2] "One of these things is not like another."

So that is a bit of a joke, but it also raises a key point. Cohesion, more than the other tools to manage complexity, is contextual. Depending on context, "All of these things may not be like the other."

We have to make choices, and these choices are intimately entangled with the other tools. I can't clearly separate cohesion from modularity or separation of concerns because those techniques help to define what cohesion means in the context of my design.

One effective tool to drive this kind of decision-making is domain-driven design.[3] Allowing our thinking, and our designs, to be guided by the problem domain helps us to identify paths that are more likely to be profitable in the long run.

---

2. A *Sesame Street* song called "One of these things is not like the other": https://youtu.be/rsRjQDrDnY8

3. *Domain Driven Design* is the title of a book written by Eric Evans and an approach to the design of software systems. See https://amzn.to/3cQpNaL.

Domain-Driven Design

Domain-driven design is an approach to design where we aim to capture the core behaviors of our code in essence as simulations of the problem domain. The design of our system aims to accurately model the problem.

This approach includes a number of important, valuable ideas.

It allows us to reduce the chance of misunderstanding. We aim to create a "ubiquitous language" to express ideas in the problem domain. This is an agreed, accurate way of describing ideas in the problem domain, using words consistently, and with agreed meanings. We then apply this language to the way that we talk about the design of our systems too.

So if I am talking about my software and I say that this "Limit-order matched," then that makes sense in terms of the code, where the concepts of "limit orders" and "matching" are clearly represented, and named `LimitOrder` and `Match`. These are precisely the same words that we use when describing the scenario in business terms with nontechnical people.

This ubiquitous language is effectively developed and refined through capturing requirements and the kind of high-level test cases that can act as "executable specifications for the behavior of the system" that can drive the development process.

DDD also introduced the concept of the "bounded context." This is a part of a system that shares common concepts. For example, an order-management system probably has a different concept of "order" from a billing system, so these are two, distinct bounded contexts.

This is an extremely useful concept for helping to identify sensible modules or subsystems when designing our systems. The big advantage of using bounded contexts in this way is that they are naturally more loosely coupled in the real problem domain, so they are likely to guide us to create more loosely coupled systems.

We can use ideas like ubiquitous language and bounded context to guide the design of our systems. If we follow their lead, we tend to build better systems, and they help us to more clearly see the core, essential complexity of our system and differentiate that from the accidental complexity that often, otherwise, can obscure what our code is really attempting to do.

If we design our system so that it is a simulation of the problem domain, as far as we understand it, then an idea that is viewed as a small change from the perspective of the problem domain will also be a small step in the code. This is a nice property to have.

Domain-driven design is a powerful tool in creating better designs and provides a suite of organizing principles that can help guide our design efforts and encourages us to improve the modularity, cohesion, and separation of concerns in our code. At the same time, it leads us toward a coarse-grained organization of our code that is naturally more loosely coupled.

Another important tool that helps us create better systems is separation of concerns, which we will talk about in considerably more detail in the next chapter, but for now it is perhaps the closest thing that I have to a rule to guide my own programming. "One class, one thing; one method/function, one thing."

I strongly dislike both of the code examples presented in this chapter so far and feel slightly embarrassed to show them to you, because my design instincts are screaming at me that the separation of concerns is so terrible in both cases. Listing 10.2 is better; at least each method now does one thing, but the class is still terrible. If you don't already see it, we will look at why that matters in the next chapter.

Finally, in my box of tools, there is testability. I started writing these bad code examples as I always start when writing code: by writing a test. I had to stop almost immediately, though, because there was no way that I could practice TDD and write code this bad! I had to dump the test and start again, and I confess that I felt like I had stepped back in time. I did write tests for my examples to check to see if they did what I expected, but this code is not properly testable.

Testability strongly encourages modularity, separation of concerns, and the other attributes that we value in high-quality code. That, in turn, helps us make an initial approximation of the contexts and abstractions that we like the look of in our design and where to make our code more cohesive.

Note, there are no guarantees here, and that is the ultimate point of this book. There are no simple, cookie-cutter answers. This book provides mental tools that help us structure our thinking when we don't have the answers.

The techniques in this book are not meant to deliver the answers to you; that is still up to you. They are rather to provide you with a collection of ideas and techniques that will allow you to safely make progress even when you don't yet know the answer. When you are creating a system of any real complexity, that is always the case; we never know the answers until we are finished!

You can think of this as a fairly defensive approach, and it is, but the aim is to keep our freedom of choice open. That is one of the significant benefits of working to manage complexity. As we learn more, we can change our code on an ongoing basis to reflect that learning. I think a better adjective than "defensive" is "incremental."

We make progress incrementally through a series of experiments, and we use the techniques of **managing complexity** to protect ourselves from making mistakes that are too damaging.

This is how science and engineering work. We control the variables, take a small step, and evaluate where we are. If our evaluation suggests that we took a misstep, then we take a step back and decide what to try next. If it looks okay, we control the variables, take another small step, and so on.

Another way to think of this is that software development is a kind of evolutionary process. Our job as programmers is to guide our learning and our designs through an incremental process of directed evolution toward desirable outcomes.

High-Performance Software

One of the common excuses for unpleasant code, like that shown in Listing 10.1, is that you have to write more complex code if you want high performance. I spent the latter part of my career working on systems at the cutting edge of high performance, and I can assure you that this is not the case. High-performance systems demand simple, well-designed code.

Think for a moment what *high performance* means in software terms. To achieve "high performance," we need to do the maximum amount of work for the smallest number of instructions.

The more complex our code, the more likely that the paths through our code are not optimal, because the "simplest possible route" through our code is obscured by the complexity of the code itself. This is a surprising idea to many programmers, but the route to fast code is to write simple, easy-to-understand code.

This is even more true as you start taking a broader system view.

Let's revisit our trivial example again. I have heard programmers make the argument that the code in Listing 10.1 is going to be faster than the code in Listing 10.2 because of the "overhead" of the method calls that Listing 10.2 adds. I am afraid that for most modern languages this is nonsense. Most modern compilers will look at the code in Listing 10.2 and inline the methods. Most modern optimizing compilers will do more than that. Modern compilers do a fantastic job of optimizing code to run efficiently on modern hardware. They excel when the code is simple and predictable, so the more complex your code is, the less help you will gain from your compiler's optimizer. Most optimizers in compilers simply give up trying once the cyclomatic complexity[4] of a block of code exceeds some threshold.

I ran a series of benchmarks against both versions of this code. They were not very good, because this code is bad. We are not sufficiently controlling the variables to really see clearly what is happening, but what was obvious was that there was no real measurable difference at this level of test.

The differences were too tiny to be distinguished from everything else that is going on here. On one run, the BadCohesion version was best; on another the ReallyBadCohesion was best. On a series of benchmark runs, for each of 50,000 iterations of the loadProcessStore method, the difference was no more than 300 milliseconds overall, so on average, that is roughly a difference of 6 nanoseconds per call and was actually slightly more often in favor of the version with the additional method calls.

This is a poor test, because the thing that we are interested in, the cost of the method calls, is dwarfed by the cost of the I/O. Testability—in this case performance testability—once again can help guide us toward a better outcome. We will discuss this in more detail in the next chapter.

There is so much going on "under the hood" that it is hard, even for experts, to predict the outcome. What is the answer? If you are really interested in the performance of your code, don't guess about what will be fast and what will be slow; measure it!

---

4. A software metric used to indicate the complexity of a program.

Link to Coupling

If we want to retain our freedom to explore and to sometimes make mistakes, we need to worry about the costs of **coupling**.

> **Coupling**: Given two lines of code, A and B, they are coupled when B must change behavior only because A changed.

> **Cohesion**: They are cohesive when a change to A allows B to change so that both add new value.[5]

Coupling is really too generic a term. There are different kinds of coupling that need to be considered (an idea that we will explore in more detail in Chapter 13).

It is ridiculous to imagine a system that has no coupling. If we want two pieces of our system to communicate, they must be coupled to some degree. So like cohesion, coupling is a matter of degree rather than any kind of absolute measure. The cost, though, of inappropriate levels of coupling is extremely high, so it is important to take its influence into account in our designs.

Coupling is in some ways the cost of cohesion. In the areas of your system that are cohesive, they are likely to also be more tightly coupled.

Driving High Cohesion with TDD

Yet again using automated tests, and specifically TDD, to drive our design gives us a lot of benefits. Striving to achieve a testable design and nicely abstracted, behaviorally focused tests for our system will apply a pressure on our design to make our code cohesive.

We create a test case before we write the code that describes the behavior that we aim to observe in the system. This allows us to focus on the design of the external API/Interface to our code, whatever that might be. Now we work to write an implementation that will fulfill the small, executable specification that we have created. If we write too much code, more than is needed to meet the specification, we are cheating our development process and reducing the cohesion of the implementation. If we write too little, then the behavioral intent won't be met. The discipline of TDD encourages us to hit the sweet spot for cohesion.

As ever, there are no guarantees. This is not a mechanical process, and it still relies upon the experience and skill of the programmer, but the approach applies a pressure toward a better outcome that wasn't there before and amplifies those skills and that experience.

---

5. Coupling and cohesion are described on the famous C2 wiki, https://wiki.c2.com/?CouplingAndCohesion.

How to Achieve Cohesive Software

The key measure of cohesion is the extent, or cost, of change. If you have to wander around your codebase changing it in many places to make a change, that is not a very cohesive system. Cohesion is a measure of functional relatedness. It is a measurement of relatedness of purpose. This is slippery stuff!

Let's look at a simple example.

If I create a class with two methods, each associated with a member variable (see Listing 10.3), this is poor cohesion, because the variables are really unrelated. They are specific to different methods but stored together at the level of the class even though they are unrelated.

Listing 10.3   **More Poor Cohesion**

```
class PoorCohesion:
    def __init__(self):
        self.a = 0
        self.b = 0

    def process_a(x):
        a = a + x

    def process_b(x):
        b = b * x
```

Listing 10.4 shows a much nicer, more cohesive solution to this. Note that as well as being more cohesive, this version is also more modular and has a better separation of concerns. We can't duck the relatedness of these ideas.

Listing 10.4   **Better Cohesion**

```
class BetterCohesionA:
    def __init__(self):
        self.a = 0

    def process_a(x):
        a = a + x

class BetterCohesionB:
    def __init__(self):
            self.b = 0
    def process_b(x):
        b = b * x
```

In combination with the rest of our principles for managing complexity, our desire to achieve a testable design helps us to improve the cohesiveness of our solutions. A good example of this is the impact of taking separation of concerns seriously, particularly when thinking about separating accidental complexity[6] from essential complexity.[7]

Listing 10.5 shows three simple examples of improving the cohesiveness of our code by consciously focusing on separating "essential" and "accidental" complexity. In each example, we are adding an item to a shopping cart, storing it in a database, and calculating the value of the cart.

Listing 10.5   Three Cohesion Examples

```python
def add_to_cart1(self, item):
    self.cart.add(item)

    conn = sqlite3.connect('my_db.sqlite')
    cur = conn.cursor()
    cur.execute('INSERT INTO cart (name, price)
    values (item.name, item.price)')
    conn.commit()
    conn.close()

    return self.calculate_cart_total();

def add_to_cart2(self, item):
    self.cart.add(item)
    self.store.store_item(item)
    return self.calculate_cart_total();

def add_to_cart3(self, item, listener):
    self.cart.add(item)
    listener.on_item_added(self, item)
```

The first function is clearly not cohesive code. There are lots of concepts and variables jumbled together here and a complete mix of essential and accidental complexity. I would say that this is very poor code, even at this essentially trivial scale. I would avoid writing code like this because it makes thinking about what is going on harder, even at this extremely simple scale.

---

6. The accidental complexity of a system is the complexity imposed on the system because we are running on a computer. It is the stuff that is a side effect of solving the real problem that we are interested in, e.g., the problems of persisting information, of dealing with concurrency or complex APIs, etc.

7. The essential complexity of a system is the complexity that is inherent to solving the problem, e.g., the calculation of an interest rate or the addition of an item to a shopping cart.

The second example is a little better. This is more coherent. The concepts in this function are related and represent a more consistent level of abstraction in that they are mostly related to the essential complexity of the problem. The "store" instruction is probably debatable, but at least we have hidden the details of the accidental complexity at this point.

The last one is interesting. I would argue that it is certainly cohesive. To get useful work done, we need to both add the item to the cart and inform other, potentially interested parties that the addition has been made. We have entirely separated the concerns of storage and the need to calculate a total for the cart. These things may happen, in response to being notified of the addition, or they may not if those parts of the code didn't register interest in this "item added" event.

This code either is more cohesive, where the essential complexity of the problem is all here and the other behaviors are side effects, or is less cohesive if you consider "store" and "total" to be parts of this problem. Ultimately, this is contextual and a design choice based on the context of the problems that you are solving.

Costs of Poor Cohesion

Cohesion is perhaps the least directly quantifiable aspect of my "tools for managing complexity," but it is important. The problem is that when cohesion is poor, our code and our systems are less flexible, more difficult to test, and more difficult to work on.

In the simple example in Listing 10.5, the impact of cohesive code is clear. If the code confuses different responsibilities, it lacks clarity and readability as add_to_cart1 demonstrates. If responsibilities are more widely spread, it may be more difficult to see what is happening, as in add_to_cart3. By keeping related ideas close together, we maximize the readability as in add_to_cart2.

In reality, there are some advantages to the style of design hinted at in add_to_cart3, and this code is certainly a nicer place to work than version 1.

My point here, though, is that there is sweet spot for cohesion. If you jumble too many concepts together, you lose cohesion at a fairly detailed level. In example 1, you could argue that all the work is done inside a single method, but this is only naively cohesive.

In reality, the concepts associated with adding an item to a shopping cart, the business of the function, are mixed in with other duties that obscure the picture. Even in this simple example, it is less clear what this code is doing until we dig in. We have to know a lot more stuff to properly understand this code.

The other alternative, add_to_cart3, while more flexible as a design, still lacks clarity. At this extreme it is easy for responsibilities to be so diffuse, so widely dispersed, that it is impossible to understand the picture without reading and understanding a lot of code. This could be a good thing, but my point is that there is a cost in clarity to coupling this loose, as well as some benefits.

Both of these failings are extremely common in production systems. In fact, they're so common that they may even be the norm for large complex systems.

This is a failure of design and comes at a significant cost. This is a cost that you will be familiar with if you have ever worked on "legacy code."[8]

There is a simple, subjective way to spot poor cohesion. If you have ever read a piece of code and thought "I don't know what this code does," it is probably because the cohesion is poor.

Cohesion in Human Systems

As with many of the other ideas in this book, problems with cohesion aren't limited only to the code that we write and to the systems that we build. Cohesion is an idea that works at the level of information, so it is just as important in getting the organizations in which we work structured sensibly. The most obvious example of this is in team organization. The findings from the "State of DevOps" report say that one of the leading predictors of high performance, measured in terms of throughput and stability, is the ability of teams to make their own decisions without the need to ask permission of anyone outside the team. Another way to think of that is that the information and skills of the team are cohesive, in that the team has all that it needs within its bounds to make decisions and to make progress.

Summary

Cohesion is probably the slipperiest of the ideas in the list of ideas for managing complexity. Software developers can, and do, sometimes argue that simply having all the code in one place, one file, and one function even, is at least cohesive, but this is too simplistic.

Code that randomly combines ideas in this way is not cohesive; it is just unstructured. It's bad. It prevents us from seeing clearly what the code does and how to change it safely.

Cohesion is about putting related concepts, concepts that change together, together in the code. If they are only "together" by accident because everything is "together," we have not really gained much traction.

Cohesion is the counter to modularity and primarily makes sense when considered in combination with modularity. One of the most effective tools to help us strike a good working balance between cohesion and modularity is separation of concerns.

---

8. *Legacy code* or *legacy systems* are systems that have been around for a while. They probably still deliver important value to the organizations that operate them, but they have often devolved into poorly designed tangled messes of code. Michael Feathers defines *legacy system* as a "system without tests."

11

Separation of Concerns

Separation of concerns is defined as "a design principle for separating a computer program into distinct sections such that each section addresses a separate concern."[1]

Separation of concerns is the most powerful principle of design in my own work. I apply it everywhere.

The simple colloquial description of separation of concerns is "One class, one thing. One method, one thing." It's a nice soundbite, but that doesn't give the functional programmers a free pass to ignore it.

This is about clarity and focus in our code and systems. It is one of the key enabling techniques to help us improve the modularity, cohesion, and abstraction in the systems that we create and, as a result, help us reduce the coupling to an effective minimum.

Separation of concerns also operates at all levels of granularity. It is a useful principle at the scale of whole systems as well as at the level of individual functions of a system.

Separation of concerns is not really the same kind of idea as cohesion and modularity. These two are properties of code, and while we can speak of code as having a "good separation of concerns," what we are really saying is that the "stuff that is unrelated is far apart, and the stuff that is related is close together." Separation of concerns is really a specific take on modularity and cohesion.

Separation of concerns is primarily a technique that we can adopt that helps us reduce coupling and improve the cohesion and modularity of our code and systems.

---

1. Source: Wikipedia, https://en.wikipedia.org/wiki/Separation_of_concerns

That does, sort of, downplay its importance to my approach to design, though. Separation of concerns is a fundamental driver of good design choices for me. It allows me to keep the code and architecture of the systems that I create clean, focused, composable, flexible, efficient, scalable, and open to change, as well as lots of other good things, too.

Swapping Out a Database

When we built our financial exchange, we adopted the engineering disciplines outlined in this book. In fact, this experience is what made me want to write this book. Our exchange was fantastic—the best large-system code base that I have ever worked on or seen.

We took a strict approach to separation of concerns from individual functions all the way to our enterprise system architecture. We could write business logic that knew nothing at all about its surroundings, was completely testable, didn't make any remote calls that it was aware of, didn't record any data that it was aware of, didn't know the addresses of its collaborators, and didn't worry about its own security, scalability, or resilience.

These services could work like this because all of these behaviors were looked after elsewhere; they were other "concerns" of the system. The pieces of behavior that provided those services to the core logic didn't know anything about the business that they operated in and didn't know what the code for which they provided these services did.

As a result, a domain-focused service in this system was secure, persistent, highly available, scalable, resilient, and very high-performance by default.

One day, we decided that we didn't like the commercial terms that we had with our relational database vendor. We used this database to store some of the contents of our data warehouse, a large data store that was growing rapidly and that stored historical details of order history and other business-critical values.

We downloaded one of the open source relational database management systems (RDBMSs), copied it to our repository for such dependencies, scripted its deployment, and made a few simple changes to the code that interacted with the RDBMS. This was simple because of the separation of concerns in our architecture. We then submitted the change to our continuous delivery deployment pipeline. A couple of tests failed; we tracked down the error and fixed the problems and then committed the new version to the pipeline. All the tests in our deployment pipeline passed on this second attempt, so we knew that our change was safe to release. Our changes were deployed into production the next time the system was released a few days later.

This whole story took a single morning!

Without good separation of concerns, this would have taken months or years and probably wouldn't even have been contemplated as a result.

Let's look at a simple example. In the previous chapter, I showed three examples of code solving the same problem; Listing 11.1 shows them again.

Listing 11.1   Three Separation of Concern Examples

```
def add_to_cart1(self, item):
    self.cart.add(item)

    conn = sqlite3.connect('my_db.sqlite')
    cur = conn.cursor()
    cur.execute('INSERT INTO cart (name, price)
    values (item.name, item.price)')
    conn.commit()
    conn.close()

    return self.calculate_cart_total();

def add_to_cart2(self, item):
    self.cart.add(item)
    self.store.store_item(item)
    return self.calculate_cart_total();

def add_to_cart3(self, item, listener):
    self.cart.add(item)
    listener.on_item_added(self, item)
```

In the previous chapter, we discussed these in the context of cohesion, but the principle that I used to achieve a more cohesive result was separation of concerns.

In the first, bad example, `add_to_cart1`, the separation is nonexistent. This code bundles together the core focus of the function, adding something to a cart, with the esoteric detail of how things are stored in a relational database. It then, as a side effect, calculates some kind of total. Nasty!

The second example, `add_to_cart2`, is a considerable step forward. Now we are initiating the storage but don't care how that works. We could imagine that the "store" was supplied to the class and could be anything. This code is considerably more flexible as a result. It still knows that storage and cart-total calculation are involved, though.

The third example represents a more complete separation of concerns. In this example, the code executes the core behavior, adding something to the cart, and then merely signals that something was added. This code doesn't know and doesn't care what happens next. It is entirely decoupled from storage and total calculation. This code is considerably more cohesive and more modular as a result.

Clearly, as with any design decision, there is choice here. I would argue that `add_to_cart1` is just bad. Separation of concerns would rule it out. The guiding principle is that this is a mix of essential and accidental complexity. That is, how and where we store something is not germane to the core shopping-cart behavior that we are trying to create. We want a clear line, a separation, between code that deals with essential and code that deals with accidental complexity.

The difference between the second two examples is more nuanced. This is more of a matter of context and choice. My personal preference is strongly in favor of add_to_cart3. This is the most flexible solution of all. I may or may not choose to achieve my separation with a method-injected listener like this, but I very much like that I have removed the concept of storage from my core domain.

This is the code that I would usually write. To my mind, version 2 of add_to_cart is still confusing concerns. I certainly think that store_item is a better abstraction than some connection and SQL stuff, but the concept itself is still in the realm of accidental complexity. If you put something in a real shopping cart, you don't then need to "persist" it!

Version 3 gives me the greatest freedom of choice, at little real penalty. A valid criticism of this approach is that you can't see here that storage may be going on, but that is not really what matters here, in this moment, for this piece of code. Storage is a side effect of how our computer works, not a core behavior of adding something to a shopping cart. In the third example, we can clearly see that when an item is added, and see that something else may be happening; we just don't care what. If we do care, we can go and look.

Think for a moment about the testability of each of these methods. Version 1 will be horrible to test. We will need a database, so the test will be difficult to establish and probably extremely fragile and slow; either the database will be shared and liable to change outside of the test, or it will be created during the setup of the test, and each test run will be very slow to execute. Both of the other two versions can be tested easily and efficiently with fakes.

The primary argument against version 3 is that it is less clear what is going on. I certainly agree that clarity is a virtue in code. Actually, though, this is really just a matter of context. I am looking at the code here that is responsible for adding an item to a cart. Why should it know what happens next?

This focus on separation of concerns has helped us improve the modularity and cohesion of this code. Depending on the degree to which the collaboration of several parts matter—listeners that store the results or calculate totals, for example—we can test the correct establishment of those relationships elsewhere.

So the "whole picture" is obscured only because we are looking in the wrong place. If we were to take that rather naive view of the world, then shouldn't the generic collection that we are using to represent our cart also know about storage and totals? Of course not!

One of the reasons that I value **separation of concerns** so highly as a guiding principle is because it reminds me to keep my focus small. I feel proud of code that I have written when you can look at each part and understand what that part does without thinking too hard about it. If you have to study it for more than a handful of seconds, I have failed. Now you may have to understand how that part is used by other parts, but those other parts will have their own concerns to deal with, and I ideally express them as clearly.

Dependency Injection

An extremely useful tool in achieving a good separation of concerns is **dependency injection**. Dependency injection is where dependencies of a piece of code are supplied to it as parameters, rather than created by it.

In our by now slightly overused example, in `add_to_cart1` the connection to the database is explicitly created and opened within the method. This means that there is no opportunity to use an alternative. We are tightly coupled to this specific implementation, even to this specifically named instance of the database. If the **store** in version 2 is passed in as a constructor parameter, then immediately this represents a step-change in flexibility. We can supply anything that implements `store_item`.

In version 3 of our `add_to_cart` method, the listener could be anything that implements `on_item_ added`.

This simple change in the relationship between the behaviors of this code is significant. In the first case, version 1, the code creates everything that it needs, so it is deeply coupled to a single, specific implementation. This code is inflexible by design. In the others, the code is a collaborator with other components of the system, so it knows, and cares, little about how they operate.

Dependency injection is often misunderstood as the function of a tool or framework, but this is not the case. Dependency injection is something that you can do in most languages, certainly in any OO or functional language, natively, and it is a powerful approach to design. I have even seen it used, to very good effect, in Unix shell scripts.

Dependency injection is a fantastic tool to minimize coupling to an appropriate, useful level, but it is also an effective way to form a line of demarcation between concerns. I will point out again how interlinked all these ideas are. This is not because of repetition, but rather that we are describing some important, deep properties of software and software development; therefore, as we approach those problems from different directions, they inevitably intersect.

Separating Essential and Accidental Complexity

An effective route into improving the quality of our design is to aim to separate concerns in a specific way—that is, to separate the essential complexity of our systems from the accidental. If the concept of "essential and "accidental" complexity is new to you, these are important ideas first described in Fred Brooks' famous paper "There is No Silver Bullet," mentioned earlier in this book.

The **essential complexity** of a system is the complexity that is inherent in solving the problem that you are trying to solve, how to calculate the value of a bank account, how to total the items in a shopping cart, or even how to calculate the trajectory of a spaceship, for example. Addressing this complexity is the real value that our system offers.

The **accidental complexity** is everything else—the problems that we are forced to solve as a side effect of doing something useful with computers. These are things like persistence of data, displaying things on a screen, clustering, some aspects of security…in fact anything that is not directly related to solving the problem at hand.

Just because it is "accidental" does not mean that it is unimportant; our software is running on a computer, so dealing with the constraints and the realities of that is important, but if we built a system that was fantastic at dealing with accidental complexity but didn't have any essential complexity, it would, by definition, be useless! So, it is in our interests to work to minimize, without ignoring, accidental complexity.

An effective approach to improving our designs through separation of concerns is to focus very clearly on separating the concerns of the accidental and essential complexities of our systems.

I want the logic of my system that cares about how to drive a car to be separate from the logic that knows how to display information on a screen, the logic that knows how to evaluate a trade to be separate from how that trade is stored or communicated.

This may or may not seem obvious, but it is important, and, subjectively, it doesn't seem to me to be how most code is written. Most of the code that I see people write decidedly conflates these two different classes of responsibility. It is common to see business logic mixed with display code and the details of persistence in the midst of the logic that deals with, or that should deal with, the core domain (the essential complexity) of the system.

This is yet another area where focusing on the testability of our code and systems can be a big help in improving our design.

Listing 10.1 demonstrated this clearly. This code is not really testable in any but the most naively complex way. Sure, I could write a test that first created a file at a specific location on disk called *words.txt* and then run the code and look for a result in another file at a specific location called *sorted.txt*, but this would be slow, annoyingly complex, and so coupled to its environment that I could trivially break the test by renaming the files or moving their location. Try running this test in parallel with itself, or something closely related, and you will quickly face some unpleasant problems!

The majority of the work going on in Listing 10.1 is not even vaguely related to the behavior of the code that matters. This is nearly all accidental complexity in the heart of the code that should be focused on doing something more important—in this case sorting a collection of words.

Listing 10.2 improved the cohesion but is still not testable as a unit. It shares the same problems as Listing 10.1 in this regard.

Listing 11.2 is an example of attempting to improve this code purely from the perspective of separating the accidental from the essential complexity. I wouldn't really pick names like "essential" or "accidental" for real code; they are just to make the example clearer.

Listing 11.2   Separating Accidental and Essential Complexity

```
public interface Accidental
{
    String[] readWords() throws IOException
    boolean storeWords(List<String> sorted) throws IOException
}
```

```
public class Essential
{
    public boolean loadProcessAndStore(Accidental accidental) throws IOException
    {
        List<String> sorted = sortWords(accidental.readWords());
        return accidental.storeWords(sorted);
    }

    private List<String> sortWords(String[] words)
    {
        List<String> sorted = Arrays.asList(words);
        sorted.sort(null);
        return sorted;
    }
}
```

Assuming that we implement the accidental complexity functions outlined in our "Accidental" interface in Listing 11.2, this code does exactly the same things as Listings 10.1 and 10.2, but it is better. By separating the concerns—in this case using the "seam" between the accidental complexity and the essential complexity of the problem that we are solving—we have improved things considerably. This code is easier to read, more focused on the problem that matters, and considerably more flexible as a result. If we wanted to supply "words" from somewhere other than a file in a specific location on a specific device, we can. If we want to store the sorted words somewhere else, we can.

This is still not great code. We could further improve its separation of concerns to improve its focus and decouple it more in terms of readability, as well as at the technical level.

Listing 11.3 shows something a bit closer; we could certainly debate some of my naming choices, which would be more context dependent, but purely from the perspective of separation of concerns, I hope that you can see a very big difference between the code in Listing 10.1 and Listings 11.2 and 11.3. Even in this simple sample, we improved the readability, testability, flexibility, and utility of this code by following these design principles.

Listing 11.3 Removing Accidental Complexity with Abstraction

```
public interface WordSource
{
    String[] words();
}

public interface WordsListener
{
```

```
        void onWordsChanged(List<String> sorted);
}

public class WordSorter
{
    public void sortWords(WordSource words, WordsListener listener)
    {
        listener.onWordsChanged(sort(words.words()));
    }

    private List<String> sort(String[] words)
    {
        List<String> sorted = Arrays.asList(words);
        sorted.sort(null);
        return sorted;
    }
}
```

The separation of essential and accidental complexity is a good starting point to help us get to code with a better separation of concerns. There is a lot of value in this approach, but it is the low-hanging fruit. What about other mixed concerns?

Importance of DDD

We can also look to guide our designs from the perspective of the problem domain. If we take an evolutionary, incremental approach to design, we can work in ways that allow us to keep a sharp look out for those moments when we may identify new concerns—concerns that may otherwise be inappropriately conflated in our designs.

Listing 11.4 shows some Python code. In it, I try to create a version of the children's game Battleship, in which we try to sink our opponent's fleet.

I have come to the point in my design where I am beginning to question it.

Listing 11.4   Missing a Concept

```python
class GameSheet:

    def __init__(self):
        self.sheet = {}
        self.width = MAX_COLUMNS
        self.height = MAX_ROWS
        self.ships = {}
        self._init_sheet()
```

```
def add_ship(self, ship):
    self._assert_can_add_ship(ship)
    ship.orientation.place_ship(self, ship)
    self._ship_added(ship)
```

In my GameSheet that represents the playing area, the grid of squares, of the game, I have come to the point where I want to add a ship to the sheet.

I was using Test-Driven Development (TDD) to create this code, and at this point I had a growing series of tests in GameSheetTest focused on the complexities of adding a ship. Out of 11 tests, 6 of them were focused on testing whether I was allowed to place a ship onto the GameSheet. I had begun adding validation code to the GameSheet to verify my additions, and I had about 9 or 10 lines of code in three extra functions.

I was feeling uneasy about my design of this code and of the tests that supported it. Both were growing in size and complexity, not by much, but enough to make me start looking for what was wrong. Then I realized that I was making a separation of concerns mistake. My problem was that my design was missing an important concept completely.

My GameSheet was responsible for the position of the ships *and* the rules of the game. Having an "and" in the description of a class or a method is a warning sign. It says that I have two concerns rather than one. In this case, it quickly seemed obvious to me that I was missing the concept of "rules" in my implementation. I refactored the code and the tests, extracting a new class called Rules. Listing 11.5 shows how the addition of Rules simplifies things.

Listing 11.5   Listening to the Code

```
class GameSheet:

    def __init__(self, rules):
        self.sheet = {}
        self.width = MAX_COLUMNS
        self.height = MAX_ROWS
        self.rules = rules
        self._init_sheet()

    def add_ship(self, ship):
        self.rules.assert_can_add_ship(ship)
        ship.orientation.place_ship(self, ship)
        self._ship_added(ship)
```

This immediately simplified the GameSheet. It removed the need for the sheet to maintain a collection of Ships, and it removed nine or ten lines of validation logic that was only the beginning of the evolution of my code focused on validating compliance with the rules.

Ultimately, this change gave me more flexibility in my design for the future, allowing me to better test the GameSheet logic and the Rules independently of one another and, potentially, as a side effect, opened the door to having this code work with different versions of the Rules one day. I didn't worry about what those rules might be. I didn't do any extra work to support some imaginary future new rules, but there was now a "seam" in my code that could possibly prove useful in the future while, in the pragmatic real world of the present, it allowed me to better test my code and improved my design. All this was driven by a simple focus on separation of concerns.

Using the problem that you are solving to help you define sensible lines of demarcation in your code is really the essence of separation of concerns. This is true at various levels of granularity. We can begin with bounded contexts to identify course-grained modules (or services) in our design and then work to refine our design over time as we learn more about the problem that we are solving and gain more insight into the readability, or otherwise, of our code.

One of the keys here is to try to maintain a very low tolerance for complexity. Code should be simple and readable, and as soon as it begins to feel like hard work, you should pause and start looking for ways to simplify and clarify the part in front of you.

In the example outlined in Listings 11.4 and 11.5, the thing that started me worrying about my design was probably down to only ten lines of code and a few test cases that I later decided were in the wrong place. This is one of the reasons that I value separation of concerns quite so highly. It provides me with a mechanism to, very early in the process, detect problems that will, if I don't react to them, lead to reduced modularity and poor cohesion in my designs.

Testability

This approach to incrementally evolving the design of your code, while keeping an eye out for poor separation of concerns, is reinforced through testing. As I have already described, dependency injection can help us improve our designs, but an even more powerful, maybe an even more fundamental, tool to help to establish an effective separation of concerns is testability.

We can use the testability of the systems that we create to drive quality into them in a way that little else, beyond talent and experience, can do.

If we work to ensure that our code is easy to test, then we **must** separate the concerns or our tests will lack focus. Our tests will also be more complex, and it will be difficult to make them repeatable and reliable. Striving to control the variables so that we can test encourages us to create systems that demonstrate the properties of high quality in software that we value: modularity, cohesion, separation of concerns, information hiding, and loose coupling.

Ports & Adapters

Our aim in focusing on separating concerns is to improve the modularity and cohesion of our systems. This, in turn, makes our systems overall less tightly coupled. Managing the coupling in our systems appropriately should be one of the primary focusses of our designs, and this is true at every level of granularity.

One level where this is perhaps most clearly evident, and of value, is at those seams in our code where one "concern" interacts with another. These are places in our systems where we should always take more care.

Let's look at a simple example (see Listing 11.6). Here we have some code that wants to store something—in this case in an Amazon AWS S3 bucket. We have some code that processes whatever it is that we want to store and some code that invokes the storage itself, which is a decent start for separating the concerns of processing and storage.

For this code to work, there will have been some setup somewhere to initialize the s3client so that it knows the necessary details of the account that owns the bucket and so on. I haven't shown that code here, on purpose; I am sure that you can imagine several different ways that s3client arrived at this point. Some of these ways demonstrate better or worse separation of concerns. In this case, let's just focus on what we have in this function.

Listing 11.6   Storing a String in S3

```
void doSomething(Thing thing) {
    String processedThing = process(thing);
    s3client.putObject("myBucket," "keyForMyThing," processedThing);
}
```

As it stands, the code in Listing 11.6 is written from two different perspectives. We are used to seeing code like this all the time, but let's think about it for a moment. Here we have two very different focuses and two very different levels of abstraction all within two lines of code.

The first line is focused on doing something that makes sense in the world of the function or method, perhaps "process (thing)'" makes sense in a business context; it doesn't really matter, except that this is, presumably, the focus, the essential part, of this code. This is the job that we want done, and it is written from that perspective. The second line is, err, alien. It is an interloper that has dumped accidental complexity into the heart of our logic.

One take on cohesion is that within a particular scope, the level of abstraction should remain consistent. So what if we improved the consistency here? Listing 11.7 is a big improvement in this respect, even if all that we have done is rename a class and a method.

Listing 11.7   Storing a String in S3 via a Port

```
void doSomething(Thing thing) {
    String processedThing = process(thing);
    store.storeThings("myBucket," "keyForMyThing," processedThing);
}
```

Now there are some implications as a result of the change from Listing 11.6 to Listing 11.7. By making the "invocation to store" more consistent with the other ideas in this function, we have increased the abstraction. We have also started to push our design in a different direction.

Remember the code that I didn't show; by making this one simple change, I have made a bunch of implementations for that initialization wrong. If I abstract storage in this way, it makes no sense at all for all of that initialization to be within the scope of this class or module. It's much better to externalize it completely.

So now I am going to hide all of that initialization somewhere else. That means I can test it, in abstract, separate from this code. It means that if I choose to use dependency injection to supply my store, I can test this code without the need for a real store. It also means that I can choose where I want to store things outside of this code, supplying different kinds of stores in different contexts so my code is more flexible.

You can think of the new abstraction as a **port**, or a vector through which information flows. Whether or not you decide to make the port polymorphic is entirely up to you and the circumstances in your code, but even where you don't, this code is better. It is better because you have improved the separation of concerns, improved the cohesion by maintaining a more consistent level of abstraction, and improved both its readability and maintainability.

The concrete implementation of this port is an **adapter** that acts as a translation service, translating ideas from, in this example, the context of "things" to the context of "AWS S3 Storage."

After this change, our code doesn't know anything about S3; it doesn't even know that S3 is being used.

The key idea here is that the code is written from a more consistent frame of reference. It maintains that more consistent abstraction.

What I have described here is sometimes called the **Ports & Adapters** pattern, also sometimes referred to as **hexagonal architecture** when applied at the level of a service or subsystem.

The value of this, in design, is very significant. It is almost never the case that your code cares about every single detail of an API that it consumes. You nearly always deal with a subset of such APIs. The port that you create only needs to expose the minimal subset that you choose to use, so it will nearly always be a simpler version of the API that you are interacting with.

The trouble with writing a book that talks about code is that to convey ideas, the code examples need to be small and simple, or the ideas get lost in the complexity of the code. But what about when you are trying to show the improvement in simplicity?

So bear with me. Imagine that we had a whole system written along the lines of Listing 11.6: tens, hundreds, maybe even thousands of interactions through an `s3client`. Then Amazon upgrades the interface to the S3 service, or at least the Java client library. Version 2 has a different programming model, so now we have to go and change tens, hundreds, or thousands of lines of code to take advantage of the new client library.

If we have created our own abstraction, our own Port & Adapter for S3, that does just, and only just, what our code needs, we can probably use that in more than just one place in the code. Maybe we use it everywhere, maybe there are some cases that are more complex, and maybe we have a different, separate Port & Adapter for those cases. Either way, we have significantly reduced our maintenance effort. We could completely rewrite the adapter to use the new client library. It wouldn't affect the code that uses it at all.

This approach embodies many of the goals of good design. By working to manage complexity, we also insulate our code against change—even unexpected or unpredictable change.

When to Adopt Ports & Adapters

When people discuss the Ports & Adapters approach, they are usually discussing it in the context of a translation layer at the boundaries between services (or modules).

This is good advice. In his book *Domain Driven Design*,[2] Eric Evans recommends:

> *Always translate information that crosses between Bounded Contexts.*

In designing a system from services, I, and others, advise that we should aim to align our services with a bounded context. This minimizes coupling and improves the modularity and cohesion of our services.

Combined, these two pieces of advice suggest a simple guideline of "Always translate information that flows between services," or to put it another way, "Always communicate between services using Ports & Adapters."

When I started writing the previous sentence, I first wrote "rule" rather than "guideline" and then quickly corrected myself. I can't, in good conscience, describe this as a rule, because there are sometimes corner cases that break the rule. However, my strong advice is to assume, as a default position, that all information exchanges between services will be translated via an adapter, whatever the technical nature of the API.

---

2. *Domain Driven Design* is a book by Eric Evans describing how to model the problem domain in software as a guiding principle in design. See https://amzn.to/2WXJ94m.

This doesn't mean the adapter needs to be lots of code or complex, but from a design perspective, each service or module should have its own view of the world and should defend that perspective. If information is sent that breaks that view, that is a serious problem for the code.

We can protect our code two ways, and we can use an adapter that translates things into our world-view as they arrive at the edges of our system, allowing us to validate our inputs to the degree to which we care about them. Or we can wrap up stuff that we don't trust and ignore it so that we can protect our systems from dubious external changes.

If we are writing a messaging system of some kind, for example, there are things that we need to know, and there are things that we should certainly not know.

We probably need to know who sent a message and where it is going. We probably need to know how big the message is and maybe whether we should retry it if there is a problem. We should certainly not know what the message is saying! That would immediately couple the technicalities of messaging to the semantics of the conversation that the messaging is being used for and would be very poor design.

This may or may not seem obvious, but I also see a lot of code that makes precisely this kind of mistake. If I were building a messaging system, I would "wrap up" the content of the message in a packet of some kind that insulates the messaging system from the content of the packets, the messages themselves.

What Is an API?

This starts to get into a bit of design philosophy: what is an API? I would argue for a fairly practical definition:

> *An application programming interface (API) is all of the information that is exposed to consumers of a service, or library, that exposes that API.*

This is different from what some developers think of when we use the term API.

There has been a morph over time in what the term "API" means. In part, this is probably due to the success of the REST approach to creating services. It is common, at least in informal conversations with developers, that the term "API" is used as a synonym for "Text over HTTP." This is certainly one form of API, but it is only one; there are many more.

Strictly any means of communication between different bits of code, meant to support programming of some kind, is an API. This is where it is important to think about the information that our code interacts with.

Imagine, for a moment, a function that takes a binary stream of data as an argument. What is the API?

Is it only the signature of the function? Well, maybe, if the function treats the binary stream as a black-box and never looks inside the stream, then yes, the signature of the function defines its coupling with its callers.

However, if the function interacts with the contents of the binary stream in any way, that is part of its contract. The level of interaction defines the degree to which it is coupled, with the information in the stream.

If the first eight bytes in the stream are used to encode its length, and that is all that the function knows or cares about the stream, then the function signature, plus the meaning of the first eight bytes and how the length is encoded within them, are "the API."

The more that the function knows of the content of the stream of bytes, the more coupled to it it is, and the greater the surface area of the API. I see many teams that ignore the fact that the data structures in its inputs that their code understands, and processes, are part of that code's public API.

Our adapters need to deal with the whole API. If that means translating, or at least validating, the content of a binary stream of inputs, then so be it. The alternative is that our code may break when someone sends us the wrong stream of bytes. This is a variable that we can control.

Designing with the assumption that we will always add Ports & Adapters at these points of communication between modules and services is a much stronger default stance than not. Even if the "adapter" is a placeholder for the future, having that placeholder in place gives us the opportunity, should the nature of the API change in any way to cope with those changes without having to rewrite all of our code.

This is the classic model of Ports & Adapters. I recommend thinking about this at finer-grained levels, too. I don't mean to suggest that you always write explicit translations, but the idea of trying to maintain a consistent level of abstraction within any piece of code, no matter how small (see Listing 11.6), is a good one.

As a default stance, or a guideline, I recommend that you always add Ports & Adapters where the code that you talk to is in a different scope of evaluation, such as a different repo or a different deployment pipeline. Taking a more defensive stance in these situations will make your code more testable, yet again, and more robust in the face of change.

Using TDD to Drive Separation of Concerns

I have already described how the ideas of designing to improve the **testability** of our code help us improve its quality, not just in the simplistic sense of "does it work," but in the more profound sense of building the kind of quality into our products that makes them capable of ongoing maintenance and development.

If we design our code using the ideas of separation of concerns as a guiding principle, including the ideas of maintaining a consistent level of abstraction within any given, even small, context, then we leave the door open to incremental change. Even if we don't yet know the details of how something will be communicated, stored, or interacted with in general, we can write code and make progress.

Later, as we learn more, we can use the code that we wrote in ways that we hadn't thought of when we wrote it. This approach allows us to take a more evolutionary approach to design, growing our systems, step-by-step, as our understanding deepens, into much more sophisticated, much more capable, versions in the future.

TDD is the most powerful tool that we can wield to achieve that testability. By driving all of our development from the perspective of testing, we dramatically change the focus of our designs.

Specifically in the context of separation of concerns, our tests become more difficult to write the more that concerns are conflated within the scope of a test. If we organize our development around testing and drive our development through testing, then we are confronted much earlier in the process by the costs and benefits of our design decisions.

This faster feedback is, naturally, a good thing, allowing us the opportunity to spot flaws in our design much sooner than any other technique, apart from us just being smarter than we are, over which we can exert only a limited degree of control. There is nothing wrong with being smart, but the best way to become "smarter" is to work in smarter ways, which is really the aim of this book. TDD is one of those important "smarter ways."

Summary

Separation of concerns is certainly an attribute of high-quality code. If you have two pieces of code that fulfil exactly the same function and one has good separation of concerns and the other doesn't, then the first is easier to understand, easier to test, easier to change, and more flexible.

Separation of concerns is also the easiest design heuristic to adopt of the collection here.

We could debate the modularity or cohesion of some code or system. As you can see, I consider these ideas to be extremely important, but ultimately their measurement is somewhat subjective. While we can probably agree on bad examples, we'd probably struggle to, at the limit, define what ideal modularity or cohesion was.

Separation of concerns is different. If your module, class, or function does more than one thing, your concerns aren't really separate. The result is that separation of concerns is a fantastic tool to guide us, definitively, in the direction of the design of better software.

12

Information Hiding and Abstraction

Information hiding and abstraction is defined as "the process of removing physical, spatial, or temporal details or attributes in the study of objects or systems to focus attention on details of greater importance."[1]

I lumped together two slightly different ideas in computer science in the title of this chapter; they are different but related, and for the purpose of thinking about fundamental principles for software engineering, they are best considered together.

Abstraction or Information Hiding

I conflate these ideas because I don't think that the difference between the two is enough to really concern us. What I am talking about here is drawing lines, or seams, in our code so that when we look at those lines from the "outside," we don't care about what is behind them. As a consumer of a function, class, library, or module, I should not need, or care, to know *anything* about how it works, only how I use it.

Some people take a much narrower view of **information hiding** than this, but I don't see that it adds anything useful. If you can't get away from worrying about "information hiding being only about data" (it's not), then whenever I say "information hiding," think "abstraction."

If you can't get away from thinking "abstraction" means only "creating abstract concept-objects," then while that is part of the definition, it is not what I mean, so maybe think "information hiding."

---

1. Source: Wikipedia, https://en.wikipedia.org/wiki/Abstraction_(computer_science)

The information that I am hiding is the behavior of the code. It includes implementation detail as well as any data that it may or may not use. The abstraction that I present to the outside world should achieve this trick of keeping secrets from other parts of the code.

It should be obvious that if our aim is to manage complexity so that we can build more complex systems than we can comfortably hold inside our heads, then we need to hide information.

We'd like to be able to focus on the work/code in front of us without worrying about what is going on elsewhere and how stuff that we don't need to care about right now works. This seems fundamental, but there is a lot of code in the world that does not look like this. Some code is fragile to change, where change in one place affects other parts of the code. There is code where the only way to make progress is to be so smart that you understand how most of the system works. That is not a scalable approach!

What Causes "Big Balls of Mud"?

We sometimes call these difficult to work on codebases *big balls of mud*. They are often so tangled, so convoluted, that people are scared to change them. Most organizations, particularly bigger organizations, that have built software for any length of time will own some tangled code like this.

Organizational and Cultural Problems

The causes are complex and diverse. One of the most common complaints that I hear from software developers and software development teams is "my manager won't let me XXX," where "XXX" is either "refactor," "test," "design better," or even "fix that bug."

There are certainly some unpleasant organizations in the world. If you work somewhere like that, my advice is to seek better employers. However, in the vast majority of cases, this complaint is simply not true, or at least not entirely true. At worst this is an excuse. I dislike blaming people, though, so a more charitable interpretation is that this is based on an important misunderstanding.

The first thing to say is why do we, as software developers, need to ask for permission to do a good job? We are the experts in software development, so we are best placed to understand what works and what doesn't.

If you hire me to write code for you, it is my duty to you to do the best job that I can. That means I need to optimize my work so that I can reliably, repeatably, and sustainably deliver code over a long period of time. My code needs to solve the problem that I am faced with, and it needs to fulfill the needs of my users and ambitions of my employers.

So, I need to create code that works, but I also need to sustain my ability to do so over time, repeatably and reliably. I need to maintain my ability to modify the code as I learn more about the problem that we are solving and the system that we are developing.

If I were a chef preparing a meal in a restaurant, I could probably prepare one meal more quickly if I decided not to clean up my tools and work area when I finished. That will probably work for one meal. It may even work for two meals; it would be disgusting, but it may work. If I worked like that all of the time, though, I'd get fired!

I'd get fired because I'd give the patrons of the restaurant food poisoning. Even if I didn't get fired, by the time I got to the third meal, I would be far slower and less productive because the mess that I had made would get in the way of my work. I'd have to clear a work area and the tools I was using for every task. I'd have to struggle with tools that were no longer sharp enough, and so on. Does this sound familiar?

If you hired me as a chef, you would never say, "you have permission to sharpen your knives" or "it is your responsibility to clean your work area," because as a professional chef, you, and I, would assume that those things are a fundamental part of being a professional. As a chef, that would be part of my **duty of care**.

As software professionals, it is our duty to understand what it takes to develop software. We need to own the responsibility for the quality of the code that we work on. It is our **duty of care** to do a good job. This is not altruistic; it is practical and pragmatic. It is in the interest of our employers, our users, and ourselves.

If we work to create and maintain the quality of our code, our employers will get the new features that they want more efficiently. Our customers will get code that makes more sense and is more usable, and we will be able to make changes without being constantly nervous of breaking things.

This matters for a variety of reasons, not the least because the data is very clear.[2] Software is not a game of short-term wins. If you are dropping testing, avoiding refactoring, or not taking time to find more modular, more cohesive designs to achieve some short-term delivery target, **you are going more slowly, not faster**.

It is reasonable for an organization creating software to want to do it efficiently. There is an economic impact that affects all of us who work for such an organization.

If we want the organizations in which we work to thrive and for us to have a more pleasant experience while building the software that helps our organizations to thrive, then we need to work effectively.

Our aim should be to do whatever it takes to build better software faster. The data is in: the *Accelerate* book describes some of what it takes, and that certainly does not involve naively cutting corners in quality. The reverse is true.

One of the key findings of the "State of DevOps" report that underpins the scientific approach to analyzing the performance of software teams outlined in the *Accelerate* book is that there is **no trade-off between speed and quality**. You don't create software faster if you do a poor job on quality.

---

2. The *Accelerate* book describes how teams that take a more disciplined approach to development spend "44% more time on new work" than teams that don't. See https://amzn.to/2YYf5Z8.

So when a manager asks for an estimate for a piece of work, it is not in your interest, your manager's interest, or your employer's interest to cut corners on quality. It will make you go slower overall, even if your manager is dumb and thinks that it will.

I have certainly seen organizations that, either intentionally or unintentionally, applied pressure on developers to speed up. Often, though, it is developers and development teams that are complicit in deciding what "speeding up" entails.

It is usually the developers that rule out quality, not the managers or organization. Managers and organizations want "better software faster," not "worse software faster." In reality, even that is not the trade-off. As we have already seen, the real trade-off, over long periods of time, is between "better software faster" and "worse software slower." "Better" goes hand in hand with "faster." This is important for all of us to recognize and to believe. The most efficient software development teams are not fast because they discard quality but because they embrace it.

It is the professional duty of a software engineer to recognize this truth and to always offer advice, estimates, and design thoughts based on a high-quality outcome.

Don't parse estimates and predictions to separate out the time to do a good job; assume that your managers, co-workers, and employers want you to do a good job, and do it.

There is a cost to doing work. In cooking, part of that cost is the time it takes to clean up and maintain your tools as you go. In software development, those costs are to refactor, to test, to take the time to create good designs, to fix bugs when they are found, to collaborate, to communicate, and to learn. These are not "nice to have" options; these are the foundations of a professional approach to software development.

Anyone can write code; that is not our job. Software development is more than that. Our job is to solve problems, and that requires us to take care in our design and consider the effectiveness of the solutions that we produce.

Technical Problems and Problems of Design

Assuming that we give ourselves permission to do a good job, the next question is, what does that take? That is really the theme for this book. The techniques that allow us to optimize for learning, outlined in Part II, and the techniques described in this part, combined, give us the tools that allow us to do a better job.

Specifically, in the context of avoiding and correcting big balls of mud, though, there is a mindset that is important to adopt. This is the mindset that it is a good thing, a sensible thing, to change existing code.

Many organizations are either afraid to change their code or have some kind of reverence for it that belies the reality. I would argue the reverse: if you can't, or won't, change the code, then the code is effectively dead. To quote Fred Brooks again:

As soon as one freezes a design, it becomes obsolete.[3]

My friend Dan North has spoken about an interesting idea. Dan has a gift for capturing an idea in a clever turn of phrase. He talked about the "software half-life of a team" as a metric for quality.

Now neither I nor Dan have any data to back up this idea, but it is an interesting one. He says that the quality of the software produced by a team is a function of its software half-life—that is, the time that it takes the team to rewrite half of the software that they are responsible for.

In Dan's model, good teams will probably rewrite half the software that they are responsible for in months; low-performing teams may never rewrite half.

Now I am pretty sure that Dan's idea is very contextual; when he came up with this, he was working in a very good, fast-paced, financial trading team. I am equally certain that there are many teams where this rule doesn't apply. Nevertheless, there is certainly a grain of truth here.

If we are, as I contend, a discipline foundationally rooted in our ability to learn, then when we learn new things that change our view on what is optimal for our design (whatever that means in our context), at that point, we should be able to change it to reflect our new, deeper understanding.

When Kent Beck picked a subtitle for his famous book on Extreme Programming, he chose *Embrace Change*. I don't know what he had in mind when he picked that subtitle, but I have come to think that it has much wider implications than I imagined when I first read his book.

If we buy in to this fundamental philosophy that we must retain our ability to change our ideas, our teams, our code, or our technology, as we learn more, then nearly everything else that I talk about in this book follows on as a natural consequence.

Working in ways that leave the door open to us making a mistake and being able to correct it; deepening our understanding of the problem that we face and reflecting our new understanding in our design; evolving our products and technologies incrementally in the direction of success wherever, or whatever, that may be—these are all targets for good engineering in software.

To be able to do this, we need to work in small steps that are easy to undo. We need our code to be a habitable space that we can revisit, maybe months or years later, and still understand. We need to be able to make a change in one part of the code and not have it affect others. We need a way to quickly and effectively validate that our changes were safe. Ideally, we'd also like to be able to change some of our architectural assumptions as our understanding, or maybe the popularity of our system, changes.

All the ideas in this book are relevant to that, but **abstraction** or **information hiding** feels to me to represent the clearest route to habitable systems.

---

3. A quote from Fred Brooks' book *Mythical Man Month*, https://amzn.to/3oCyPeU

Raising the Level of Abstraction

What would it take to get a Brooksian order-of-magnitude improvement? One avenue to explore is to raise the level of abstraction of programming.

The most common theme, in this line of thinking, has been to strengthen the relationship between the high-level diagrams that we sometimes use to describe our systems. "Wouldn't it be good if when I draw a picture of my system, I can use that picture to program my system, too?"

Over the years there have been lots of attempts at implementing this, and periodically new versions of this idea tend to crop up. At the time of writing, the current incarnation of this approach is called *low code development*.

However, there are several problems that seem to get in the way of this approach.

One common approach to diagram-driven development is to use the diagram to generate source code. The idea here is to use the diagrams to create the broad structure of the code, and then the detail can be filled in, by hand, by a programmer. This strategy is pretty much doomed to failure by one difficult-to-solve problem. The problem is that you are almost always going to learn more as the development of any complex system evolves.

At some point, you will need to revisit some of your early thinking. This means that your first version of your diagram and so the skeleton structure of your system is wrong and will need to change as your understanding deepens. The ability to "round-trip" or create a skeleton for your code, modify the detail by hand, change your mind, regenerate the diagram from the code, modify it, but keep the detailed changes is a tricky problem. It is the hurdle at which all such efforts, so far, have fallen.

So how about doing away with the manual coding step altogether? Why not use the diagrams as the code? This too has been tried lots of times. These sorts of systems usually demo extremely well. They look really nice and easy when building some simple, sample system.

However, there are two big problems. It is actually hard to raise the level of abstraction to a degree where you gain, by drawing pictures rather than writing code. You lose all of the benefits that, over time, we have evolved to support more conventional programming languages such as exception handling, version control, debugging support, library code, automated testing, design patterns, etc.

The first problem is the reason why these things demo so well but don't really scale to real-world systems. The problem is that while it is easy to create a graphical "language" that lets us express simple problems succinctly, it is much more difficult to create a similar visual "language" that provides general-purpose tools that allow you to create any old piece of logic. Turing-complete languages are really built out of some extremely common but quite low-level ideas. The level of detail that we require to describe and encode a working, complex software system seems to be inherently intricate and fine-grained.

Consider the need to add a graph to a spreadsheet. Most spreadsheet programs offer tools that allow you to add a graph, err, graphically. You can select some rows and columns of data in your spreadsheet and select a picture of the type of graph that you would like to add, and for simple cases, the program will generate a graph for you. These are good tools.

It gets trickier, though, if the data doesn't easily fit one of the simple, predefined patterns. The more specific your graph requirements are, the more detailed your instructions to the graphing system in your spreadsheet need to become. There comes a point where the limitations of the tools make them harder to use rather than easier. Now, you not only need a clear idea of how you want your graph to work but also a deep understanding of how to get around, or apply, the programming model that was in the head of the graphing-system developer.

Text is a surprisingly flexible, concise way of encoding ideas.

Fear of Over-Engineering

Many factors push developers to abdicate responsibility for quality. One of them is pressure, real or perceived, to get the job done efficiently. I have heard commercial people worry about software developers and teams "over-engineering." This is a real fear, and we technical professionals are to blame. We have been guilty of over-engineering sometimes.

Abstraction vs. Pragmatism

I once worked on a project for a client, a big insurance company. This was a "rescue project." I worked for a consultancy that was pretty well known for being able to go in and deliver effective solutions to projects that were stuck or had failed in previous attempts.

This project had failed fairly spectacularly, twice. It had been in development for more than three years, and they had nothing to show for it that was usable.

We started work and were making decent progress on a replacement. We were approached by an architect from the "strategy group" or some such name. He insisted that our software must comply with the "global architecture." So I, as the tech lead for the project, looked into what that would entail.

They had a grand plan for a distributed, service-based component architecture that abstracted their entire business. They had services for technical things as well as domain-level, useful behaviors. Their infrastructure would look after security and persistence, as well as allow the systems in the enterprise to be fully integrated with each other.

As by now, I am sure you suspect, this was all vapor-ware. They had lots of documents and a fair amount of code that didn't work as far as I could see. This project was being built by a team of more than 40 people and was about three or four years late. All projects were mandated to use this infrastructure, but no project ever did!

It sounded like magic because it was magic; it was imaginary.

We politely declined and finished the system that we were building without using the ideas or tech from this architecture.

On paper the architecture looked fine, but in practice, it was only theory.

We are technologists. As a result, we share certain tendencies. One of those tendencies that we should be aware of, and guard against, is chasing "technically shiny ideas." I am as guilty as anyone of being interested in technical ideas. This is part of the appeal of our discipline, the kind of learning that we value. However, if we are to be engineers, we must adopt a degree of pragmatism, skepticism even. Part of my definition for engineering, at the start of this book, included the phrase "within economic constraints." We should always be thinking of the simplest route to success, not the coolest, not the one with the most tech that we can add to our CVs or résumés.

By all means, keep up-to-date with new ideas. Be aware of new technologies or approaches to our work, but always evaluate their use honestly in the context of the problem that you are trying to solve. If you are applying this tech, or idea, to learn if it is useful, then recognize that fact and carry out your exploration quickly and efficiently as trial, prototype, or experiment, not as the cornerstone of your new architecture on which the future of the company depends. Be prepared to discard it if it doesn't work out, and don't risk the entire development on tech that looks cool.

In my experience, if we take this idea of "striving for simplicity" seriously, we are more, rather than less, likely to end up doing something cool. We are more, rather than less, likely to enhance the value of our CVs and résumés, too.

There is another way in which we are often lured to over-engineer our solutions. That is to make them **future-proof**. If you have ever said or thought, "We may not need this now, but we probably will in the future," then you were "future-proofing." I was as guilty of this as anyone else in the past, but I have come to regard it as a sign of design and engineering immaturity.

We attempt this kind of design future-proofing to give us some insurance that we will be able to cope with future enhancements, or changes in requirements. This is a good aim, but the wrong solution.

Referring to Kent Beck's *Extreme Programming Explained* book again, he introduced me to the following concept:

YAGNI: *You Ain't Gonna Need It!*

Kent's advice was that we should write code to solve the problem that faces us right now and only that. I strongly reiterate that advice, but it is part of a larger whole.

As I have already said many times in this book, software is weird stuff. It is almost infinitely flexible and extremely fragile. We can create any construct that we want in software, but we run the risk of damaging that construct when we change it. The problem that people are trying to address when they over-engineer their solutions, by attempting to future-proof them, is that they are nervous of changing their code.

In response to that nervousness, they are trying to fix the design in time now, while they are paying attention to it. Their aim is that they won't need to revisit it in the future. If you have made it this far through this book, you will know by now that I think that this is a very bad idea, so what could we do instead?

We could approach the design of our code so that we can return to it at any point in the future when we have learned something new and change it. We can take advantage of that nearly infinite flexibility. Now the problem that we need to fix is that of the fragility of our code.

What would it take to give us confidence that we can safely change our code in the future? There are three approaches, and one of them is stupid.

We could be so smart that we completely understand the code and all of its implications and dependencies so that we can safely make changes. This is the hero-programmer model, and although this is the stupid one, this is also one of the more common strategies as far as I can tell.

Most orgs have a usually small number of people "heroes"[4] who are called on to "save the day" when things go wrong or who are called on for the tricky changes that need to be made. If you have a hero in your organization, she needs to be working to spread her knowledge and to work with others to make the system more understandable. This is profoundly more valuable than the more usual firefighting that "heroes" more commonly undertake.

The real solutions to the problem of being afraid to change our code are **abstraction** and **testing**. If we abstract our code, we are, by definition, hiding the complexity in one part of the system from another. That means that we can more safely change code in one part of the system, with a much higher level of confidence that our change, even if wrong, will not adversely affect other parts. To be even more sure of this, we also need the testing, but as usual the value of testing is not that simple.

Improving Abstraction Through Testing

In Figure 4.2, I showed a flattened Cost of Change graph, representing the ideal situation in which we would like to be able to make any change at any time, for roughly the same cost in terms of time and effort.

---

4. There is a lovely, fictional example of this in Gene Kim's book *The Phoenix Project*, where the character Brent Geller is the only person who can save the day.

To achieve this flat Cost of Change curve, we'd need an effective, efficient strategy for regression testing, which really means a wholly automated strategy for regression testing. Make a change, and run the tests so that you can see where you broke things.

This idea is one of the cornerstones of continuous delivery, the most effective starting point for an engineering approach that I know of. We work so that our software is "always in a releasable state," and we determine that "releasability" through efficient, effective, automated testing.

However, there is another aspect of testing that is important, beyond merely catching our mistakes, and it is much harder for people to spot if they have never worked this way.

That is the impact of testability on design that I have described previously. We will explore this idea in more depth in Chapter 14. Specifically, though, in the context of abstraction, if we approach our tests as mini-specifications for the desirable behavior of our code, then we are describing that desirable behavior from the outside-in.

You don't write specification after you have completed the work; you need them before you start. So we will write our specifications (tests) before we write the code. Since we don't have the code, our focus is more clearly fixed on making our life easier. Our aim, at this point, is to make it as simple as possible to express the specification (test) as clearly and simply as we can.

Inevitably then, we are, or at least should be, expressing our desires for the behavior that we want, from our code from the perspective of a consumer of it, as clearly and simply as we can. We should not be thinking about the implementation detail that will be required to fulfill that mini-specification at this point.

If we follow this approach, then, by definition, we are abstracting our design. We are defining an interface to our code that makes it easy to express our ideas so that we can write our test case nicely. That means that our code is also easy to use. Writing the specification (test) is an act of design. We are designing how we expect programmers to interact with our code, separate from how the code itself works. All this before we have gotten to the implementation detail of the code. This approach, based on abstraction, helps us separate what the code needs to do from how it does it. At this point, we say little or nothing about how we will implement the behavior; that comes later.

This is a practical, pragmatic, light weight approach to design by contract.[5]

Power of Abstraction

As software developers, we are all familiar with the power of abstraction, as consumers. When we become software producers though many developers pay abstraction too little attention in their own code.

Early operating systems didn't have much in the way of hardware abstraction compared to their modern successors. These days if I want to change the video card in my PC, there are a whole stack

---

5. Design by contract is an approach to software design focused on the contracts, which are specifications that the system, or components of it, support. See https://en.wikipedia.org/wiki/Design_by_contract.

of abstractions that insulate my applications from such changes, so I can make that change in the confidence that my apps will most likely continue to work and display things.

Modern cloud vendors are busy working on abstracting away much of the operational complexity of running complex, distributed, scalable applications. An API like that of Amazon Web Service's S3 is deceptively simple. I can submit any sequence of bytes along with a label that I can use to retrieve it and the name of a "bucket" to place it in, and AWS will distribute it to data centers around the world and make it available to anyone who is allowed to access it and provide service-level agreements that will ensure that access in all but the most catastrophic of events is preserved. This is abstracting some fairly complex stuff!

Abstractions can also represent an organizing principle on a broader front. Semantically tagged data structures like HTML, XML, and JSON are extremely popular for communications. Some people say that they prefer them because they are "plain text," but that is not really true. After all, what does *plain text* mean for a computer? It's all electron flows through a transistor in the end, and electrons and transistors are abstractions, too!

The appeal of HTML or JSON for messages sent between different code modules is that the structure of the data is explicit in the communication, and the schema is transmitted along with the content. We could do that with other, much higher-performance mechanisms, like Google's Protocol Buffers[6] or SBE,[7] but mostly we don't.

Developers really like the (in practice) horribly inefficient mechanisms like JSON or HTML because everything can work with them. That is because of another important abstraction: plain text. Plain text isn't plain, and it isn't text; it is a protocol and an abstraction that allows us to deal with information without worrying too much about how that information is organized other than at some pretty basic level of it being represented as a stream of characters. Nevertheless, it is still an abstraction that is hiding information from us.

This "plain text" ecosystem is pervasive in computing, but it isn't natural, or inevitable. People designed it, and it has evolved over time. We needed to agree on things like byte ordering and encoding patterns. All of that is before we even begin to think about the underlying abstractions, through which we understand the hardware that our software runs on.

The "plain text" abstraction is an extremely powerful one. Another extremely powerful abstraction is that of "files" in computing, brought to its height in the Unix model of computing in which everything is a file. We can connect logic to build up new, more complex systems, by "piping" files from the output of one module to the input of another. All of this is "made up" and is just a useful way of imagining and organizing what is really going on.

---

6. Google's Protocol Buffers are meant to be a smaller, faster, more efficient version of XML. Read more at https://bit.ly/39QsPZH.

7. Simple Binary Encoding (SBE) is used in finance. It is a binary data encoding approach that allows you to define data structures and have code generated to translate them at either end. It shares some of the properties of other semantic data encoding approaches, but with lower performance overhead. Read more here: https://bit.ly/3sMr88c.

Abstractions are fundamental to our ability to deal with computers. They are fundamental to our ability to understand and deal with the systems that we create to add value to our computers, too. One way of looking at what it is that we do when we write software (and it is the only thing that we do in some ways) is to create new abstractions. The key is to create good ones.

Leaky Abstractions

Leaky abstractions are defined as "an abstraction that leaks details that it is supposed to abstract away."

This idea was popularized by Joel Spolsky, who went on to say this:

> All non-trivial abstractions are leaky.[8]

I have occasionally heard people excuse terrible code by saying something along the lines of "all abstractions are leaky, so why bother?" Well, this completely misses the point of both the original post and of abstraction in general.

Computers and software would not exist without abstraction. The idea of "leaky abstractions" is not an argument against them; rather, it describes that abstractions are complex things that we need to take care over.

There are also different kinds of "leaks." There are leaks that are impossible to avoid, for which the most effective course is to think about them carefully and work to minimize their impact. For example, if you want to build a low-latency system that processes data at "as close to the limits of the hardware as you can get," then the abstractions of "garbage collection" and "random access memory" will get in the way because they leak in terms of time, by making the latency a variable. Modern processors are hundreds of times faster than RAM, so access is not random if you care about time. There is a different cost, in time, depending on where the information that you want to process comes from. So you need to optimize to take advantage of the hardware; you need to understand its abstractions, caches, prefetch cycles, and so on, and allow for them in your design, if you want to minimize the impact of the leak.

The other kind of leak is really a point at which the illusion that your abstraction attempts to convey breaks down because you ran out of time, energy, or imagination to cater for that break in your design.

An authorization service that reports functional failures as HTML errors and a business logic module that returns `NullPointerExceptions` are both breaking business-level abstractions with technical failures. Both of these are a kind of break in the continuity of the illusion that the abstraction is intended to convey.

In general, try to cope with this second kind of leak by trying to maintain a consistent level of abstraction as far as possible. It may be acceptable that a remote component exposed as a web

---

8. You can read Joel Spolsky's original post here: https://bit.ly/2Y1UxNG.

service of some kind reports communications failures via HTML; that is a problem in the technical realm of abstraction of networking and communications, not in the world of the service itself. The mistake is using HTML error codes for business-level failures of the service. This is a break in the abstraction.

One take on this is that abstraction, all abstraction, is fundamentally about modeling. Our aim is to create a model of our problem that helps us reason about it and helps us to do work. I like this quote from **George Box**:

> All models are wrong, some models are useful.[9]

This is always the situation that we are in. However good our models, they are representations of truth, not the truth itself. Models can be enormously useful even when fundamentally untrue.

Our aim is not to achieve perfection but to achieve useful models that we can use as tools to solve problems.

Picking Appropriate Abstractions

The nature of the abstractions that we choose matters. There is no universal "truth" here; these are models.

A good example of this are maps (the human kind of "map," not the computer language data structure). All maps are abstractions of the real world, of course, but we have different types of abstraction depending on our needs.

If I want to navigate a boat or a plane to a destination, it is useful to have a map that allows me to measure a course between two points. (This kind of map is, strictly, called a *chart*, which means that I can measure a "bearing" on a chart, and if I steer that course, I will get to the right place.) The idea of the constant bearing chart was invented by Mercator in 1569.

Without boring you with too much detail, constant-bearing charts are based on things called *Rhumb-lines*. You can measure a bearing on this kind of map, and if you start off at point A and sail (or fly) that bearing, you will end up at point B.

Now, as we all know, the world isn't a flat plane. It is a globe, so in reality this is not the shortest distance between A and B because on the surface of a sphere the shortest distance between two points is a curve, and that means that the bearing changes constantly. So the abstraction of a chart hides the more complex math of curved planes and provides a practical tool that we can use to plan our course.

This abstraction leaks in the fact that the distance that you travel is longer than absolutely necessary, but since we are optimizing for ease of use, while planning and sailing, all is good.

---

9. A quote from statistician George Box, though the idea is older. See https://bit.ly/2KWUgbY.

A completely different abstraction is used for most underground train maps. This was invented by Harry Beck in 1933.

Harry's map has become a design classic, and the idea is used all over the world to depict how to get around on an underground train network. Harry realized that when navigating the London Tube (London's underground system), you don't care where you are when you are in transit. So he built a topologically accurate map of the network that bore no real relationship to the physical geography.

This style of map, this abstraction, allows passengers to see which trains go to which stations and which stations have connections to other lines extremely clearly. But if you try to use it to walk between the stations, the abstraction breaks down. Some stations are within a few paces of each other but look far apart; others look close but are distant.

My point is that it is fine to have different abstractions—even different abstractions—for the same thing. If we were tasked to thread a network cable between stations on the London Underground, we'd be stupid to choose Harry's map. But if we wanted to travel from Arsenal Tube Station to Leicester Square for dinner, we'd be stupid to choose a geographical chart.

Abstraction, and the modeling that is at its heart, is a fundamental of design. The more targeted the abstractions are to the problem that you are trying to solve, the better the design. Note, I didn't say "the more accurate the abstraction." As Harry's Tube map so clearly demonstrates, the abstraction doesn't need to be accurate to be enormously useful.

Yet again, testability can give us early feedback and inspiration in our attempt to come up with useful abstractions.

One of the common arguments against unit testing, and sometimes against TDD, too, is that the tests and the code become "locked together," and everything becomes more difficult to change. This is much more a criticism of unit testing, where the tests are written after the code is complete. Inevitably, such tests are tightly coupled to the system under test, because they were written as tests rather than as specifications. TDD suffers less from this problem because we write the test (specification) first and are led to abstract the problem, as I have described.

The subtlety here, though, and the enormous value that TDD delivers, is that if I have written my abstract specification, focusing on what the code should do and not how it achieves that outcome, then what my test is expressing is my abstraction. So if the test is fragile in the face of change, then my abstraction is fragile in the face of change. So I need to think harder about better abstractions. I know of no other way of getting this kind of feedback.

The next chapter talks about coupling. Inappropriate coupling is one of the most significant challenges for software development. This entire section of the book is really about the strategies that allow us to manage coupling. The problem is that there is no free lunch. Overly abstract designs can be as big a pain as under-abstracted designs. They can be inefficient and impose unwanted developmental and performance costs. So, there is a sweet spot to hit, and the testability of our system is a tool that we can use to hit it.

In general, our objective should be to retain our ability to change our mind about implementation, and as far as we can our design, without too much extra work. There is no fixed recipe here. This is the real skill of good software development, and it comes with practice and experience. We need to build up our instincts to be able to spot design choices that will limit our ability to change our minds later and that allow us to keep our options open.

What this means is that any advice I offer here is contextual. However, here are a few guidelines, rather than rules.

Abstractions from the Problem Domain

Modeling the problem domain will give your design some guide rails. This will allow you to achieve a **natural for the problem domain separation of concerns** as well as helping you, maybe even forcing you, to better understand the problem that you are attempting to solve. Techniques like **event storming**[10] are a great starting point to mapping out the territory of a problem.

Event storming can help you identify clusters of behavior that may represent concepts of interest, and the interesting concepts are good candidates for modules or services in your design. It can highlight bounded contexts and natural lines of abstraction in the problem domain that will tend to be more decoupled from one another than other, more technical divisions.

Domain-Specific Languages

One idea that certainly is more promising in raising the level of abstraction is the idea of the domain-specific language (DSL). However, by definition a DSL is not general purpose. It is, intentionally, more narrowly focused and can be more abstract, hiding detail.

This is the effect that we really see when we see diagram-driven development systems demonstrated. We are seeing the impact of a DSL—in this case a graphical one—on solving narrowly scoped problems. In this space, these more constrained ways to represent ideas are extremely powerful and useful.

DSL is an extremely useful tool and has an important role to play in developing powerful, maybe even "user-programmable" systems, but it is not the same thing as general-purpose computing, so it is not really the topic of this book; therefore, we will leave it there, but as a brief aside, there is no better way to create effective test cases than to create a DSL that allows you to express the desirable behaviors of your system as "executable specifications."

---

10. Event storming is a collaborative analysis technique invented by Alberto Brandolini that allows you to model interactions within a problem domain. See http://bit.ly/3rcGkdt.

Abstract Accidental Complexity

Software runs on computers. The way that computers work presents its own series of abstractions and constraints that we are forced to contend with. Some of these are deep, at the level of information and information theory, like concurrency and sync versus async communications. Others are a bit more hardware-implementation-specific like processor caching architecture, or the difference between RAM and offline storage.

Except for the most trivial of systems, you can't ignore these things, and depending on the nature of your system, you may have to consider them very deeply. However, these are abstractions that will inevitably leak. If the network is down, your software will be affected, eventually.

In general, in my designs, I aim to abstract the interface between the accidental complexity realm and the essential complexity (problem domain) realm as far as I can. This does take a bit of good design thinking and a bit of thinking like an engineer.

The starting question is, how do I represent the accidental-complexity world in the essential complexity domain? What does the logic of my system need to know about the computer it is running on? We should be striving to make that knowledge minimal.

Listing 12.1 shows the three examples of cohesion from Chapter 10. If we look at these from the perspective of abstraction and the separation of accidental and essential complexity, we can gain more insight.

Listing 12.1   Three Cohesion Examples (Again)

```python
def add_to_cart1(self, item):
    self.cart.add(item)

    conn = sqlite3.connect('my_db.sqlite')
    cur = conn.cursor()
    cur.execute('INSERT INTO cart (name, price) values (item.name, item.price)')
    conn.commit()
    conn.close()

    return self.calculate_cart_total();

def add_to_cart2(self, item):
    self.cart.add(item)
    self.store.store_item(item)

    return self.calculate_cart_total();

def add_to_cart3(self, item, listener):
    self.cart.add(item)
    listener.on_item_added(self, item)
```

The first example, `add_to_cart1`, doesn't abstract at all and is a bit of a mess as a result.

The next, `add_to_cart2`, is better. We have added an abstraction for storing information. We have created a "seam" in our code called `store`, and this allows the code to be more cohesive, drawing a clean line in the separation of concerns between the essential functions of our domain, adding items to carts, and calculating totals and the accidental complexity caused by the fact that our computer makes a distinction between volatile but quick RAM and slower but nonvolatile disk.

Finally, in `add_to_cart3`, we have an abstraction that leaves our essential complexity code uncompromised. Our abstraction is intact, with the very slight concession of the introduction of the idea of something that is interested in what happened, a `Listener`.

In terms of the consistency of the abstraction, `add_to_cart3` is, to my mind, the best. Even the concept of storage has been removed.

The beauty of this abstraction is how clean the model is of accidental concerns and, as a result, how easy it would be to test it or to enhance this code with new behavior `on_item_added`.

The cost to this abstraction, the leak that may get in the way of `add_to_cart3` being the best choice, raises the question, what happens if the attempt to store fails? What happens if our database runs out of connections in the connection pool or our disk runs out of space or the network cable between our code and the database is dug up by accident?

The first example is not modular, it lacks cohesion, it conflates accidental and essential complexity, and there is no separation of concerns; this is still just bad code!

The other two are better, not for any artificial notion of beauty or elegance but for practical, pragmatic reasons.

Versions 2 and 3 are more flexible, less coupled, more modular, and more cohesive because of the separation of concerns and because of the abstractions that we have chosen. The choice of abstraction between these two is really a design choice that should be driven by the context in which this code exists.

We could imagine several ways that this could work.

If, for example, the lack of storage is transactional with the addition of the item to the cart, then we'd need to undo the change to the cart. This is unpleasant, because the technicalities of the storage are intruding into our previously pure abstraction. Perhaps we could work to limit the extent of the leak; take a look at Listing 12.2.

Listing 12.2   Reducing the Abstraction Leak

```
def add_to_cart2(self, item):
    if (self.store.store_item(item))
        self.cart.add(item)

    return self.calculate_cart_total();
```

In Listing 12.2, we stepped back from our fully abstracted version 3 and allowed the concept of "storage" to exist in our abstraction. We have represented the transactional nature of the relationship between storing and adding the item to the cart with a success or failure return value. Note we aren't confusing our abstraction by returning implementation-specific error codes and leaking those into our domain-level abstraction. We have limited the technical nature of the failure to a Boolean return value. This means that the problems of capturing and reporting the errors are dealt with somewhere else, inside our implementation of "storage" in this case perhaps.

This is a further example of us trying to minimize the impact of the inevitable leaks in our abstraction. We are modeling the failure cases and abstracting them, too. Now we can once again imagine all kinds of implementation of "store." Our code is more flexible as a result.

Alternatively, we could take a more relaxed, decoupled view. In `add_to_cart3` in Listing 12.1, we could imagine that behind the event `on_item_added` there are some "guarantees."[11] Let's imagine that if, for some reason `on_item_added` fails, it will be retried until it works. (In reality we'd want to be smarter than that, but for the sake of keeping my example simple, let's stick to that!)

Now we are sure that, at some point in the future, the "store" or anything else that is responding to `on_item_added` will be updated.

This certainly adds complexity to the communication underneath `on_item_added`, but it more strongly preserves our abstraction and, depending on context, may be worth the extra complexity.

My objective with these examples is not to exhaustively explore all the options but rather to demonstrate some of the engineering trade-offs that we may choose to make, depending on the context of our system.

The "thinking like an engineer" that I alluded to, and ideally demonstrated here, is in thinking about the ways in which things can go wrong. You may recall that Margaret Hamilton described this as a cornerstone of her approach when she invented the term *software engineering*.

In this example, we imagined what would happen if the storage failed. We found that in that situation our abstraction leaked. So we were forced to think a bit more and thought of a couple of different ways that we could cope with that leak.

Isolate Third-Party Systems and Code

The other clear difference between version 1 of `add_to_store` and versions 2 and 3 is that version 1 exposes and couples our code to specific third-party code, in this case `sqlite3`. This is a common library in the Python world, but even so, our code is now concretely tied to this specific third-party library. Yet another reason for this code being the worst of the three is because of this coupling to this third-party code.

---

11. Computer scientists will, quite correctly, tell you that it is impossible to offer "guaranteed delivery." What they mean is that you can't guarantee "exactly once delivery," but we can work with that. See https://bit.ly/3ckjiwL.

The tiny, insubstantial cost of cutting out the block of code that talks about `sqlite3`, connections, and insert clauses, and moving it to somewhere else, away from my code that doesn't care about any of that stuff, is a big step forward toward greater generality. It's a big gain for so little work.

As soon as we allow third-party code into our code, we are coupled to it. In general, my preference and advice is to always insulate your code from third-party code with your own abstractions.

Some caveats before we proceed with this idea. Obviously, your programming language and its common supporting libraries are "third-party code," too. I am not suggesting that you write your own wrapper for `Strings` or `Lists`, so as usual my advice is a guideline rather than a hard-and-fast rule. However, I advise that you think carefully about what you allow "inside" your code. My default position is that I will allow language concepts and libraries that are standard, but not any third-party libraries that don't come with my language.

Any third-party libraries that I use will be accessed through my own facade or adapter that will abstract, and so simplify, my interface to it and provide a usually pretty simple layer of insulation between my code and the code in the library. For this reason I tend to be wary of all-encompassing frameworks that try to impose their programming model on me.

This may sound a little extreme, and it may be extreme, but this approach means that as a result my systems are more composable and more flexible.

Even in the trivial example we have been looking at here, `add_to_cart2` presents an abstraction that makes sense in the context of my implementation of storage. I can provide a version that is in essence the block of code implementing storage in `sqlite3` from `add_to_store1`, but I can also write a completely different kind of store, without needing to modify the `add_to_cart2` implementation in any way. I could use the same code in different scenarios, and I could even write some kind of composite version of store that stored my items in multiple places if the need arose.

Finally, we can test our code to this abstraction, which will always be a simpler version than the real thing. As a result, my solution will be dramatically more flexible, and easier to change if I make a mistake, for very little extra work.

Always Prefer to Hide Information

Another strong guideline to help us steer our code in a direction that will keep the doors to future-change open, without breaking YAGNI, is to prefer the more general representations rather than more specific, but this is slightly overly simplistic advice. The clearest demonstration of this idea is probably through functions and method signatures.

Listing 12.3 shows three versions of a function signature. One of these looks a lot better to me than the others, though as usual, it is contextual.

Listing 12.3   Prefer to Hide Information

```
public ArrayList<String> doSomething1(HashMap<String, String> map);

public List<Sting> doSomething2(Map<String, String> map);

public Object doSomething3(Object map);
```

The first is overly specific. When I collect the return value, do I really ever care that it is an ArrayList rather than any other kind of List? I suppose that I can imagine vanishingly rare cases when I care, but in general I'd prefer not to care. The stuff I am almost certainly interested in is the List-yness, not the ArrayList-yness!

"OK," I hear you cry. "So always prefer the most abstract, most generic, representation." Well, yes, but within sensible bounds that maintain your abstraction. I would be dumb to follow this advice and create the rather unpleasant function signature of version doSomething3. This is generic to the point of being probably unhelpful. Again, there may be times when Object is the correct level of abstraction, but those are, or should be, rare and always in the realm of accidental, rather than essential, complexity.

So, in general, doSomething2 is probably my most common target. I am abstract enough that I am not too tied to the technical specificity of doSomething1, yet I am also specific enough to be helpful in presenting and maintaining some pointers about how to consume the information that I produce and my expectations for the information that I consume.

I am sure that you will be tired of me repeating this by now, but once again, our ability to identify a sweet spot for our abstractions is enhanced by designing for **testability**. Attempting to write a test and simulating the use of the interface that we are creating gives us an opportunity to experience and exercise our understanding of that interface to the code under test.

This, in combination with our preference to hide information in general and to prefer the more generic representations of the information that we deal with that make sense in our context will, once again, help us keep the doors to future change open.

Summary

Abstraction is at the heart of software development. It is a vital skill to develop for the aspiring software engineer. Most of my examples are probably rather object oriented, which is because that is how I tend to think about code. However, this is just as true of functional programmer or even assembler programming. Our code, whatever its nature, is better when we construct seams in it that hide information.

13

Managing Coupling

Coupling is one of the most important ideas to think about when we start to think about how to manage complexity.

Coupling is defined as "the degree of interdependence between software modules; a measure of how closely connected two routines or modules are; the strength of the relationships between modules."[1]

Coupling is an essential part of any system, and in software we are often lax in discussing it. We often talk about the value of more loosely coupled systems, but let's be clear: if the components of your software system are perfectly decoupled, then they can't communicate with one another. This may, or may not, be helpful.

Coupling is not something that we can, or should, aim to always wholly eliminate.

Cost of Coupling

However, coupling is the thing that impacts most directly on our ability to reliably, repeatably, and sustainably create and deliver software. Managing the coupling in our systems, and in the organizations that create them, is front and center in our ability to create software at any kind of scale or complexity.

The real reason why attributes of our systems like **modularity** and **cohesion** and techniques like **abstraction** and **separation of concerns** matter is because they help us reduce the **coupling**

---

1. Source: Wikipedia, https://en.wikipedia.org/wiki/Coupling_(computer_programming)

in our systems. This reduction has a direct impact on the speed and efficiency with which we can make progress and on the scalability and reliability of both our software and our organizations.

If we don't take the issues and costs of coupling seriously, then we create big balls of mud in software, and we create organizations that find it impossible to make or release any change into production. Coupling is a big deal!

In the previous chapter, we explored how abstraction could help us break some of the chains that bind even tiny pieces of software together. If we decide not to abstract, then our code is tightly coupled, forcing us to worry about changes in one part of the system and compromising the behavior of code in another.

If we don't separate the concerns of essential and accidental complexity, then our code is tightly coupled and now we must worry about sometimes horribly complex ideas like concurrency, while also being comfortable that our account balance adds up correctly. This is not a nice way to work!

This does not mean that tight coupling is bad and loose coupling is good; I am afraid it is not that simple.

In general, though, by far the most common way for developers and teams to make a big mistake is in the direction of overly tight coupling. There are costs to "too loose coupling," but they are generally much lower costs than the costs of "too tight coupling." So, in general, we should aim to **prefer looser coupling over tighter coupling**, but also to understand the trade-offs that we make when we make that choice.

Scaling Up

Perhaps the biggest commercial impact of coupling is on our ability to scale up development. The message may not have reached everyone that it should yet, but we learned a long time ago that you don't get better software faster by throwing people at the problem. There is a fairly serious limit on the size of a software development team, before adding more people slows it down (refer to Chapter 6).

The reason for this is coupling. If your team and my team are **developmentally coupled**, we could maybe work to coordinate our releases. We could imagine tracking changes, and each time I change my code, you are informed of it in some way. That may work for a very small number of people and teams, but it quickly gets out of hand. The overhead of keeping everyone in step rapidly spirals out of control.

There are ways in which we can minimize this overhead and make this coordination as efficient as possible. The best way to do this is through **continuous integration**. We will keep all our code in a shared space, a repository, and each time any of us changes anything, we will check that everything is still working. This is important for any group of people working together; even small groups of people benefit from the clarity that continuous integration brings.

This approach also scales significantly better than nearly everyone expects. For example, Google and Facebook do this for nearly all of their code. The downside of scaling up in this way is that you have to invest heavily in the engineering around repositories, builds, CI, and automated testing to get feedback on changes quickly enough to steer development activities. Most organizations are unable or unwilling to invest enough in the changes necessary to make this work.[2]

You can think of this strategy as coping with the symptoms of coupling. We make the feedback so fast and so efficient that even when our code, and our teams, are coupled, we can still make efficient progress.

Microservices

The other strategy that makes sense is to decouple or at least reduce the level of coupling. This is the **microservices** approach. Microservices are the most scalable way to build software, but they aren't what most people think they are. The microservice approach is considerably more complex than it looks and requires a fair degree of design sophistication to achieve.

As you may have gathered from this book, I am a believer in the service model for organizing our systems. It is an effective tool for drawing lines around modules and making concrete the seams of abstraction that we discussed in the previous chapter. It is important to recognize, though, that these advantages are true, independently of how you choose to deploy your software. They also predate, by several decades, the idea of microservices.

The term *microservices* was first used in 2011. There was nothing new in microservices. All of the practices and approaches had been used, and often widely used before, but the microservice approach put them together and used a collection of these ideas to define what a microservice was. There are a few different definitions, but this is the list that I use.

Microservices are as follows:

- Small
- Focused on one task
- Aligned with a bounded context
- Autonomous
- Independently deployable
- Loosely coupled

I am sure that you can see that this definition closely aligns with the way that I describe good software design.

---

2. My other book *Continuous Delivery* describes the practices that are necessary to scale up these aspects of software engineering. See https://amzn.to/2WxRYmx.

The trickiest idea here is that the services are "independently deployable." **Independently deployable** components of software have been around for a long time in lots of different contexts, but now they are part of the definition of an architectural style and a central part.

This is the key defining characteristic of microservices without this idea; they don't introduce anything new.

Service-based systems were using semantic messaging from at least the early 1990s, and all of the other commonly listed characteristics of microservices were also in fairly common use by teams building service-based systems. The real value in microservices is that we can build, test, and deploy them independently of other services that they run alongside, and even of other services that they interact with.

Think what this means for a moment. If we can build a service and **deploy it independently** of other services, that means we don't care what version those other services are at. It means that we don't get to test our service with those other services prior to its release. This ability wins us the freedom to focus on the now simple module in front of us: our service.

Our service will need to be cohesive so that it is not too dependent on other services or other code. It needs to be very loosely coupled with respect to other services so that it, or they, can change without either one breaking the other. If not, we won't be able to deploy our service without testing it with those other services before we release, so it isn't **independently deployable**.

This independence, and its implications, are commonly missed by teams that think that they are implementing a microservice approach but have not decoupled them sufficiently to trust that their service can be deployed without testing it first with other the services that collaborate with it.

Microservices is an organizational-scaling pattern. That is its advantage. If you don't need to scale up development in your organization, you don't need microservices (although "services" may be a great idea).

Microservices allow us to scale our development function by decoupling the services from one another and vitally decoupling the teams that produce those services from one another.[3]

Now your team can make progress at its own pace, irrespective of how fast or slow my team is moving. You don't care what version my service is because your service is sufficiently loosely coupled to allow you not to care.

There is a cost to this decoupling. The service itself needs to be designed to be more flexible in the face of change with its collaborators. We need to adopt design strategies that insulate our service from change in other places. We need to break **developmental coupling** so that we can work independently of one another. This cost is the reason that microservice may be the wrong choice if you don't need to scale up your team.

Independent deployability comes at a cost, like everything else. The cost is that we need to design our service to be better abstracted, better insulated, and more loosely coupled in its interactions with other services. There are a variety of techniques that we can use to achieve this, but all of them add to the complexity of our service and to the scale of the design challenge that we undertake.

---

3. In 1967, Mervin Conway created something called Conway's law that said, "Any organization that designs a system (defined broadly) will produce a design whose structure is a copy of the organization's communication structure."

Decoupling May Mean More Code

Let's try to pick some of these costs apart so that we can better understand them. As ever, there is a cost to pay for the decisions that we make. That is the nature of engineering; it is always a game of trade-offs. If we choose to decouple our code, we are almost certainly going to write more code, at least to start with.

This is one of the common design mistakes that many programmers make. There is an assumption that "less code is good" and "more code is bad," but that is not always the case, and here is a key point at which that is decidedly not the case. Let's revisit once again the trivial example that we have used in previous chapters. Listing 13.1 shows once again the code to add an item.

Listing 13.1   One Cohesion Example (Yet Again)

```
def add_to_cart1(self, item):
    self.cart.add(item)

    conn = sqlite3.connect('my_db.sqlite')
    cur = conn.cursor()
    cur.execute('INSERT INTO cart (name, price) values (item.name, item.price)')
    conn.commit()
    conn.close()

    return self.calculate_cart_total();
```

Here we have eight lines of code, if we ignore the blank lines. If we make this code better by abstracting a method, I hope that we'd all agree that it is better, but we do need to add some more lines of code.

In Listing 13.2, the reduction in coupling, improved cohesion, and better separation of concerns has cost us two additional lines of code. If we took the next step—of introducing a new module or class that we passed as a parameter—we'd add several more lines to further improve our design.

Listing 13.2   Reducing Coupling

```
def add_to_cart1(self, item):
    self.cart.add(item)
    self.store_item(item)
    return self.calculate_cart_total();

def store_item(self, item):
    conn = sqlite3.connect('my_db.sqlite')
    cur = conn.cursor()
    cur.execute('INSERT INTO cart (name, price) values (item.name, item.price)')
    conn.commit()
    conn.close()
```

I have heard programmers reject the approach to design that I describe in this book, and I have heard others reject the use of automated testing because "I have to type more." These programmers are optimizing for the wrong things.

Code is a means of communication, and it is primarily a means of communication to other human beings, not to computers.

Our aim is to make our lives and the lives of other humans who interact with our code easier. This means that the readability isn't an effete, abstract property of code that is only meaningful for people who nerd out about style and aesthetics. Readability is a fundamental property of good code. It has a direct economic impact on the value of that code.

So taking care so that our code and systems are understandable is important. It's more than that, though. The idea that taking a dumb, naive approach to evaluating efficiency by counting the characters that we type is ridiculous. The kind of unstructured, coupled code in Listing 13.1 may be fewer lines of code if we are looking at eight lines. If this function was 800 lines, though, it is much more likely that there will be duplication and redundancy. Managing the complexity of our code is important for many reasons, but one of those reasons is that it significantly helps us in spotting redundancy and duplication and removing it.

In real systems, we end up with less code by thinking carefully, designing well, and communicating clearly through code, not by counting how many characters we type.

We should optimize for thinking, not for typing!

Loose Coupling Isn't the Only Kind That Matters

Michael Nygard[4] has an excellent model to describe coupling. He divides it into a series of categories (see Table 13.1).

Table 13.1   The Nygard Model of Coupling

Type	Effect
Operational	A consumer can't run without a provider
Developmental	Changes in producers and consumers must be coordinated
Semantic	Change together because of shared concepts
Functional	Change together because of shared responsibility
Incidental	Change together for no good reason (e.g., breaking API changes)

This is a useful model, and the design of our systems has an impact on all of these types of coupling. If you can't release your changes into production unless I am finished with mine, then we are developmentally coupled. We can address that coupling by the choices we make in our design.

---

4. Michael Nygard is a software architect and author of *Release It*. He presented his model of coupling at several conferences in this excellent talk: https://bit.ly/3j2dGIP.

If my service can't start unless yours is already running, then our services are operationally coupled, and, once again, we can choose to address that through the design of our systems.

Recognizing these different kinds of coupling is a good step forward. Thinking about them and deciding which to address and how to address them is another.

Prefer Loose Coupling

As we have seen, loose coupling comes at a cost, and the cost of more lines of code can also end up being a cost in performance.

Coupling Can Be Too Loose

Many years ago I did some consultancy for a large finance company. They had a rather serious performance problem with an important order-management system that they had built. I was there to see if I could help them improve the performance of the system.

The architect responsible for the design was very proud of the fact that they had "followed best practice." His interpretation of "best practice" was to reduce coupling and increase abstraction, both good things in my opinion, but one of the ways that the team had done this was to create a completely abstract schema for their relational database. The team was proud of the fact that they could store "anything" in their database.

What they had done was, in essence, create a "name-value pair" store mixed with a kind of custom "star schema" that used a relational database as the store. More than that, though, each element in a "record" as far as their application was concerned was a separate record in the database, along with links that allowed you to retrieve sibling records. This meant that it was highly recursive.

The code was very general, very abstract, but if you wanted to load almost anything, it involved hundreds, and sometimes thousands, of interactions with the database to pull the data out before you could operate on it.

Too much abstraction and too much decoupling can be harmful!

It is important then to be aware of these potential costs and not take our abstraction and decoupling too far, but as I said earlier, the vastly more common failure is the inverse. Big balls of mud are much more common than overly abstract, overly decoupled designs.

I spent the latter part of my career working in very high-performance systems, so I take performance in design seriously. However, it is a common mistake to assume that high-performance code is messy and can't afford too many function or method calls. This is old-school thinking and should be dismissed.

The route to high performance is simple, efficient code, and these days, for most common languages and platforms, it's simple, efficient code that can be easily and, even better, predictably, understood by our compilers and hardware. Performance is not an excuse for a big ball of mud!

Even so, I can accept the argument that within high-performance blocks of code, tread a little carefully with the level of decoupling.

The trick is to draw the seams of abstraction so that high-performance parts of the system fall on one side of that line or another so that they are cohesive, accepting that the transition from one service, or one module, to another will incur additional costs.

These interfaces between services **prefer looser coupling** to the extent that each service hides details from another. These interfaces are more significant points in the design of your system and should be treated with more care and allowed to come at a little higher cost in terms of runtime overhead as well as lines of code. This is an acceptable trade-off and a valuable step toward more modular, more flexible systems.

How Does This Differ from Separation of Concerns?

It may seem that **loose coupling** and **separation of concerns** are similar ideas, and they are certainly related. However, it is perfectly reasonable to have two pieces of code that are tightly coupled, but with a very good separation of concerns or loosely coupled with a poor separation of concerns.

The first of these is easy to imagine. We could have a service that processes orders and service that stores the orders. This is a good separation of concerns, but the information that we send between them may be detailed and precise. It may require that both services change together. If one service changes its concept of an "order," it may break the other, so they are tightly coupled.

The second, loose coupled but with a poor separation of concerns, is probably a little more difficult to imagine in a real system, though easy enough to think of in the abstract.

We could imagine two services that manage two separate accounts of some kind and one account sending money to credit the other. Let's imagine that our two accounts exchange information asynchronously, via messages.

Account A sends message "Account A Debited by X, Credit Account B." Sometime later, Account B sees the message and credits itself with the funds. The transaction here is divided between the two distinct services. What we want to happen is that money moves from one account to the other. That is the behavior, but it is not cohesive; we are removing funds in one place and adding them in another, even though there needs to be some sense of overall "transaction" going on here.

If we implemented this as I have described, it would be a very bad idea. It's overly simplistic and doomed to failure. If there was a problem in transmission somewhere, money could vanish.

We'd definitely need to do more work than that. Establish some kind of protocol that checked that the two ends of the transaction were in step perhaps. Then we could confirm that if the money was removed from the first account, it certainly arrived in the second, but we could still imagine doing this in a way that was loosely coupled, technically if not semantically.

DRY Is Too Simplistic

DRY is short for "Don't Repeat Yourself." It is a short hand description of our desire to have a single canonical representation of each piece of behavior in our system. This is good advice, but it is not always good advice. As ever, it is more complex than that.

DRY is excellent advice within the context of a single function, service, or **module**. It is good advice; beyond that, I would extend DRY to the scope of a version control repository or a deployment pipeline. It comes at a cost, though. Sometimes this is a very significant cost when applied between services or modules, particularly if they are developed independently.

The problem is that the cost of having one canonical representation of any given idea across a whole system increases coupling, and the cost of coupling can exceed the cost of duplication.

This is a balancing act.

Dependency management is an insidious form of developmental coupling. If your service and my service share the use of a library of some kind and you are forced to update your service when I update mine, then our services and our teams are developmentally coupled.

This coupling will have a profound impact on our ability to work autonomously and to make progress on the things that matter to us. It may be a problem for you to hold your release until you have changed to consume the new version of the library that my team imposed upon you. Or it may be a pain because you were in the middle of some other piece of work that this change now makes more difficult.

The advantage of DRY is that when something changes, we need to change it in only one place; the disadvantage is that every place that uses that code is coupled in some way.

From an engineering standpoint, there are some tools that we can use to help us. The most important one is the deployment pipeline.

In continuous delivery, a **deployment pipeline** is meant to give us clear, definitive feedback on the releasability of our systems. If the pipeline says "everything looks good," then we are safe to release with no further work. That implicitly says something important about the scope of a deployment pipeline; it should be "an independently deployable unit of software."

So, if our pipeline says all is good, we can release; that gives us a sensible scope to use for DRY. DRY should be the guiding principle within the scope of a deployment pipeline but should be actively avoided between pipelines.

So if you are creating a microservice-based system, with each service being independently deployable, and each service having its own deployment pipeline, you should not apply DRY between microservices. **Don't share code between microservices**.

This is interesting and sort of foundational to the thinking that prompted me to write this book. It is not random chance or an accident that my advice on coupling is related to something that may seem distant. Here is a line of reasoning that goes from a fairly basic idea in computer science, coupling, and links it, through design and architecture, to something that is seemingly to do with how we build and test our software: a deployment pipeline.

This is part of the engineering philosophy and approach that I am attempting to describe and promote here.

If we follow a line of reasoning—from ideas like the importance of getting great feedback on our work, creating efficient, effective approaches to learning as our work proceeds and dividing our work into parts that allow us to deal with the complexity of the systems that we create, and the human systems that allow us to create them–then we end up here.

By working so that our software is always in a releasable state, the core tenet of continuous delivery, we are forced to consider deployability and the scope of our deployment pipelines. By optimizing our approach so that we can learn quickly and fail fast if we make a mistake, which is the goal of the first section of this book, then we are forced to address the testability of our systems. This guides us to create code that is more modular, more cohesive, has better separation of concerns, and has better lines of abstraction that keep change isolated and loosely coupled.

All of these ideas are linked. All reinforce one another, and if we take them seriously and adopt them as the foundations for how we approach our work, they result in us creating better software faster.

Whatever software engineering is, if it doesn't help us create better software faster, it doesn't count as "engineering."

Async as a Tool for Loose Coupling

The previous chapter discussed the leakiness of abstractions. One of those leaky abstractions is the idea of synchronous computing across process boundaries.

As soon as we establish such a boundary, whatever its nature, any idea of synchrony is an illusion, and that illusion comes at a cost.

The leakiness of this abstraction is most dramatic when thinking about distributed computing. If service A communicates with service B, consider all the places where this communication can fail if a network separates them.

The illusion, the leaky abstraction, of synchrony can exist, but only to the point where one of these failures happens—and they will happen. Figure 13.1 shows the places where a distributed conversation can go wrong.

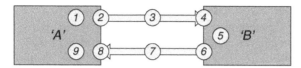

Figure 13.1
Failure points in synchronous communications

1. There may be a bug in **A**.

2. **A** may fail to establish a connection to the network.

3. The message may be lost in transmission.

4. **B** may fail to establish a connection to the network.

5. There may be a bug in **B**.

6. The connection to the network may fail before **B** can send a response.

7. The response may be lost in transmission.

8. **A** may lose the connection before it has the response.

9. There may be a bug in **A**'s handling of the response.

Apart from 1 and 9, each of the points of failure listed is a leak in the abstraction of synchronous communications. Each adds to the complexity of dealing with errors. Nearly all of these errors could leave A and B out of step with one another, further compounding the complexity. Only some of these failures are detectable by the sender, A.

Now imagine that A and B are communicating about some business-level behavior as though this conversation was synchronous. At the point that something like a connection problem or a dropped message on the network happens, this technical failure intrudes into the business-level conversation.

This kind of leak can be mitigated significantly by more closely representing what is really going on. Networks are really asynchronous communications devices; communication in the real world is asynchronous.

If you and I converse, my brain doesn't freeze awaiting a response after I have asked you a question; it carries on doing other things. A better abstraction, closer to reality, will leak in less unpleasant ways.

This is not really the place to go into too much detail of specific approaches to design, but I am a believer in treating process boundaries as asynchronous and communicating between distributed services and modules via only asynchronous events. For complex distributed systems, this approach significantly reduces the impact of abstraction leaks and reduces the coupling to the underlying accidental complexity that sits beneath our systems.

Imagine for a moment the impact of a reliable, asynchronous messaging system on the list of failure points in Figure 13.1. All of the same failures can occur, but if Service A only sends asynchronous messages, and some time later receives only a new async message, then now Service A doesn't need to worry about any of them after step 2. If a meteorite has hit the data center that contains Service B, then we can rebuild the data center, redeploy a copy of Service B, and resubmit the message that Service A sent originally. Although rather late, all the processing continues in precisely the same way as though the whole conversation had taken only a few microseconds.

This chapter is about coupling, not asynchronous programming or design. My intent here is not to convince you of the merits of asynchronous programming, though there are many, but rather to use it as an example to show that by smart use of the ideas of reducing coupling, in this case between the accidental complexity of networks and remote comms and the essential complexity of the business functions of my services, then I can write one piece of code that works when the system is working well and when it is not. This is a well-engineered answer to a particular class of problem.

Designing for Loose Coupling

Yet again, striving for testable code will provide a useful pressure on our design that encourages us, if we pay attention, to design more loosely coupled systems. If our code is hard to test, it is commonly as a result of some unfortunate degree of coupling.

So we can react to the feedback from our design and change it to reduce the coupling, make testing easier, and end up with a higher-quality design. This ability to amplify the quality of our code and designs is the minimum that I would expect of a genuine engineering approach for software.

Loose Coupling in Human Systems

I have grown to think of coupling, in general, as being at the heart of software development. It is the thing that makes software difficult.

Most people can learn to write a simple program in a few hours. Human beings are extremely good at languages, even weird, grammatically constrained, abstract things like a programming languages. That isn't the problem. In fact, the ease with which most people can pick up a few concepts that allows them to write a few lines of code is a different kind of problem altogether, in that it is sufficiently simple to lull people into a false sense of their own capabilities.

Professional programming isn't about translating instructions from a human language into a programming language. Machines can do that.[5] Professional programming is about creating solutions to problems, and code is the tool that we use to capture our solutions.

---

5. GPT3 is a machine learning system trained on the Internet, all of it. Given instructions in English, it can code simple apps. See https://bit.ly/3ugOpzQ.

There are a lot of things to learn about when learning to code, but you can get started quickly and, while working on easy problems on your own, make good progress. The hard part comes as the systems that we create, and the teams that we create them with, grow in size and complexity. That is when coupling begins to have its effect.

As I have hinted, this is not just about the code, but vitally, it is about coupling in the organizations that create it, too. Developmental coupling is a common, expensive problem in big organizations.

If we decide to solve this by integrating our work, then however we decide to deal with that, the integration will come at a cost. My other book, *Continuous Delivery*, is fundamentally about strategies to manage that coupling efficiently.

In my professional life, I see many large organizations hamstrung by organizational coupling. They find it almost impossible to release any change into production, because over the years they have ignored the costs of coupling, and now making the smallest change involves tens, or hundreds, of people to coordinate their work.

There are only two strategies that make sense: you take either a coordinated approach or a distributed approach. Each comes with costs and benefits. This is, it seems, part of the nature of engineering.

Both approaches are, importantly, deeply affected by the efficiency with which we can gather feedback, which is why continuous delivery is such an important concept. Continuous delivery is built on the idea of optimizing the feedback loops in development to the extent that we have, in essence, continuous feedback on the quality of our work.

If you want consistency across a large, complex piece of software, you should adopt the coordinated approach. In this you store everything together, build everything together, test everything together, and deploy everything together.

This gives you the clearest, most accurate picture but comes at the cost of your needing to be able to do all of these things quickly and efficiently. I generally recommend that you strive to achieve this kind of feedback multiple times per day. This can mean a significant investment in time, effort, and technology to get feedback quickly enough.

This doesn't prevent multiple teams from working on the system, nor does it imply that the systems that the teams create this way are tightly coupled. Here we are talking about the scope of evaluation for a production release. In this case, that scope is an entire system.

Where separate teams are working semi-independently, they coordinate their activities through the shared codebase and a continuous delivery deployment pipeline for the whole system.

This approach allows for teams working on code, services, or modules that are more tightly coupled to make good progress, with the minimum of costs in terms of feedback, but, I repeat, you have to work hard to make it fast enough.

The distributed approach is currently more in favor; it is a microservices approach. In microservices organizations, decision-making is intentionally distributed. Microservice teams work independently of one another, each service is independently deployable, and there is no direct coordination cost between teams. There is, though, an indirect cost, and that cost comes in terms of design.

To reduce organizational coupling, it is important to avoid the need to test services together later in the process. If services are independently deployable, that means they are tested independently too, since how can we judge deployability without testing? If we test two services together and find out that version 4 of one works with version 6 of another, are we really then going to release version 4 and version 17 without testing them? So they aren't independent.

A microservice approach is the most scalable strategy for software development. You can have as many teams as you want, or at least as many as you can find people to populate and funds to pay them.

The cost is that you give up on coordination, or at least reduce it to the simplest, most generic terms. You can offer centralized guidance, but you can't enforce it, because enforcement will incur coordination costs.

Organizations that take microservices seriously consciously loosen control; in fact, a microservices approach makes little or no sense in the absence of that loosening of control.

Both of these approaches—the only two that make any real sense—are all about different strategies to manage the coupling between teams. You manage coupling by speeding up the frequency with which you check for mistakes when coupling is high, or you don't check at all, at least prior to release, when coupling is low.

There are costs to this either way, but there is no real middle ground, though many organizations mistakenly attempt to forge one.

Summary

Coupling is the monster at the heart of software development. Once the complexity of your software extends beyond the trivial, then getting the coupling right, or at least working to manage whatever level of coupling you have designed into it, is often the difference between success and failure.

If your team and mine can make progress without needing to coordinate our activities, the "State of DevOps" reports say that we are more likely to be supplying high-quality code more regularly.

We can achieve this in three ways. We can work with more coupled code and systems but through continuous integration and continuous delivery get fast enough feedback to identify problems quickly. We can design more decoupled systems that we can safely, with confidence, change without forcing change on others. Or we can work with interfaces that have been agreed on and fixed so that we never change them. These are really the only strategies available.

You ignore the costs of coupling, both in your software and in your organization, at your peril.

IV

TOOLS TO SUPPORT ENGINEERING IN SOFTWARE

14

The Tools of an Engineering Discipline

When I think about what a genuine engineering discipline for software should mean, I don't think much in terms of specific tools, programming languages, processes, or diagramming techniques. Rather, I think of outcomes.

Any approach worth the name of **software engineering** must be built around our need to learn, to explore, and to experiment with ideas. Most importantly, if it doesn't help us build better software faster, it is "fashion" rather than engineering. Engineering is the stuff that works; if it doesn't work, we will change it until it does.

Although I may not be thinking of specific tools, that doesn't mean there are none. This book is built on the idea that there are some intellectual "tools" that we can apply universally to software development that significantly improve our chances of building better software faster. All ideas are not equal; there are some ideas that are simply bad, and we should be able to discard them.

In this chapter, I examine some ideas that I have spoken about throughout this book. These ideas pull together everything else in the book. If you ignored everything else that I have written, adopted only these ideas, and treated them as the founding principles on which you undertook software development, then you would find that you got better results and that you would, over time, discover all of the other ideas that I have written about here, because they follow as a logical consequence.

What Is Software Development?

Software development is certainly more than simply knowing the syntax and libraries associated with a programming language. The ideas that we capture are in many ways more important than the tools that we use to capture them. After all, we get paid to solve problems, not wield tools.

What does it mean to write software, for any purpose, if we don't know if it works?

If we carefully examine the code that we wrote but never run it, then we are placing ourselves as hostages to fortune. Humans just don't work like that. Even for loosely interpreted languages like a human spoken language, we make mistakes all the time. Have you ever written anything—an email, perhaps—sent it without proofreading it, and then, only too late, spotted all the grammatical errors or spelling mistakes?

My editors and I have worked very hard to eliminate mistakes in this book, but I am pretty sure that you have found a few nonetheless. Humans are error-prone. We are particularly bad at checking things over, because we often tend to see what we expect to see, rather than what is really there. This is not a criticism of our laziness as much as a recognition of the limitations of our biology. We are built to jump to conclusions, a very good trait for wild humans in hostile environments.

Software is intolerant of errors; proofreading and code review are not enough. We need to test it to check that it works. That testing can take a variety of forms, but whether it is us informally running the code and watching what happens or running it in a debugger to watch how things change or running a battery of behavior-driven development (BDD) scenarios, it is all just us attempting to get feedback on our changes.

As discussed in Chapter 5, feedback needs to be fast and efficient to be valuable.

If we must test it then, the only question now is, how should we do that as efficiently and effectively as possible?

We could decide to wait until we think that we are finished with our work and then test everything together. Maybe we could just release our software into production and let our users test it for us for free? That's not the most likely route to success! There is a commercial cost to low-quality work; this is why taking an engineering approach to software development matters.

Instead of crossing our fingers and hoping that our code works, we should probably do some form of evaluation before we release changes into production. There are a few different ways that we could organize that.

If we wait until we think we are finished, we are clearly not getting high-quality, timely **feedback**. We will probably forget all the little nuances of what we did, so our testing will be somewhat cursory. It is also going to be quite the chore.

At this point, many organizations decide to hire people to do that chore for us. Now we are back to square one, hostages to fortune, guessing that our software will probably work and relying on others to tell us that it didn't. This is certainly a step forward compared to waiting to hear the wails of our users in production, but it is still a low-quality outcome.

Adding separate steps into the process, in the form of separate groups of people, does not improve the speed or quality of the feedback that we can collect. This is not criticism of the people involved; all people are too slow, too variable in what they do, and too expensive to rival an automated approach to gathering the feedback that we need.

We are also going to receive this feedback too late and have no idea of how good or bad our software is while we are developing it. This means we will miss out on the valuable learning opportunities that we could have benefited from if the feedback had been more timely. Instead, we wait until we think that we are finished and then get low-quality, slow feedback from people, however skilled and however diligent they are, who don't know the inner workings of a system that wasn't designed with testing in mind.

I suppose that it is possible that we may end up being pleasantly surprised at the quality of our software, but I suspect that it is much more likely that we will be shocked by the dumb errors that we left in. Remember, we have done no other testing, not even run it until now.

I am sure you can tell that I don't think this is anywhere close to good enough.

This is a bad idea, so we *must* build some kind of checks into our process before we get this far. This is much too late to find out that users can't log in and that our cool new feature actually corrupts the disk.

So if we must do some testing, let's be smart about it. How can we organize our work in a way that minimizes the amount of work that we need to do and maximizes the insight that we can gain as we proceed?

In Part II, we talked about optimizing for learning, so what is it that we wish to learn, and what is the most efficient, effective way to do it?

There are four categories of learning relevant at the point where we are about to write some code:

- "Are we solving the right problem?"

- "Does our solution work as we think?"

- "What is the quality of our work?"

- "Are we working efficiently?"

These are certainly complex questions to answer, but fundamentally that is all we are interested in when we develop software.

Testability as a Tool

If we are going to test our software, then it makes sense that, to make our lives easier, we should make our software easy to test. I already described (in Chapter 11) how **separation of concerns** and **dependency injection** can make our code more testable. In fact, it is hard to imagine code that is testable that is not also modular, is cohesive, has a good **separation of concerns**, and exhibits information hiding. If it does all these things, then it will inevitably be **appropriately coupled**.

Let's look at a simple example of the impact of making our code more **testable**. In this example, I am not going to do anything other than follow the line of reasoning that I want to be able to test something. Listing 14.1 shows a simple Car class.

Listing 14.1   Simple Car Example

```
public class Car {
  private final Engine engine = new PetrolEngine();

  public void start() {
      putIntoPark();
      applyBrakes();
      this.engine.start();
  }

  private void applyBrakes() {
  }

  private void putIntoPark() {
  }
}
```

This class has an engine, a PetrolEngine. When you "start the car," it does a few things. The engine puts the Car into park, applies the brakes, and starts the Engine. That looks OK; lots of people would write code that looks something like this.

Now let's test it, as shown in Listing 14.2.

Listing 14.2   Test for a Simple Car

```
@Test
public void shouldStartCarEngine() {
    Car car = new Car();
    car.start();
    // Nothing to assert!!
}
```

Immediately, we run into a problem. Unless we decide to break the encapsulation of our car and make the private field engine public, or provide some other nasty, backdoor hack that allows our test to read a private variable (both of which are terrible ideas by the way), then we can't test the Car! This code is simply not testable because we can't see the effect of "starting the car."

The problem here is that we have hit some kind of endpoint. Our last point of access to the Car is to call the start method. After that, the internal workings are invisible to us. If we want to test the Car, we need to allow access in some way that isn't just a special case for testing. We'd like to be able to see the engine.

We can address that, in this case, by adding a measurement point through **dependency injection**. Here is an example of a better car; in this example, instead of hiding the Engine, we will pass the BetterCar an Engine that we'd like it to use. Listing 14.3 shows the BetterCar, and Listing 14.4 shows its test.

Listing 14.3   BetterCar

```
public class BetterCar {
    private final Engine engine;

    public BetterCar(Engine engine) {
        this.engine = engine;
    }

    public void start() {
        putIntoPark();
        applyBrakes();
        this.engine.start();
    }

    private void applyBrakes() {
    }

    private void putIntoPark() {
    }
}
```

Listing 14.3 injects an Engine. This simple step completely changes the coupling with the PetrolEngine; now our class is more abstract because it deals in terms of Engine instead of PetrolEngine. It has improved the separation of concerns and cohesion because now the BetterCar is no longer interested in how to create a PetrolEngine.

In Listing 14.4, we see the test for the BetterCar.

Listing 14.4   Test for a BetterCar

```
@Test
public void shouldStartBetterCarEngine() {
    FakeEngine engine = new FakeEngine();
    BetterCar car = new BetterCar(engine);
    car.start();
    assertTrue(engine.startedSuccessfully());
}
```

This `BetterCarTest` uses a `FakeEngine`, shown for completeness in Listing 14.5.

Listing 14.5   FakeEngine to Help Test a BetterCar

```java
public class FakeEngine implements Engine {
    private boolean started = false;

    @Override
    public void start() {
        started = true;
    }

    public boolean startedSuccessfully() {
        return started;
    }
}
```

The `FakeEngine` does nothing except record that `start` was called.[1]

This simple change made our code testable and, as we have seen, better. However, as well as the perhaps seemingly abstract attributes of quality, such as modularity and cohesion, it is better in a simpler, more practical way.

Because we made our code testable, it is now more flexible. Creating a `BetterCar` with a `PetrolEngine` is simple, but so is creating a `BetterCar` with an `ElectricEngine` or a `FakeEngine` or even, if we are a bit crazy, a `JetEngine`. Our `BetterCar` is better code, and it is better code because we focused on making it easier to test.

Designing to improve the **testability** of our code makes us design higher quality code. It is, of course, no panacea. If you are bad at coding, your coding may still be bad, but it will be better than you'd normally achieve if you work to make it testable. If you are great at coding, your code will be greater because you made it testable.

Measurement Points

The `FakeEngine` in our example demonstrates another important idea: **measurement points**. If we want our code to be testable, we need to be able to control the variables. We want to be able to inject precisely the information that we need and only that information. To get our software into a state where we can test it, we invoke some behavior, and then we need the results to be visible and measurable.

---

1. In a real test, we'd choose to use a Mocking library rather than write this code ourselves. I included the *FakeEngine* code here to make the example clear.

This is really what I mean when I say "design for testability." We are going to design our systems so that there are many measurement points, places where we can examine the behavior of our system without compromising its integrity. These measurement points will take different forms, depending on the nature of the component and the level at which we are thinking about testability.

For fine-grained testing, we will rely on parameters and return values from functions or methods, but we will also use **dependency injection**, as demonstrated in Listing 14.4.

For larger-scale, system-level testing, we will fake external dependencies so that we can insert our **measurement point probes** into the system allowing us to inject test inputs or collect test outputs, as I described in Chapter 9.

Problems with Achieving Testability

Many teams struggle to achieve the kind of testability that I am describing here, and there are two primary reasons for that. One is a technical difficulty; the other is a more cultural problem.

As we have already explored, any form of testing needs us to have access to some sensible measurement points. This is fine for most of our code. With techniques like dependency injection and good modular design, we can organize our code to be testable, but this becomes difficult at the edges of our system, the points at which our system interacts in some way with the real world (or at least a close computer facsimile of it).

If we write code that writes to disk, draws on a screen, or controls or reacts to some other hardware device, then that edge of the system is difficult to test, because how do we inject some test code to either inject test data or collect test results?

The obvious answer to this problem is to design our systems so that these "edges" in our code are pushed to the margins and minimized in their complexity. This is really about reducing the coupling of the bulk of the system with respect to these edges. This, in turn, reduces our dependence on third-party software elements and leaves our code more flexible, for little extra work.

We create some suitable abstraction that represents our interaction at this edge, write tests that evaluate the interaction of our system to a fake version of this abstraction, and then write some simple code to translate the abstraction into a real interaction with the edge technology. That is a lengthy way of saying that we add a level of indirection.

Listing 14.6 shows a simple example of some code that needs to display something. We could create a robot with a camera to record the output on a screen of some kind, but that would be overkill. Instead, we abstract the act of showing some result by injecting a piece of my code that provides the ability to "display" some text.

Listing 14.6   Stuff to Display

```java
public interface Display
{
    void show(String stringToDisplay);
}

public class MyClassWithStuffToDisplay
{
    private final Display display;

    public MyClassWithStuffToDisplay(Display display)
    {
        this.display = display;
    }

    public void showStuff(String stuff)
    {
        display.show(stuff);
    }
}
```

By abstracting the act of displaying information, I have gained the nice side effect that my class with stuff to display is now decoupled from any actual display device, at least outside of the bounds of the abstraction that I have provided. Obviously, this also means that now we can test this code in the absence of a real Display. I have included an example of such a test in Listing 14.7.

Listing 14.7   Testing Stuff to Display

```java
@Test
public void shouldDisplayOutput() throws Exception
{
    Display display = mock(Display.class);
    MyClassWithStuffToDisplay displayable = new MyClassWithStuffToDisplay(display);

    displayable.showStuff("My stuff");

    verify(display).show(eq("My stuff"));
}
```

Finally, we can create a concrete implementation of Display. In this simple case shown in Listing 14.8, it's a ConsoleDisplay, but we could imagine replacing this with all kinds of different options if the need arose, such as LaserDisplayBoard, MindImprintDisplay, 3DGameEngineDisplay, and so on.

Listing 14.8   Displaying Stuff

```java
public class ConsoleDisplay implements Display
{
    @Override
    public void show(String stringToDisplay)
    {
        System.out.println(stringToDisplay);
    }
}
```

Listings 14.5 to 14.8 are trivial, and the abstraction would clearly need to be more complex if the technology that we are interacting with at this edge was more complex, but the principle remains.

> **Testing at the Edges**
>
> On one project that I worked on, we abstracted the web DOM in this way in order to make our web page logic unit testable.
>
> There are better options now, but at the time it was tricky to unit test web applications in the absence of a real browser. We didn't want to slow down our testing by having to start up a browser instance for each test case, so we changed how we wrote our UI.
>
> We wrote a library of UI components that "sat in front of the DOM" (Ports & Adapters for the DOM), so if we needed a table, we created a JavaScript Table via our own DOM factory. At runtime, that gave us a thin facade object that gave us a table we could use. At test time, it gave us a stub we could test against but didn't require the presence of a real browser or DOM.

You can always do this. It is really only a matter of how easy, or difficult, the tech that you are trying to abstract is and the degree to which you think this is important enough to expend the effort.

For these "edges of the system," it is nearly always worth the effort. Sometimes, in a web UI or mobile app testing, for example, other people may have done the work for you, but this is how to unit test to the edges.

The problem with this approach, and any approach to solving this problem really, is cultural. If we take testability seriously and adopt it in our approach to design from the outset, this is all pretty easy.

It gets much more difficult when we hit code that wasn't built with testability in mind, or people don't think it's important. This clash of cultures is a tough problem.

The code is probably the easier part of the problem to deal with, though easier does not necessarily mean "easy." We can always add our own abstractions, even if they are leaky ones, and make it easier to test. If we really must, we can include the intransigent "edge" code within the scope of our test. This is an unpleasant compromise, but it's workable in some circumstances.

The difficult problem is people. I am not arrogant enough to state that there has never been a team that has practiced true TDD, in the sense of "Write a test before you write the code-driven development," and found it didn't work, but I have never met one.

I have met lots of teams that have told me that "We tried TDD, and it didn't work," but what all of the groups that I have met meant when they said that was that they had tried writing unit tests after they had written the code. This is not the same thing by a long margin.

The difference is that TDD encourages the design of **testable code** and unit testing does not. Unit testing, after the code is written, encourages us to cut corners, break encapsulation, and tightly couple our test to the code that we already wrote.

TDD is essential as a cornerstone for an engineering approach to software development. I don't know of any other practice that is as effective at encouraging and amplifying our ability to create good design in line with the ideas in this book.

The strongest argument against TDD that I sometimes hear is that it compromises the quality of design and limits our ability to change code, because the tests are coupled to the code. I have simply never seen this in a codebase created with "test-first TDD." It is common—I'd say inevitable—as a result of "test-after unit testing," though. So my suspicion is that when people say "TDD doesn't work," what they really mean is that they haven't really tried TDD, and while I am sure that this is probably not true in all cases, I am equally certain that it is true in the majority and so a good approximation for truth.

The criticism on the quality of design is particularly close to my heart because, as I suspect you can see from this book, I care very much about the quality of design.

I would be disingenuous if I pretended that I don't have some skill at software development, software design, and TDD. I am pretty good at it, and I can only guess at the reasons why. I am experienced, sure. I probably have some natural talent, but much more importantly than all these things, I have some good habits that keep me out of trouble. TDD gives me clearer feedback on the quality of my design as it evolves than anything else that I am aware of and is a cornerstone of the way that I work and recommend others to work.

How to Improve Testability

Part II describes the importance of optimizing for learning. I don't mean this in some grandiose, academic sense. I mean it in the fine-grained, practical sense of everyday engineering. So we will work iteratively, adding a test for the piece of work in front of us. We want fast, efficient, clear feedback from our test so that we can learn quickly, on tiny timescales, every few minutes that our code is doing exactly what we expect.

To do that, we want to compartmentalize our system so that we can clearly see what that feedback means. We will work incrementally on small, separate pieces of code, limiting the scope of our evaluations so that it is clear what is happening as we proceed.

We can work experimentally, structuring each test case as a small experiment that predicts and verifies the behavior that we want of our code. We write a test to capture that hypothesis of how the software should behave. We predict how the test will fail before we run it so that we can verify that our test is in fact testing what we expect it to. Then we can create code that makes the test pass and use the stable, passing combination of code and test as a platform to review our design and make small, safe, behavior-preserving changes to optimize the quality of our code and our tests.

This approach gives us deep insight into our design as it progresses in a much more profound sense than merely "does it pass a test?" If we pay attention, the testability of our code guides us in the direction of a higher-quality outcome.

We don't have enough tools that do this kind of thing for us, and we ignore this one at our peril. Too many developers and development teams ignore this and produce worse software, more slowly, than they could and should.

If the test before you is difficult to write, the design of the code that you are working with is poor and needs to be improved.

The testability of our system is fractal. We can observe it and use it as a tool, at both the level of whole enterprise systems and at the narrow focus of a few lines of code, but it is one of the most powerful tools in our tool chest.

At the fine-grained level of functions and classes, the most important aspect of testability to focus on is the measurement points. They define the ease with which we can establish our code in a particular state and the ease with which we can observe and evaluate the results of its behavior.

At a more systemic and multisystemic level, the focus is more on the scope of evaluation and testing. The fundamentals of measurement points still matter, but the scope of evaluation is an important tool.

Deployability

In my book *Continuous Delivery*, we described an approach to development based on the idea of working so that our software is always in a releasable state. After each small change, we evaluate our software to determine its releasability, and we gain that feedback multiple times per day.

To achieve this, we employ a mechanism called a *deployment pipeline*. The deployment pipeline is intended to determine releasability, as far as practical, through high levels of automation.

So what does "releasable" mean? Inevitably that is somewhat contextual.

We'd certainly need to know that the code did what the developers thought it did, and then it would be good to know that it did what the users needed it to do. After that, we'd like to know if the software was fast enough, secure enough, resilient enough, and maybe compliant with any applicable regulations.

These are all tasks for a deployment pipeline. So far I have described the deployment pipeline in terms of releasability, but there is a small nuance that I want to get out of the way before we move on.

Actually, when describing deployment pipelines, I make a distinction between **releasable** and **deployable**. It is a subtle point, but from a development perspective, I want to separate the idea of being "ready to **deploy** a change into production" from "releasing a feature to users."

In continuous delivery we want the freedom to create new features over a series of deployments. So at this point I am going to switch from talking about **releasability**, which implies some feature completeness and utility to users, to **deployability**, which means that the software is safe to release into production, even if some features are not yet ready for use and are hidden in some way.

So the **deployability** of our system consists of a number of different attributes; the unit of software must be capable of deployment, and it must fulfil all of the properties of releasability that make sense in the context of that system: fast enough, secure enough, resilient enough, working, and so on.

This idea of deployability is an extremely useful tool at the system and architectural level. If the deployment pipeline says that the system is deployable, it is ready to be deployed into production.

Lots of people misunderstand this about continuous delivery, but this is what a deployment pipeline is for. If the deployment pipeline says that the change is good, there is no more testing to be done, no more sign-offs, and no further integration testing with other parts of the system before we deploy the change into production. We don't have to deploy into production, but if the change was approved by the pipeline, it is ready, if we choose to.

This discipline says something important. It defines deployability as there being "no more work to do," and that means to achieve a deployable outcome, we must take the ideas of modularity, cohesion, separation of concerns, coupling, and information hiding seriously at the level of **deployable units of software**.

The scope of our evaluation should always be an **independently deployable unit of software**. If we can't confidently release our change into production without further work, then our unit of evaluation, the scope of our deployment pipeline, is incorrect.

There are a variety of ways to approach this. We can choose to include everything in our system within the scope of evaluation, within the scope of our deployment pipeline, or we can choose to decompose our system into independently deployable units of software, but nothing else makes sense.

We can organize multiple components of our system to be built in separate places, from separate repos, but the scope of evaluation is driven by the demands of deployability. So if we choose this path and feel it essential to evaluate these components together before release, then the scope of evaluation, the scope of the deployment pipeline, is still the whole system. This is important because however fast the evaluation of a small part of the system, it is the time it takes to evaluate the deployability of a change that really matters. So this is the scope that should be the target for our optimization.

This means that deployability is a vital concern in creating systems. Thinking in these terms means that it helps to focus us on the problem that we must address. How do we get feedback in a sensible timeframe that allows us to direct our development efforts?

Speed

This brings us to **speed**. As we discussed in Part II, the speed and quality of the feedback that we get in our development process are essential to allowing us to optimize for learning. In Chapter 3 we discussed the importance of measurement and focused on the use of **stability**, and **throughput**. Throughput, as a measure of the efficiency of our development process, is clearly speed-related.

When I consult with teams to help them adopt continuous delivery, I advise them to focus on working to reduce the time it takes to gain feedback.

I usually offer some guidelines: I tell them to work to optimize their development process so that they can achieve a releasable outcome, a production-quality deployable unit of software, multiple times per day, with a strong preference for shorter times. As a target, I generally recommend aiming to have something that you could deploy into production in less than one hour from the commit of any change.

This can be a challenging target, but just consider what such a target implies. You can't have teams that are too large, because the communication overhead will slow them down too much. You can't have siloed teams, because the cost of coordination between teams will be too slow. You have to have a great position on automated testing, you need feedback mechanisms like continuous integration and continuous delivery, you have to have good architecture to support these kinds of strategies, and you need to be evaluating independently deployable units of software and many more things to get to a releasable outcome in less than one hour.

If you take an iterative, experimental approach to only improving the speed of feedback in your development process, it acts as a kind of fitness function for all of agile theory, all of lean theory, and all of continuous delivery and DevOps.

This focus on speed and feedback leads you inexorably to these ideas. That is a much more powerful, measurable guide in the direction of better outcomes than following some rituals or recipes from some off-the-shelf development process. This is the kind of idea that I mean when I talk about *engineering for software*.

Speed is a tool that we can use to guide us toward higher-quality, more efficient outcomes.

Controlling the Variables

If we want to be able to quickly, reliably, and repeatably test and deploy our systems, we need to limit variance, and we need to **control the variables**. We want the same results every time that we deploy our software, so we need to automate the deployment and manage the configuration of the systems that we deploy as far as we are able to do so.

Where we can't exert control, then we have to treat those margins of the system that touch on the uncontrolled world with great care. If we are deploying software to an environment outside of our control, we want to depend on it to the least degree that we can. Abstraction, separation of concerns, and loose coupling are key ideas to limit our exposure to anything outside of our direct control.

We want the tests that we create to give precisely the same results every time that we run them for the same version of the software under test. If test results vary, then we should work to exert greater control to better isolate the test from outside influences or to improve the determinism in our code. Modularity and cohesion, separation of concerns, abstraction, and coupling are yet again key ideas in allowing us to exert this control.

Where there is a temptation to have long-running tests, or manual tests, these are often symptoms of an inappropriate lack of controlling variables.

We often don't take this idea sufficiently seriously.

Cost of Poor Control

I once consulted for a large organization building a large complex, distributed software system. They had more than 100 teams of developers working on the project. They asked me to advise them on performance testing.

They had created a large complex suite of end-to-end performance tests for the whole system.

They had attempted to run their performance test suite on four occasions, but now they didn't know what the results meant.

The results were so variable that there was no way to compare them between test runs.

One of the reasons for this was that they had run the test on the corporate network, so depending on what else was going on at the time, the results were completely skewed.

All the work to create these tests and to execute them was essentially waste because no one could tell what the results meant.

Computers give us a fantastic opportunity. Ignoring cosmic rays and neutrino collisions with our NAND gates (both catered for by hardware error-correction protocols), computers, and the software that runs on them, are deterministic. Given the same inputs, computers will generate the same outputs every time. The only limit to this truth is concurrency.

Computers are also incredibly fast, providing us with an unprecedentedly fantastic, experimental platform. We can choose to give up these advantages or to take control and make use of them to our advantage.

How we design and test our systems has a big impact on the degree of control that we can exert. This is yet another advantage of driving our designs from tests.

Reliably testable code is not multithreaded within the scope of a test, except for some very particular kinds of test.

Concurrent code is difficult to test because it is not deterministic. So if we design our code to be testable, we will think carefully about concurrency and work to move it to controlled, well-understood edges of our system.

In my experience, this results in code that is much easier to test because it is deterministic, but also code that is much easier to understand and, certainly in the places where I work, code that is, computationally, much more efficient.

Continuous Delivery

Continuous delivery is an organizing philosophy that helps us bring these ideas together into an effective, efficient, workable approach to development. Working so that our software is always releasable focuses our minds on the scope of evaluation in a deployment pipeline and the deployability of our software. This gives us some tools that we can use to structure our code and our organizations to create these **independently deployable units of software**.

Continuous delivery is not about automating deployment, though that is part of it; it is about the much more important idea of organizing our work so that we create a semi-continuous flow of changes.

If we take this idea seriously, then it demands of us that we structure all aspects of our development approach to achieve this flow. It has impacts on the structures of our organizations, minimizing organizational dependencies and promoting the autonomy of small teams that can work quickly and with high quality without the need to coordinate their efforts with others.

It demands that we apply high levels of automation, particularly in testing our software, so that we can understand quickly and efficiently that our changes are safe. As a result, it encourages us to take this testing very seriously so we end up with testable software and can benefit from all of the advantages that that brings.

Continuous delivery guides us to test the deployment and configuration of our systems and forces us to take seriously the ideas of controlling the variables so that we can achieve repeatability and reliability in our tests and, as a side effect, in our production deployments.

Continuous delivery is a highly effective strategy around which to build a strong engineering discipline for software development.

General Tools to Support Engineering

These are general tools. These ideas are applicable for any problem in software.

Let's look at a simple example. Imagine that we want to add some software to our system—a third-party component, subsystem, or framework perhaps. How do we evaluate it?

Of course, it is going to have to work and deliver some kind of value to our system, but before that, I believe that you can use the ideas in this chapter, and the rest of the book, as qualifiers.

Is the tech deployable? Can we automate the deployment of the system so that we can deploy it reliably and repeatably?

Is it testable? Can we confirm that it is doing what we need it to do? It is not our job to test third-party software exhaustively; if we have to do that, it is probably not good enough, not of sufficient high quality, for us to use. However, to the degree that we want to test that it is doing what it needs to in the context of our system, is it configured correctly, is it up and running when we need it to be, and so on? Can we test it?

Does it allow us to control the variables? Can we reliably and repeatably deploy this? Can we version control the deployment and any configuration?

Is it fast enough to work in a continuous delivery setting? Can we deploy it in a reasonable amount of time and get things up and running quickly enough to be able to use it and evaluate it multiple times per day?

If it is a software component that we will be writing code to interface to, does it allow us to maintain a modular approach to the design of our code, or does it force a programming model of its own on us that compromises our design in some way?

The wrong answer to any of these questions should almost certainly disqualify the technology for us before we even look at whether it did a good job and was useful in other contexts.

Unless the service this third-party tech provides is indispensable, I recommend that we seek alternatives. If the service is indispensable, we will need to do work to try to achieve these properties despite the tech. This is a cost that needs to be factored in to the cost-benefit calculation for this tech.

This little example is meant to give a model for the generality of this style of thinking. We can use the tools of learning, the tools of managing complexity, and these tools to support an engineering approach to inform decisions and choices in every aspect of our work.

Summary

This chapter brings together the interlinked ideas that I have presented in this book into a coherent model for developing software more effectively. By adopting the ideas in this chapter as organizing principles for the way that we approach software development, we will get a better outcome than if we ignore them.

That is the best that we can ever hope for from any tool, process, or discipline. There is no guarantee of success, but by applying the thinking that I have described here and throughout this book, I believe that you will create higher-quality code more quickly.

15

The Modern Software Engineer

All the ideas in this book are deeply intertwined. There is crossover and redundancy everywhere. You can't really separate concerns without improving modularity.

Modularity, **cohesion**, and **separation of concerns** enhance our ability to gather **feedback** and so facilitate **experimentation**.

As a result, I have looped through each of these topics many times during the course of this book. That is both intentional and inevitable, but I also think that it says something more important about these ideas.

Not only are these ideas deeply linked, but they apply nearly everywhere, and that is kind of the whole point.

It is too easy to get lost in the detail of ephemera. Which language, operating system, text editor, or framework we choose is detail that, ultimately, should matter less to us than those skills that are transferable across all of these things.

As I have said elsewhere, the best software developers I have worked with wrote good software whatever tools they chose to apply. Certainly, many of them had deep expertise and skill with their chosen tools, but this wasn't the core of their skill, talent, or value to the organizations that employed them.

All these ideas are probably familiar to you, but perhaps you haven't thought of them as an approach to organizing your work. That has been my intent with this book. I don't mean only to remind you that these things are there, but to recommend that you adopt them as the driving principles beneath all that you do.

These ideas, organized around the principles of optimizing everything that we do to maximize our ability to learn and to manage the complexity of the systems that we create, genuinely form the foundation of a discipline that we can justifiably refer to as an engineering approach to solving problems with software.

If we do these things, we have a higher likelihood of success than if we don't.

This isn't a "crank the handle" kind of approach. You are not going to get great software by simply following my, or anyone else's, recipe, any more than you will create a great car by following some mythical dot-to-dot-car-builder's manual.

This requires you to be thoughtful, diligent, careful, and intelligent. Software development is not an easy thing to do well. Some forms of coding may be, but as I have already described, there is a lot more to software development than only coding.

This is a simple model for software engineering, but one that it is difficult to apply.

It is simple in that there are ten fundamental ideas in two groups and then a few tools like testability, deployability, speed, controlling the variables, and continuous delivery that can help us achieve those fundamentals, and that is all that there is. However, the implications of these ten things are often thought-provoking and complex, so that can make them difficult to apply.

Mastering the use of these tools and using these ideas as the foundational principles that underpin our designs and decisions amplify our chances of success. Using them as the basis on which we make decisions about the software that we create seems to me to be at the heart of the discipline of software development.

My objective with this book is not to say "software is easy" but rather to admit that "software is difficult, so let's approach it thoughtfully."

For me, that means we need to approach it with a bit more care, within a framework of thinking that enables us to find better answers to questions that we haven't thought of yet. It's a approach to finding solutions to problems that we have no idea how to solve.

These ten things give me this framework, and I have seen many individuals and teams benefit from applying them.

Understanding the nature of our discipline affects our ability to make progress. Recognizing the reality of the complexity of the systems that we build, and of the very nature of software itself, is important to success. Treating it lightly as a trivial exercise in coding a semi-linear sequence of instructions is always doomed to failure in all but the most trivial of programming exercises.

We need to apply mental tools that we can adapt to whatever circumstances we face. This seems to me to be at the heart of anything that we could think of as a true engineering discipline for software.

Engineering as a Human Process

The term *engineering* can be slippery, as it is often misapplied in the context of software development.

Most definitions of *engineering* begin with something like "The study of the work of an engineer" and then go on to describe the use of math and science that informs that work. So it is really about the process, our approach to doing work.

The working definition that I introduced at the start of this book hits the target for me.

> *Engineering is the application of an empirical, scientific approach to finding efficient, economic solutions to practical problems.*

Engineering is empirical, in that we are not attempting to apply science to the degree that we expect perfect results every time. (Actually, science doesn't work like that either; it just strives to approach it.)

Engineering is about making rationally informed decisions, often with incomplete information, and then seeing how our ideas play out in reality based on the feedback that we gather from real-world experience.

It is based on a scientific style of reasoning. We want to measure what we can sensibly measure. Take an experimental approach to making changes. Control the variables so that we can understand the impact of our changes. Develop and maintain a model, a hypothesis, against which we can continually evaluate our understanding as that understanding grows.

It is important that the solutions we find and the way in which we work to achieve them are efficient.

We want the systems we create to be as simple as they can be and run as quickly as they can while consuming the minimum resources they need to succeed.

We also want to be able to create them quickly and with the least amount of work. This is important for economic reasons, but it is also crucially important if we want to be able to learn effectively. The timeliness of feedback is a good measure of the efficiency with which we do work. The timeliness of feedback, as we explored in Chapter 5, is also fundamental to our ability to learn effectively.

In addition to the general applicability of engineering thinking to development, it is important to recognize that the organizations and teams we work in are information systems too, so the ideas of managing complexity apply equally, if not more, to those things, too.

Digitally Disruptive Organizations

It is common for businesses and business leaders to talk about ideas like digital disruption, by which they mean digital technologies applied to re-imagining and disrupting traditional businesses. Think Amazon disrupting the retail supply chain, Tesla changing the fundamentals of how you approach car production, or Uber turning taxi services into a gig economy. These ideas are challenging to traditional businesses and to traditional business thinking.

One of the defining characteristics of organizations like these is that they are nearly always engineering-led. Software development is not a cost center or a support function; it is the "business." Even a company like Tesla, whose product is a physical device, has shaped its organization around software ideas.

Tesla is a continuous delivery company to the extent that if someone thinks of a new idea, they can reconfigure the factory, often through software, to apply the new idea.

Software is changing how business is conducted, and to do this, it challenges many traditional assumptions.

One of my favorite models comes from Jan Bosch; he describes it as "BAPO versus OBAP."[1] Figure 15.1 and Figure 15.2 help to explain his idea.

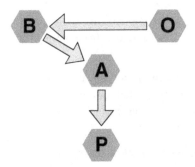

Figure 15.1
How most businesses plan (OBAP)

Most firms follow an OBAP model (see Figure 15.1). They first fix the organization, departments, teams, responsibilities, and so on. Then they decide on a business strategy and how to generate revenue and profit or other business outcomes, based on the constraints of those organizational decisions. Next they decide on a suitable architecture to base their systems on, and finally on a process that can deliver that system architecture.

This is kind of crazy. The business vision and goals are constrained by organizational structure.

A more sensible model is to treat the structure of our organizations as a tool: BAPO.

We identify business vision and goals, decide how we could achieve that technically (architecture), figure out how we could build something like that (process), and then pick an organizational structure that will support the necessary activities.

---

1. Jan Bosch describes these ideas in his blog post "Structure Eats Strategy" at https://bit.ly/33GBrR1 and in his book *Speed, Data and Ecosystems*. See https://amzn.to/3x5Ef6T.

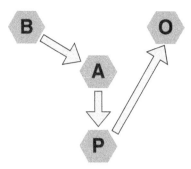

Figure 15.2
How business should organize (BAPO)

When we start thinking about the ways that we organize groups of people as a tool to achieve an end, applying the kind of engineering thinking described in this book is central to the successful wielding of that tool.

As with any other information system, managing the coupling within our organizations is one of the keys to success. In the same way that this is true for software, it is true for organizations. Modular, cohesive organizations with a sensible separation of concerns and teams that are abstracted in a way that allows them to hide information from other parts of the organization are more scalable and more efficient than highly coupled groups that can make progress only in lock-step.

This is one of the reasons that it is so difficult to scale organizations. As they grow, the costs of the coupling increase. Designing organizations to minimize the coupling between different groups of people is the modern strategy for large, fast-growing companies.

It is not an accident that the research behind the *Accelerate* book found that one of the defining characteristics of high-performing teams, based on measures of stability and throughput, is that they can make decisions within the team, without seeking permission from, or coordination with, other groups. Such teams are informationally decoupled.

This is important stuff. It is the difference between an organization like Amazon, which more than doubles in productivity when it doubles in size, and a more traditionally structured firm that increases productivity by only 85 percent as it doubles in size.[2]

---

2. James Lewis, inventor of the term *microservices*, has an interesting presentation that touches on the work of the Santa Fe Institute on Non-Linear Dynamics. See https://youtu.be/tYHJgvJzbAk.

Outcomes vs. Mechanisms

As I approached writing the conclusions of this book, I became involved in an online debate about the importance of outcomes and mechanisms. I started from a position of absolute certainty that everyone would agree with me that outcomes are more important than mechanism. I was quickly disabused of this assumption.

However, I don't think that my interlocutors were stupid because they disagreed with me. Looking at their responses, I think they ultimately agreed with my point. They weren't dismissing the importance of "outcomes"; what they were worrying about were some implicit things that they valued, or the mechanisms that they preferred, that helped them achieve their desired outcomes.

A successful outcome for software development is a complex idea. There are some obvious things that are easy to measure that we can begin with. We can measure commercial outcomes for some kinds of businesses and software; this is one measure of success. We can measure usage numbers, and the success of an open source software project is often measured in the number of downloads that the software accrues.

We can apply the DORA measures of productivity and quality, **stability**, and **throughput**, which tell us that successful teams produce very high-quality software, very efficiently. We can also measure customer satisfaction with our products through a variety of metrics.

Good "scores" in all of these dimensions are to some degree desirable outcomes. Some of them are contextual, and some are not, and working efficiently with quality (having good scores in **stability and throughput**) is going to be more successful in any context than not, which is why I consider these measures to be such an effective tool.

The context in which I had my discussion about "outcomes being more important than mechanisms" was a debate about continuous delivery as an idea compared to DevOps as an idea.[3]

My point was that I thought continuous delivery defines a desirable outcome, rather than a mechanism, so it is more useful as a general, organizing principle to guide development strategy and approach.

DevOps is an extremely useful collection of practices; if you adopt all of the practices and do them well, then you will be able to continuously deliver value into the hands of your users and customers. However, if a circumstance arises that is outside the scope of DevOps for some reason, because it is more a collection of practices, then it is less obvious how to cope.

Continuous delivery, though, says "work so that your software is always in a releasable state," "optimize for fast feedback," and "our aim is to have the most efficient feedback from idea to valuable software in the hands of our users."

If we take these ideas seriously, we can use them to come up with unique, innovative solutions to problems that we haven't encountered before.

---

3. If you are interested in my thoughts on CD versus DevOps, watch this video on my YouTube channel: https://youtu.be/-sErBqZgKGs.

When I, and others, began work on codifying continuous delivery, we had never built a car or a spaceship or a telecoms network. Each of these activities presents very different challenges to the kinds of systems that we were building when Jez Humble and I wrote our book.

When I work as a consultant, I give my clients specific advice on targets and goals that they should strive to achieve in terms of feedback from their deployment pipelines. I generally advise my clients to aim for a result in five minutes from the commit stage and in less than one hour for the whole pipeline. "Aim to create something releasable every hour."

If you are Tesla building a car or SpaceX building a rocket or Ericsson building a global mobile phone infrastructure, this is probably not possible because the physics of burning silicon or making things out of metal gets in the way.

However, the principles of continuous delivery still hold.

"Work so that your software is always releasable." You can still test your software thoroughly, rejecting any change immediately if a single test fails. "Optimize for fast feedback." Automate everything: automate tests to do the vast majority of testing in simulation so that feedback is always fast and efficient.

More deeply than this, the ideas that we can take from science, the ideas that continuous delivery is founded upon, are the most durable of all.

- **Characterize**: Make an observation of the current state.

- **Hypothesize**: Create a description, a theory that may explain your observation.

- **Predict**: Make a prediction based on your hypothesis.

- **Experiment**: Test your prediction.

To make sense of what we learn from this approach, we must control the variables. We can do this in a few different ways. We can work in small steps so that we can understand the impact of each step. We can exercise complete control over the configuration of our systems and limit the scope of change with the techniques of managing complexity that we have discussed.

This is what I mean by engineering—the ideas, methods, and tools that give us a demonstrably higher chance of success.

You may not be able to hit the feedback targets that I generally recommend, but you can use them as a target and work toward them within physical, or maybe economic, constraints.

Durable and Generally Applicable

If we were to succeed in defining an engineering discipline for software development, then it would be agnostic of technology. The principles on which it was built would be long-lasting and useful, helping us answer questions that we hadn't foreseen and understand ideas and technologies that we haven't invented yet.

We can try this!

My career has been spent developing software that my colleagues and I have designed, but could we apply this kind of thinking to a different form of software development? Do these engineering principles still apply to machine learning (ML)?

Figure 15.3 shows a typical ML workflow. Time is spent organizing training data, cleansing it, and preparing it for use. Suitable machine learning algorithms are selected, fitness functions are defined to apply to the input data, and then the ML algorithms are let loose on the training data. They cycle around trying out different solutions to the problem until the desired accuracy of a match to the fitness function is achieved. At this point, the generated algorithm can be deployed into production.

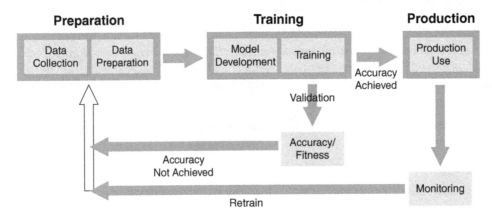

Figure 15.3
Typical ML workflow

If the accuracy isn't achieved, the process cycles around with the developers/data scientists changing the training data and fitness functions to try to target an effective solution.

Once the algorithm makes it into production, it can be monitored, and if any problems are noticed, it can go back into the cycle to be retrained.

How does our engineering model fit?

Clearly, the development of machine learning systems is all about learning, and not just for the machine. Developers need to optimize their work, and approach, to allow them to learn what data to use to train their systems and what works in fitness functions to guide that training.

Training machine learning systems involves lots of data, so thinking about and actively adopting techniques to manage that complexity is essential to making good progress. It is easy and quite common, I am told, for data scientists to get lost in morasses of data and make no reproducible progress.

The development process itself is obviously going to work best as an iterative one. The assembly and preparation of training data and the establishment and refinement of suitable fitness-functions are fundamentally iterative processes. Feedback is delivered in the form of the accuracy of matches to the fitness function. Clearly, this will work best when the iterations are short and the feedback fast and clear. The whole process is one of experimental iteration and refinement.

Thinking of it that way gives us opportunities to do a better job. It will be sensible to optimize the process so that developers can cycle through it quickly to improve the quality of the learning at each iteration. That means working in smaller steps and being clear about the nature and quality of the feedback.

Thinking about each small step as an experiment encourages us to take greater control of the variables, such as version controlling our scripts and training data.

It seems somewhat bizarre to even imagine this part of the process being planned and working in anything other than a dynamic, iterative, feedback-driven process of empirical discovery.

Why empirical? Because the data is messy and the outcomes are complex enough to be not deterministic at the levels of control that are typically exercised in ML development.

That suggests another interesting question. Could you exercise more control? I had interesting conversations with an ML expert. He questioned my simple picture (refer to Figure 15.3). "What do you mean by monitoring? How can we possibly know the result?"

Well, if we took an engineering approach, then we would approach the release of our model into production as an experiment. If it is an experiment, then we are making a prediction of some kind and need to test our prediction. At the point that we create our ML system, we could imagine describing what it is that are we attempting to do. We could predict the kind of outcomes that we might expect to see. This is more than the fitness function. This is more like defining some error-bounds, a range, within which we would expect sensible answers to fall.

If our ML system is designed to sell more books, it is probably not doing a good job if the answer drifts into the territory of "try to take over the world."

What about managing complexity? Well, one of the problems in ML is that the people doing it often don't come from a software background. As a result, many of the techniques that have become normal for software development—even basic ones like version control—are not the norm.

Nevertheless, it is easy to see ways that the engineering principles in this book might be applied. Taking a modular approach to writing the scripts to assembly, cleansing the data, and defining fitness functions is obvious. This is code, so use the tools necessary to allow us to write good code. Control the variables, keep related ideas close together with cohesion, and keep unrelated ideas apart with modularity, separation of concerns, abstraction, and reductions in coupling. This is just as true of the data involved, though.

Applying these ideas to the data and selecting training data that is modular (in the sense that it focuses on the right aspects of the problem) allow developers of ML systems to iterate more quickly. This limits changes and focuses the training process and perhaps facilitates a more effective, more scalable approach to managing training data. This is one take on what *data cleansing* really means.

Ensuring a separation of concerns within the data and the fitness functions is also important. You can sensibly think of problems like ML systems making bad decisions based on built-in "assumptions" between things like economic circumstances and ethnic groupings or salaries and gender as representing a poor separation of concerns in the training data, as well as a sad statement on our society.

I will stop at this point, before I expose even more of my ignorance about machine learning. My point here is that if these mental tools are generally applicable, they will provide us with useful ways to approach problems, even when we are ignorant of them.

In my example here, I don't claim that I have come up with any correct answers, but my model has allowed me to pose some questions that aren't, as far as I understand it, commonly asked in ML circles. They are questions that we could investigate and that could possibly help us optimize the process, improve the quality of the production of ML systems, and even improve the systems themselves.

This is what we should expect from a real engineering process. It will not give us the answers, but it will provide us with an approach that guides us toward better answers.

Foundations of an Engineering Discipline

The ideas in this book form the foundations for an engineering discipline that can amplify our chances of success.

The programming language that you choose doesn't really matter. The framework that you employ doesn't really matter. The methodology that you pick matters less than the ideas that I have outlined in this book.

It is not that these other things have no bearing on our work; they do. They matter to the degree that the model of hammer that a carpenter chooses to wield matters.

For software, this sort of choice is a bit more than a personal preference because it has an impact on how a team works together, but in essence the choice of one tech over another has less impact on the outcome than how that technology is applied.

My intention with this book is to describe ideas that, in general, offer us guidance on how to wield our tools more effectively.

By focusing on the fundamentals of optimizing for learning and managing complexity, we increase our chances of success, whatever technology we choose to use.

Summary

The ideas in this book have formed the basis of my approach to software development for many years now. Inevitably, the process of writing this book has helped me crystallize my thinking in a way that, I hope, makes it easier to communicate them to other people.

In the latter stages of my career, I have worked, almost exclusively, on complex systems. I have been fortunate to work on a few problems that few people, if anyone, had solved before. Whenever my team and I became stuck, these are the fundamentals that we turned to. They worked as guide rails to steer us to better outcomes, whatever the nature of the problem, even when we had no clue at all about how to make progress.

These days I make my living advising mostly big multinational firms, often doing innovative things, sometimes on unprecedented scales. These ideas still hold true and guide us to solving genuinely difficult problems.

When I get to write code for myself, still something that I take great pleasure in, I apply these same ideas at the smallest and often simplest of scales.

If you always optimize your work and how you undertake it to maximize your ability to learn efficiently, you will do a better job.

If you always work, at every scale, to manage the complexity of the work in front of you, you will be able to sustain your ability to do a better job indefinitely.

These are the hallmarks of a genuine engineering discipline for software development. When we apply that discipline, we dramatically improve our chances of building better software faster.

There is something important and valuable here. I hope that I have been able to express it in a way that you will find helps you in your work.

Index

Software Architecture
Books, eBooks & Video

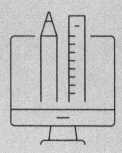

Creating great software architecture today requires effective methods and tools, an understanding of DevOps, continuous delivery, and integration, design, as well as services. Check out our books, eBooks, and video that will help you improve your software architecture.

- Official guides from the Software Engineering Institute (SEI)
- Design patterns
- Guides for Domain-Driven Design (DDD)
- System and project design guidance

Visit **informit.com/swarchcenter** to read sample chapters, shop, and watch video lessons from featured products.

Extra value: Take advantage of free ground shipping on all U.S. orders. Most eBooks are available as DRM-free EPUB, MOBI, and PDF—all together for one price so you can learn on your desktop or preferred device!

Photo by izusek/gettyimages

Register Your Product at informit.com/register

Access additional benefits and **save 35%** on your next purchase

- Automatically receive a coupon for 35% off your next purchase, valid for 30 days. Look for your code in your InformIT cart or the Manage Codes section of your account page.

- Download available product updates.

- Access bonus material if available.*

- Check the box to hear from us and receive exclusive offers on new editions and related products.

Registration benefits vary by product. Benefits will be listed on your account page under Registered Products.

InformIT.com—The Trusted Technology Learning Source

InformIT is the online home of information technology brands at Pearson, the world's foremost education company. At InformIT.com, you can:

- Shop our books, eBooks, software, and video training
- Take advantage of our special offers and promotions (informit.com/promotions)
- Sign up for special offers and content newsletter (informit.com/newsletters)
- Access thousands of free chapters and video lessons

Connect with InformIT—Visit informit.com/community

the trusted technology learning source

Addison-Wesley • Adobe Press • Cisco Press • Microsoft Press • Pearson IT Certification • Que • Sams • Peachpit Press

 Pearson

Printed in the United States
By Bookmasters

Hello, Singularity
...shall we have another go..?